RUSKINIAN GOTHIC

EVE BLAU

RUSKINIAN GOTHIC

THE ARCHITECTURE OF

DEANE AND WOODWARD

1845-1861

PRINCETON UNIVERSITY PRESS

Copyright © 1982 by Princeton University Press
Published by Princeton University Press, 41 William Street, Princeton, New Jersey
In the United Kingdom: Princeton University Press, Guildford, Surrey

This book has been composed in Linotron Bodoni
Designed by Barbara Werden

Clothbound editions of Princeton University Press books
are printed on acid-free paper, and binding materials are
chosen for strength and durability

Printed in the United States of America by Princeton University Press,
Princeton, New Jersey

LIBRARY OF CONGRESS CATALOGING IN PUBLICATION DATA

Blau, Eve.
Ruskinian Gothic.

Bibliography: p.
Includes index.
1. Deane, Thomas, 1792-1871.   2. Wood-
ward, Benjamin, 1816-1861.   3. Gothic revival
(Architecture)—Great Britain.   I. Title.
NA997.D43B5   720′.92′2   81-7302
ISBN 0-691-03984-4   AACR2
ISBN 0-691-10127-2 (pbk.)

*Eve Blau has taught at Yale and Brown universities and is now
Assistant Professor of the History of Art at Wesleyan University.
In addition to this book, she has lectured and published on various
aspects of Victorian architecture.*

To my mother and my father

CONTENTS

[vii]

ACKNOWLEDGMENTS

Of the many people who helped me in the preparation and writing of this book I owe a special debt of gratitude to George L. Hersey for his support, advice, and friendship in my years as his student at Yale, where work on this project began. I am deeply grateful for his guidance and encouragement at every stage and his assistance with the preparation of the manuscript. No one could have done more. I am also indebted to Vincent Scully, whose work has been an inspiration to all students of architectural history, and who has been for me an invaluable teacher, mentor, and friend for many years. I would also like to thank Sir Nikolaus Pevsner and Sir John Summerson, both of whom encouraged my research plans and were generous with their time and advice when I consulted them at an early stage in the project. I am further indebted to Henry-Russell Hitchcock and Allan Greenberg, who read the manuscript and provided many valuable suggestions for its improvement.

Much of the work was done in London and could not have been accomplished without the assistance of several people who directed me to sources, supplied information, and made important material available. I owe thanks to John Gordon Christian, Michael Darby, Irene K. Falkiner, Geoffrey Fisher, Mark Girouard, Peter Howell, Lady Rosalie Mander, John Newman, John O'Callaghan, Andrew Saint, Helen Smith, Raleigh Trevelyan, and Clive Wainwright. I am also under obligation to the librarians and staff of the British Library, Greater London Council, Guildhall Library, Public Record Office, Royal Institute of British Architects, and the Victoria and Albert Museum for their services.

In Oxford I was assisted by several individuals and institutions. In particular, I would like to thank Mr. Turner (Secretary of the Oxford Museum), David Vaizey and Ruth Vyse (of the Oxford University Archives), Malcolm Graham (City Library, Oxford), Morna R. Chichester (Christ Church College, Library), R. Walters (Librarian of the Oxford Union), and the staff of the Bodleian Library, who were especially helpful and offered every courtesy. I am also obliged to Francis Haskell, Howard Colvin, Dr. H. C. Harley, John D. Renton, and J. M. Edmonds for their help.

In Dublin I am particularly indebted to Edward MacParland and Jeanne Sheehy for supplying me with information and for their suggestions, help, and friendship on many occasions. I also owe thanks to Mark Bence-Jones, Colonel Boydell, Philip Cassidy, Maurice Craig, Desmond Fitzgerald Knight of Glin, Desmond Guinness, Charles Lysaght, Freddie O'Dwyer, Nicholas Shaeff, and David Tomkin; and a special note of gratitude

[ix]

ACKNOWLEDGMENTS

to Michael Hewson of the National Library and William O'Sullivan of the Manuscripts Room, Trinity College Library.

Elsewhere in Ireland I wish to thank T. F. MacNamara, City Architect in Cork for his assistance, friendship, and generosity in sharing information from his own work-in-progress on the history of Cork architecture. Further thanks go to Patrick Madden (County Librarian), Edward McCarthy (College Engineer, University College, Cork), and Richard Wood, all of whom helped with my research in Cork; Mrs. Kathleen Lanigan and Mrs. Peggy Haughton for their kind assistance in Kilkenny; and Anne Healy and Tom Lynch in Killarney.

To the Bodleian Library, Cork City Library, National Gallery and National Library of Ireland, Royal Irish Academy, Trinity College Library, the Marquis of Ormonde, the Trevelyan Family, and Violet Sparrow I am indebted for allowing me to quote and reproduce material from unpublished manuscripts in their possession.

The nature of this project required large amounts of time visiting and photographing buildings in Ireland and England. I am sincerely grateful in every case to the owners and trustees for their essential courtesies.

The Kress Foundation and the Institute for International Education supported my research in Britain for two years, and I am particularly grateful to Mary K. Davis of the Kress Foundation for her personal support and interest.

Finally, I owe a great debt of thanks to friends and family; Mr. and Mrs. Roger Ellis for their generous hospitality, kindness, and care during my final months in London; my parents and sister for their good counsel and many intangibles which sustained me throughout the preparation of this book. My greatest thanks go to Nicolas Sanderson, who accompanied me to Ireland, on innumerable smaller trips within England, and took almost all the photographs for this book. Without his help, insights, and good-humored support this work could not have been done.

EVE BLAU
Middletown, Connecticut
September 1980

LIST OF ILLUSTRATIONS

Each monument is identified fully at its first appearance. Since the illustrations for any given monument are grouped together in most cases, a brief form of reference is employed for subsequent illustrations of the same work.

Photographs by Nicolas Sanderson unless otherwise indicated.

LIST OF ILLUSTRATIONS

LIST OF ILLUSTRATIONS

LIST OF ILLUSTRATIONS

LIST OF ILLUSTRATIONS

LIST OF ILLUSTRATIONS

LIST OF FREQUENTLY USED ABBREVIATIONS

Crofton Croker Correspondence	Thomas Crofton Croker Correspondence, Cork City Library
DNB	*Dictionary of National Biography*
JCHAS	*Journal of the Cork Historical and Archaeological Society*
JRIBA	*Journal of the Royal Institute of British Architects*
JRIAI	*Journal of the Royal Institute of the Architects of Ireland*
JSAH	*Journal of the Society of Architectural Historians*
MS. Acland	Acland Manuscripts, Bodleian Library, Oxford
MS. TOP. OXON. D. 144	Letter from D. G. Rossetti to Alexander Gilchrist, June 1861, Bodleian Library, Oxford
OUM Committee	Oxford University Museum Committee
Papers of OUM	Papers of the Oxford University Museum, Oxford University Archives, Oxford
Pembroke Estate Office	Papers and Correspondence, Pembroke Estates, Pembroke Estate Office, Dublin
RHA	Royal Hibernian Academy
RIA	Royal Irish Academy
RIBA	Royal Institute of British Architects
TCD	Trinity College Museum, Dublin
WCT 70, Newcastle	W. C. Trevelyan Papers, University Library Newcastle
Works of Ruskin	E. T. Cook and A. Wedderburn (eds.). *The Works of John Ruskin*. 39 vols. London, 1903-1912.

RUSKINIAN GOTHIC

INTRODUCTION

When a revival of Irish progress came after the famine of 1847, and was marked by a hopeful national exhibition in 1853, it found a circle of architects, practitioners trained in local works, not of first class, and practically unconcerned with Gothic revivals or controversies of their calling in an outside world. It was such a complacent community that the two young architects of Cork, Benjamin Woodward and Thomas Newenham Deane, invaded about 1852, shocking proprieties of established methods of practice, and preaching a new gospel of architecture of an unknown Ruskinite cult. Mr. Ruskin himself visited Dublin, and in his lectures and writings lauded the young architects as men of the future dispensation.[1]

Indeed, before the decade was over Deane and Woodward, working with the gifted stone carvers James and John O'Shea had created what is here analyzed in detail as a truly Ruskinian architecture. The earliest significant exponents of Ruskin's precepts, the firm was responsible for shaping a Ruskinian Gothic style in the early 1850s that was distinct both in form and theoretical basis from the concurrently evolving High Victorian Gothic.

Yet, paradoxically, Deane and Woodward remain among the most understudied architects of significant stature in the mid-Victorian period. While a great deal of scholarly research and writing has been devoted to Ruskin's influence on Victorian architecture, the role of his self-avowed disciples has received only a narrow and highly repetitive treatment. Since Charles Eastlake's pioneering *History of the Gothic Revival* in 1872, historians in dealing with Deane and Woodward have been content to reiterate the by now well-known story of the Oxford Museum. In all of these accounts it is Ruskin who dominates the foreground while Deane and Woodward, the Museum's architects, remain shadowy and obscure. Otherwise, two of the firm's other buildings of the mid-fifties—the Oxford Union, with

[3]

its ill-fated mural paintings by the Pre-Raphaelites, and the Crown Life Company office building in London—are generally discussed in the context of Victorian painting and commercial architecture respectively. But the firm's work in other areas and the architects themselves remain largely ignored, and Deane and Woodward's career and oeuvre as a whole have never received comprehensive treatment.[2]

The reasons for this neglect are threefold. First, the relative inaccessibility of information on the architects and many of their works has made study of their achievement difficult. While some of their most important and influential works were built in England, and while for a time they opened offices in Oxford and London, the firm's headquarters and the majority of their buildings were in Ireland. Because of the relative remoteness of the Dublin-based practice these Irish works received little contemporary notice in the British building press and were virtually unknown in England. Like much other Irish architecture of the period these buildings have remained obscure, though recently some (notably Trinity College Museum and the Kildare Street Club in Dublin) have been resurrected by Douglas Richardson in his important study, *Gothic Revival Architecture in Ireland*.[3]

Furthermore, over the years the buildings themselves and their documentation have fared badly also. In Ireland the Troubles in 1916 and 1922 took their toll in the destruction of both records and buildings. Since then, mostly through carelessness or for economic reasons, other buildings by the firm have been demolished or altered beyond recognition and today the future of even more is threatened. In England Deane and Woodward's work has fared little better. All of their buildings in London have been destroyed, some within a few years of their completion. In 1960 even the Oxford Museum was threatened and as recently as 1975 the firm's only house in Wales was demolished.

The second reason for the neglect of the firm's work is the suppression of the Woodward memoir.[4] Following the death of the latter, who was the designer of the partnership, in 1861, a committee was formed to raise subscriptions and gather material for a memorial to him. This was to include a comprehensive biographical and critical sketch of his life and work and a photographic record of the firm's buildings. Nothing, however, came of the project and the memoir was never written, largely because of strong opposition to the scheme by the Deanes. Over time the documentation gathered and other Woodward papers disappeared. These have still not come to light, though in 1973 five private sketchbooks of Woodward's, containing information on the design of some of the firm's major buildings, were discovered in the collection of Thomas Newenham Deane papers in the National Gallery of Ireland.[5]

The third reason is more complex and must be examined in some detail, for it involves a key aspect of the present book and indeed the whole question of the constituents of Ruskinian Gothic. This is that the question of Ruskin's influence on Victorian architecture in the 1850s has remained an unresolved and highly controversial issue.

Early writers on the Gothic Revival tended to endorse Ruskin's much-quoted claim in 1872 that "I have had indirect influence on nearly every cheap villa-builder between this [Denmark Hill] and Bromley; and there is scarcely a public house near the Crystal Palace but sells its gin and bitters under pseudo-Venetian capitals copied from the Church of the Madonna of Health or of Miracles. And one of my principal notions for leaving my present house is that it is surrounded everywhere by the accursed Frankenstein monsters of, indirectly, my own making."[6] Thus, Charles Eastlake considered Ruskin to have initiated the mature phase of the Gothic Revival in the 1850s and gave him the responsibility for introducing Italian Gothic and for freeing the Revival from its earlier ecclesiastical, nationalistic, and picturesque associations.[7] This view of Ruskin's central role in the development of High Victorian Gothic was commonly accepted, even exaggerated, as Kenneth Clark recalled in 1927, "In Oxford it was universally believed that Ruskin had built Keble . . . [he] was believed also to have designed Balliol Chapel and Meadow Buildings at Christ Church."[8] Clark himself was called a liar in a public meeting at the time for denying Ruskin's part in these buildings. But nevertheless, he too claimed that Ruskin, by introducing Italian Gothic into Britain had sown the seeds of destruction in the Ecclesiologists' "tidy garden and immediately it became a tangle of exotic weeds."[9] Before Ruskin, the Revivalists had been inspired and guided by a religious/patriotic vision. As Clark pointed out, Ruskin opposed the first and effectively destroyed the second by introducing Italian Gothic modes. It should be pointed out that in sharp distinction to Pugin and the Ecclesiologists Ruskin could be wholeheartedly anti-English. The result was the international confusion of styles which characterized Victorian architecture of the 1850s.[10]

The decisive turning point in this debate came in 1954 when Henry-Russell Hitchcock readdressed the question of Ruskin's influence on Gothic Revival architecture in the 1850s in terms of "Ruskin or Butterfield?" By isolating the distinctive characteristics of High Victorian Gothic as an increasing use by architects of ideas and details of Continental origin—primarily Italian, but also German and Flemish; the introduction of new materials, especially iron, brick, and tiles, both for structural and ornamental purposes; the extension of Gothic beyond ecclesiastical uses; and structural polychromy, Hitchcock pointed out that Ruskin's influence on these developments was hardly as significant as had hitherto been accepted.[11] Instead, he concluded that it was William Butterfield rather than Ruskin who was primarily responsible for initiating High Victorian Gothic. It was not Ruskin's *Seven Lamps of Architecture*, of 1849, but Butterfield's All Saints, Margaret Street, begun in the same year and consecrated by 1856 (a building not even mentioned in the early editions of Clark's book), which became the High Victorian model with its harsh outlines, accented vertically, irregularity, "brutal" juxtaposition of simplified forms, and powerful detail.[12] Indeed, Hitchcock saw Ruskin's role in High Victorian Gothic in the 1850s as confirming the propriety of following Butterfield's stylistic lead, and asserted that "no architect of the 50's attempted to mold his methods of design step by step upon [Ruskin's] precepts."[13]

In recent years a number of significant studies of mid-Victorian architecture have appeared, which, following Hitchcock's lead, have tended to focus on the essentially "Butterfieldian" High Victorian Gothic of the 1850s while underplaying the significance of Ruskin's writings and dealing only summarily, if at all, with Deane and Woodward's architecture. In 1971 Paul Thompson agreed with Hitchcock in seeing Butterfield as the originator of the High Victorian phase of the Gothic Revival with the introduction in All Saints of constructional polychromy, the latter being, for him, the "hallmark of High Victorian architecture."[14] Butterfield, Thompson maintained, was influenced to a certain extent by Ruskin's *Seven Lamps*, but much more of the church is non-Ruskinian, if not anti-Ruskinian.[15]

Georg Germann, in 1972, saw Ruskin's contribution to architectural theory as merely echoing and enforcing views already expressed by Butterfield's patrons, the Ecclesiological Society. Germann isolated as the "one really independent and fertile argument" in Ruskin's *Seven Lamps* and "Nature of Gothic" in *Stones of Venice*, II: the importance of independent creative effort on the part of the workmen. But he skipped over the work of Deane and Woodward in the 1850s and instead linked this concept with the social idealism of William Morris over a decade later.[16]

Like Germann, Stefan Muthesius in his monograph on the High Victorian

Movement of the same year, claimed that Ruskin's "comments hardly stood out from the mass of architectural criticism of the day."[17] At the same time, however, he noted that Ruskin's views on architectural sculpture and painting were influential from the mid- to late 1850s on, largely through Deane and Woodward's works. But Muthesius dealt neither with Ruskin's influence nor with Deane and Woodward's work in any detail.[18]

Finally, again in 1972, George Hersey turned the question around and found evidence of Butterfield's influence on Ruskin's later writings after the *Seven Lamps*.[19] That is, he agreed with Hitchcock in assigning Ruskin a subsidiary role in the genesis of High Victorian Gothic, but carried the argument further by asserting that Ruskin's precepts of 1849 were actually in opposition to the new style of Butterfield's All Saints.[20] Hersey recognized not only the disparity between Ruskin's early architectural principles and the High Victorian Gothic of the Ecclesiologists, but also saw Ruskin's writings as formulating an independent style which was neither High Victorian Gothic nor specifically Venetian Gothic. He identified this essentially symmetrical, classicizing, polychromatic Ruskinian ideal of the *Seven Lamps* with Deane and Woodward's Oxford Museum.[21]

But Hersey also suggested that this classicizing style had already appeared in England, independently of Ruskin's influence, in J. W. Wild's St. Martin's Northern Schools, in Soho of 1849. Though St. Martin's was built in an Italian Gothic mode, and direct sources for the design can be found in northern and central Italian civic architecture of the fourteenth and fifteenth centuries—it is hardly Ruskinian.

Furthermore, Hersey's primary concern was nevertheless with High Victorian Gothic. He saw Ruskinian Gothic as a counter-style, antithetical to High Victorian Gothic, and which "even helped to denature it."[22] Consequently he was only concerned with those elements of Ruskinism and, by extension, Deane and Woodward's architecture, which contributed to the dissolution of the mainstream High Victorian Gothic style. Thus Hersey too left the central question of Ruskin's role in the formation of the Ruskinian Gothic style identified with Deane and Woodward's work unanswered.

This book attempts to take the next step: to trace the development of Deane and Woodward's individual Ruskinian style as it evolved in the sixteen-year period of the partnership and to determine the separate roles played by Ruskin and Woodward in its formation. It will be seen that Ruskin's influence—both that which came about through his books and that which he exercised more or less on the site in visits to Oxford as well as through his letters and conversations with the architects and his friends associated with the firm—stands well apart from the practical design and building of the structures which they affected. Ruskin's principles alone were too limited to engender a distinctive architectural style. That is, while he was responsible for advocating the use of particular materials, surface patterns, and an independent role for the decorative carvers, it was Woodward, not Ruskin, who provided the program, planning, siting, composition, structural engineering, fenestration—in short, most of what a building truly is—for the key "Ruskinian" Gothic buildings at Oxford and elsewhere. And it was Woodward who was primarily responsible for actually shaping the Ruskinian Gothic style and for putting into practice Ruskin's most important ideas concerning workmanship, craft, and the liberty of the craftsman.

The firm of Deane and Woodward was an outgrowth of the original Cork-based practice of Sir Thomas Deane (1792-1871).[23] The Deanes had been in the building trade in Cork since the middle of the eighteenth century. Originally from Ayreshire, in Scotland, they emigrated in the seventeenth century to Ulster as Protestant settlers in Donaghadee, County Down, and from there to Cork where, altogether within five generations, at least fifteen Deanes were builders, architects, or surveyors.[24]

Thomas Deane (Fig. 1) began practicing as an architect and builder in 1806, when at the age of fourteen following his father's death he took over the family business with his mother.[25] He possessed a precocious talent for both business and design. In 1811 he won his first major commission for the Cork Commercial Buildings in a competition against William Wilkins. In the 1820s and 1830s Deane became the principal architect and builder in the county. Active in local politics, he was twice elected High Sheriff (Mayor) of Cork, in 1815 and 1830, at which time he was knighted for his public services by the Duke of Northumberland, then Lord Lieutenant of Ireland. In partnership with his brothers he executed a number of banks and other civic structures, notably the Old Savings Bank (1824), the portico of the County Court House (1835), the Bank of Ireland (1838-1840), and the New Savings Bank (1840-1842). Competent but essentially conventional Neo-classical works, the sound functional planning, solid construction, and keen sense of economy and utility which all these buildings exhibit, show Deane's skill in dealing with the more pragmatic aspects of design. These qualities of Deane's work as well as the bold but finely detailed architectural ornament and evident sensitivity to materials, continued to characterize the firm's later buildings designed by Woodward. On the other hand, Deane's one Gothic work of this period, Dromore Castle (1831-1836) in County Kerry, was a great rambling castellated Neo-Tudor pile. Its crude detail, falsity of scale, mock battlements, sham vaults and archways place it firmly within the tradition of late Georgian "Gothick" castles and Sir Thomas among the lesser provincial practitioners in the mode.[26]

But when Benjamin Woodward (Fig. 2) entered the office in 1845 the style and quality of the firm's Gothic work underwent a dramatic change. Woodward's passionate interest in medieval architecture, and the deeply earnest commitment which he brought to his art, infused the firm's designs with a vitality, intensity, and originality that made them unique in the Victorian age.

Little is known of Benjamin Woodward's early life. He was born on November 16, 1816, in Tullamore, County Offaly (then Kings County). His father, Charles Woodward, a captain in the Meath Militia, had married Mary Atkinson of Kells, County Meath, shortly before moving to Tullamore in about 1810 where the Militia was quartered at the time.[27]

The Woodwards were a Cromwellian family, that is, Anglo-Irish Protestants who had settled in Ireland in the seventeenth century. The original English settler was a Major Benjamin Woodward, an officer in Cornwall's Horse serving in Ireland in the Commonwealth period, who had come over with the victorious Parliamentary Army to crush the Irish insurrection in 1649-1650. Listed as an adventurer for lands in Ireland, Woodward, like many other English soldiers of the Commonwealth, was granted lands in County Meath by Cromwell in the 1650s. By the end of the seventeenth century the Woodwards, whose property and seat were in Drumbaragh, near Kells, were among the principal Anglo-Irish families in Ireland.[28]

No record of Benjamin Woodward's training and early career has survived. His obituary in the *Dublin Builder* records that he received his professional education in Ireland, where he was articled to a civil engineer.[29] It is unlikely that he trained in Tullamore, as the family did not remain there long. He was probably educated in Dublin or Cork and served his articles with an engineer in the latter city.[30] It is possible that the family was connected to the Woodwards of Cork; the most notable of whom was Richard Woodward, Bishop of Cloyne from 1781 to 1794. His son, Benjamin Blake Woodward (1769-1841), was a prominent barrister and Member of Parliament for Middleton, County Cork, and may well have had connections in the building trade there.[31]

The *Dublin Builder* further noted that while training as a civil engineer Woodward "zealously cultivated an acquaintance with the artistic department of architecture, particularly with the branches of Medieval art. In the walk in which he has become distinguished, he was, therefore, self-taught."[32] Woodward's interest in medieval art may well have been stimulated by the resurgence of Irish archaeological and antiquarian publications in the 1830s and 1840s which accompanied the rise of political nationalism in these years.[33] At this time A.W.N. Pugin, who also encouraged the study of Irish medieval architecture, began his ecclesiastical work in Ireland.[34] As will be seen Woodward's own work was to be influenced by Pugin's conventual buildings in Ireland, and he was deeply impressed by Pugin's published writings, some of which appeared in the *Dublin Review* in 1841. Woodward undertook his own antiquarian studies in the early 1840s in a series of extant measured drawings of the buildings at Cashel and the Abbey of Holycross in County Tipperary, dated June 1844.[35]

It is possible that Woodward, after a brief association with the Cork architects Richard and William Vitruvius Morrison in the late 1830s, was already affiliated with the Deanes at this time.[36] However, it would seem most probable that he was first brought into the firm to help with the working drawings for Queen's College, Cork in 1845-1846, the firm's most important commission to date. Deane was particularly worried about the Queen's College designs which were to be Gothic, a mode in which he had little experience or talent.[37] Thus it is not surprising that he took on Woodward, the as yet unknown young architect with a passionate interest in medieval architecture and a "mind burning to excel," to help him.[38]

The new association of Deane and Woodward was a union of opposites. The *Builder* described Sir Thomas Deane as "of a hopeful, cheerful spirit, with a kindliness of disposition and happy wit characteristic of his country."[39] He had an expansive personality and was naturally gregarious and aggressive, even bombastic. Possessed of great personal drive and energy, Deane was a shrewd businessman, politician, financier, and something of an opportunist who thrived in the competitive world of business and public life. Physically robust, he married three times, on the third occasion when he was over sixty, and fathered six children.

Woodward, on the other hand, was quiet, reserved, and diffident. D. G.

Rossetti described him as "the stillest creature that ever breathed out of an oyster shell."[40] William Rossetti noted that "he was the very reverse of what Irish men are currently assumed to be and was the most modest, retiring and shyly taciturn man of noticeable talent whom it was ever my fortune to meet. He was of handsome and stately presence, eminently gentle and courteous."[41] Richard Brash, a Cork architect, called him "a man of most refined and cultivated taste, a scholar and a gentleman, one of the most amiable and unselfish of men."[42] Throughout his life Woodward suffered from recurring bouts of the consumption which finally killed him in his forty-sixth year. Perhaps for this reason he never married, and though his friendships were, in Rossetti's words, "of that faithful kind which is love for life," few of them were intimate.[43] Woodward's only passion would seem to have been for his work, to which he was "unalterably devoted," and "the art which he loved . . . more dearly than his life."[44]

Together, Sir Thomas Deane and Benjamin Woodward formed a formidable team. Initially it was through Deane's connections, long experience, and high standing in the profession that the firm obtained the commissions which provided Woodward with opportunities for exercising his talent. But the firm's later success was chiefly due to Woodward. After Thomas Newenham Deane (Fig. 3), who had neither his father's business acumen nor Woodward's creative ability, joined the firm in the early 1850s, and Sir Thomas ceased to play an active role in the business, Woodward assumed the lead in the partnership. We can now begin the process of assessing the contribution of this gifted architect, bringing him out of obscurity to assign him his rightful place as one of the more original minds in Victorian architecture.

I

THE BEGINNINGS IN IRELAND

QUEEN'S COLLEGE, CORK

The 1840s in Ireland were a time of violent political and economic upheaval. The decade began with the struggle for repeal of the Union with Great Britain led by Daniel O'Connell. This movement collapsed in October 1843 and O'Connell died in 1847. The cause was taken up by Young Ireland, a militant movement of romantic nationalists, but this too ended in failure with the abortive insurrection of 1848. At mid-decade Ireland was further hit by devastating famine and widespread rural unemployment. The final years of the decade were a period of gradual reconciliation and reconstruction in the form of government relief projects.[1]

As part of the British government's relief effort, a series of building projects was organized by the Board of Public Works in Ireland, with the purpose of providing labor and wages for the local population as well as to answer the pressing need for new roads, hospitals, asylums, schools, and colleges.[2]

One of the first of these projects was the building of three provincial colleges, called the Queen's Colleges, to serve the south in Cork, the north in Belfast, and the west in Galway. The Commissioners of Public Works in Ireland charged with the responsibility to select sites, appoint architects, and prepare plans,[3] chose three local Irish architects to design the colleges—Sir Thomas Deane for Cork, Charles Lanyon for Belfast, and J. B. Keane for Galway. The colleges were incorporated on December 30, 1845, and a single set of specifications was drafted for all three buildings.

Following the example of the Scottish Universities, the Queen's Colleges were all nonsectarian, without theological faculties, nonresidential, and professorial rather than tutorial. They were essentially middle-class institutions with a strong professional and scientific bias.

The sites chosen, all on the periphery of the towns, measured approximately ten acres each. The accommodation requirements were a Great Hall for public and ceremonial purposes, a museum of natural history and geology, a library, a botanic garden, a chemical laboratory, a "cabinet" for philosophical and mechanical apparatus, six lecture theaters holding two hundred persons each, residences for the President and Vice-President, and a cloister for exercise in wet weather. The specifications were changed many times until various compromises were reached in the different colleges and the plans and elevations were published in the Parliamentary "Blue Books" in 1847-1848.[4]

The one thing not set down in the Commissioner's specifications was the architectural style of the buildings; presumably this was left to the individual architects involved. In December 1848, *The Builder* reported that "the style of architecture adopted in each case is the Gothic."[5] The *Ecclesiologist*, chief architectural voice of High Church Anglicanism, was also quick to comment on the new designs—dubbing the Queen's Colleges the "Godless Colleges" and noting ironically, "It is a curious 'fact' that all these structures have put on the garb of Christian architecture, and try to look like 'Colleges,' as of old the word was known; although by a curious sort of unconscious symbolism, the style in every case is the most mundane of its sort, the Third Pointed."[6]

Both Keane and Lanyon looked to Oxford for their models.[7] Deane and Woodward, however, attempted instead to find a more resourceful solution. As a result, Cork is the most advanced of the colleges and closest in spirit and execution to the "real" Victorian Gothic of Pugin and Butterfield in the 1840s.

The firm received the commission in Cork in December 1845. The work progressed rapidly and preliminary drawings were sent to London for approval by the Treasury before May 1846. Approval to proceed was granted in June and working drawings were made in January 1847. It was at this point that Sir Thomas Deane probably brought Benjamin Woodward into the firm. Kearns Deane (Sir Thomas' brother and partner until his death in January 1847) may have had a hand in preparing the preliminary drawings but since these have not survived it is impossible to tell how much they were subsequently altered by Woodward. In any case, a completely new set of drawings (later published in the Board of Works Sixteenth Report) was made with Woodward's assistance in 1847.[8] Construction began early in 1847. The college was substantially complete by the end of 1848 and was officially opened on November 7, 1849.[9]

The building is well situated on the top of a hill overlooking the river Lee, on the site of the ancient Gill Abbey, a school founded in the seventh century by the patron saint of Cork, from whom it derived its motto: Where Finbarr taught let Munster learn. The initial prospect can be best appreciated from a contemporary lithograph which hangs in the college (Fig. 4). Viewed from below, the imposing buttressed and battlemented pile of brilliant white limestone, quarried on the site, is first seen rising from the crest of the hill. The library juts forward at right angles to the main block. Beyond this, the Aula Maxima dominates the eastern ridge of the hill. Then, to the west of the library, the composition falls back along the contour of the hill to the vertical axis of the gate tower on the northwest. The college is entered through an arched passage at the base of this tower. Once inside the courtyard (Fig. 5), the mood and scale of the building change dramatically. Enclosed on three sides by low two-story wings, the quadrangle is open to the south. The effect is one of soft sunlight, peace, and regularity, a marked contrast to the large jutting masses on the exterior.

The external massing of the college directly expresses the spatial arrangement of the interior in a way that shows that Woodward had absorbed the principles of functional associationism being practiced in Britain at the time. The examination hall and library, the most important and largest single elements, are given prominence along the principal north range. Set off from the main quad in elevation and plan (Figs. 6, 7), they form a separate block of individually articulated units. This arrangement has both a symbolic and functional rationale. As the intellectual fountainhead of the university, the library occupies the focal point of the complex and is clearly differentiated from the contiguous buildings by its north-south axis and freestanding gable ends. The examination hall functions primarily as a place of assembly on ceremonial occasions and for administering examinations. Symbolically it is the most significant part of the institution and at the same time the least-used space. Deane and Woodward's design takes account of both considerations. Away from the main circulation area, on the north-east corner of the complex, the hall is also the largest and most imposing element of the composition.

Similarly, the difference in status of the President's and Vice-President's houses (Figs. 8, 9) in the east wing is expressed not only by the sizes of the respective residences and the treatment of the doorways on the entrance front, but also associationally. The President's house, with the elegantly balanced symmetry of its central block evokes the restrained dignity and authority of the manor house. The Vice-President's house, on the other hand, with its asymmetrical front and dormered kitchen wing, alludes to something less grand and more dependent in character though equally dignified: the country vicarage.

Deane and Woodward's design is also structurally expressive. The buttresses are purely functional, never superfluous or ornamental. There are also masonry diaphragm arches in the cloister of the west wing and a true transverse rib vault in the entrance arch under the gate tower.

Some of the most notable structural features are the wide variety of wooden beam roofs used throughout the college. Meticulously measured and designed, these structures were separately diagrammed in a series of drawings preserved in the college archives.[10] The most impressive of these is the hammer beam roof in the examination hall. The central arched braces follow the outline of the east window, thus effectively lowering the ceiling and forming a continuous arcade down the length of the hall. From the sectional drawing of the hall (Fig. 10) it is easy to see the way in which the interior hammer beams and wall posts lock into and form a unified support system with the masonry buttresses on the exterior. In general, the structural simplicity of these roofs, showing Deane and Woodward's skill in combining sound engineering with effective design, were to remain an outstanding characteristic of the firm's subsequent work.

Such wooden roofs were important features of Gothic Revival architecture generally in the 1840s. The more elaborate hammer beam roofs, with their explicit associations with the banqueting or great hall of the medieval manor, were revived in domestic architecture along with the Neo-Tudor and Elizabethan styles. Gothic Revival churches of the 1840s tended toward simpler structures. But all in all, the emphasis was on constructional truthfulness, materials, and craftsmanship associated with medieval building.[11]

Stylistic sources for Queen's College, such as the colleges at Oxford have been mentioned as well as unspecified Elizabethan and Tudor prototypes.[12] But the clearest influence came from A.W.N. Pugin. In 1843 Pugin called at length for a revival in new college construction of "that scholastic gravity of character, the reverend and solemn appearance, that is found in the ancient erections."[13] Where

> every portion of these edifices had its distinguishing character and elevation in order to give due effect to the gate-house, refectory and other important parts of the building, the chambers never exceeded the height of one storey above the ground floor. A very characteristic feature of the old collegiate building is the position of the chimneys, which are made to project from the front walls of the building.[14]

Woodward was no doubt familiar with this, and it is possible that he made a conscious attempt to follow, at least partially, Pugin's suggestions. As the College was nondenominational and nonresidential, the chapel and refectory are naturally absent from the design, which nevertheless alludes to these features in the examination hall and library and incorporates much of the rest of Pugin's college program, including the central courtyard, cloister, and domestic range.

Other similarities derive from Woodward's knowledge of Pugin's illustrations of collegiate and related buildings in his published writings. In particular, Pugin's "Ancient Residences for the Poor" (Fig. 11) relate very closely to Queen's College, with its three-sided cloistered quadrangle and gate tower.[15]

In the last analysis, however, the College is closest in spirit to Pugin's Irish conventual work. Pugin designed two complete convents in Ireland, the Presentation Convent in Waterford of 1842-1848 and the Convent of Our Lady of Mercy, Birr, County Offaly, of 1845-1847. A design of the latter was published in the *Catholic Directory* in 1845. These were both rather severe structures, with blocks grouped around rectangular cloisters. The buttresses and projecting chimneys were the only irregular features on the otherwise unornamented walls. Here also Pugin purposely adopted a more indigenous vernacular style that was "rude and simple, massive and solemn," like the true medieval architecture of Ireland prior to the Norman invasion. The emphasis is on the materials (usually the local limestone and granite) with broad planes and varied textures. Queen's College displays a similar sense of wall plane and materials.

But the functional articulation and cranky detailing of the President's, and especially the Vice-President's, residences are closer to Butterfield's early work of this period, such as the vicarage at Coalpit Heath, Gloucestershire, 1844-1845, which was published in the *Ecclesiologist* in 1845, and St. Augustine's Missionary College, Canterbury (1845-1848), illustrations of which appeared in the *Builder* in 1848 and the *Illustrated London News* in 1847.[16] Indeed, this free manipulation of forms for functionally expressive purposes never appears in Pugin's collegiate or conventual work. Instead, Pugin used a recognizable vocabulary of Gothic forms which embody their function in their form. The references are only to the medieval prototypes. These historical associations also operate at Queen's College; but whereas in Pugin's work functionalism is symbolic, implicit in the forms themselves, at Queen's College it is practical and explicit.

Of course, far more important than the identification of possible sources for Queen's College is the essential independence of the work. The design owes something to the influence of Pugin and Butterfield, but an equal amount is due to practical adjustments to functional demands. Furthermore, certain qualities of the work, including the emphasis on structure and materials, and the tendency toward simple functional design were already there in Deane's earlier buildings.[17]

But the most remarkable feature of Queen's College—the newly sharp understanding of the principles of Gothic architecture—is probably due to Woodward alone. Unlike Pugin and Butterfield, Woodward did not have opportunities to study a wide variety of well-preserved English medieval work at first hand. Much of his early knowledge of medieval architecture and ornament must have been acquired from books and illustrations. However, he had studied Irish medieval architecture at first hand and was an early member of the Royal Society of Antiquaries of Ireland, to which he was elected in 1852 when it was known as the Kilkenny Archaeological Society.[18] We know that he undertook his own antiquarian studies in the early 1840s and made measured drawings of the buildings at Cashel and Holy Cross Abbey in County Tipperary.[19] These carefully executed line drawings reveal Woodward's early preoccupation, independent of the influence of Ruskin, with architectural ornament. Over half of the drawings are precise renderings of sculptural detail, one of which Woodward submitted to the *Builder* (it appeared on May 6, 1848).[20] However, Woodward's antiquarian study and architectural practice were never independent activities; as we will see, the drawings of Holy Cross Abbey became the source for much of the architectural ornament at Queen's College.

In this regard a group of tracings in the college archives are most interesting for the information they give about the firm's method of design. They show that the decorative features were conceived separately from the basic design of the architecture and added as the construction of the building proceeded.[21] This method allowed for considerable flexibility and in part accounts for the aptness, spontaneity, and diversity of the architectural ornament here as in all of Deane and Woodward's subsequent buildings.

This will become a hallmark of Ruskinian Gothic. Another hallmark has to do with the independence of the decorative carvers. The stone carving at Queen's College is probably the work of the brothers John and James O'Shea, and their nephew Edward Whellan (sometimes spelled Whelland), who later followed Deane and Woodward to Dublin, Oxford, and London and continued to work for the firm until Woodward's death in 1861.[22] Though no record of the O'Sheas' employment at Queen's College exists, it seems possible for a number of reasons to conjecture that they were responsible for the high quality of the stone carving at Cork.

The O'Sheas came from Ballyhooly, County Cork, just fifteen miles north of

Cork itself. They could have learned their trade as stonecutters in any of the numerous limestone quarries that were worked in that part of the County. During the famine years many new quarries were opened and provided employment for large numbers of laborers and stonecutters. Sir Thomas Deane, who was also active in the building trade, is said to have discovered one of the O'Sheas "as a boy, carving a piece of wood so cleverly, he had him trained."[23] Whatever the case may be, it seems probable that they were taken on by Deane and were trained as stone carvers in his employ, the usual way in Ireland that masons and carvers learned their trade. Later, the O'Sheas became known for the originality of their lively naturalistic carvings of plant and animal forms. They are reputed to have followed their own inclinations with a minimum of supervision and to have worked directly from nature copying specimens which they collected and brought with them into the stoneyard. At Queen's College, however, they were not yet given such a free hand, for it appears that the design and execution of the carved ornament was closely supervised by Woodward.

This ornament is sparse, confined on the exterior mostly to the label steps, hood moldings, and corbels. The motifs are predominantly Irish and heraldic. Characteristically Irish are the nobbly "seaweed" forms, the human heads, the grotesques, and "vegetation" heads (Fig. 12). Many are similar to those that Woodward had studied and drawn in 1844 at Holy Cross Abbey and Cashel. A good example, directly borrowed from Holy Cross, is the termination of a hood molding over the tower window carved with delicately intertwining tendrils (Fig. 13). Several of the corbels on the cloister windows are carved into bolder leaf clusters and plant forms, which also have precedents in the medieval carving at Holy Cross (Fig. 14). In fact, included in Woodward's drawings of the Abbey is a careful study of one of these corbels in the Chapel of the South Transept (Fig. 15). Other borrowings from Holy Cross are the spandril decorations on the entrances to the President's and Vice-President's residences and the carved frieze on the library fireplace copied from the Waking Bier in the Abbey (Figs. 16, 17).[24] The human heads used as label stops on the library and examination hall are familiar motifs at both Cashel and Holy Cross, as are the grotesques and "vegetation" heads. The best known Gothic Revival precedent in Ireland for such rich carving with associative meaning is Francis Johnston's Chapel Royal in Dublin, of 1807-1814, decorated with the busts and heads of Irish kings and saints by the Dublin carver Edward Smyth.

Some of the carving of foliage suggests another possible source. In 1848 the *Builder* published a series of illustrations of carved "Ornamentation From Natural

Types" by James K. Colling,[25] including a number of French Gothic examples but also some from the Chapter House at Southwell Minster. Like the stone used at Southwell, the Cork limestone allowed for deep undercutting—and many of the corbels and label stops at Queen's College closely resemble the foliage carvings in the Chapter House illustrated in the *Builder*.

Two corbels are interesting for their combination of heraldry and naturalism (Fig. 18). One shows a hart springing from the gate of a battlemented tower, the crest of Ireland since the reign of George III. But here the wreath, which on the crest surrounds the tower, has been replaced by naturalistic leafage. On the right the chained and collared wolf is an heraldic attribute of the Barrymores, one of the oldest landowning families in Cork, whose estates comprised most of the County. Here, too, naturalistic foliage has been added and the heraldic image made more likelife. Finally Sir Thomas Deane signed his own work with his monogram "T.D." on one of the cloister corbels.

Equally individual is the wood carving at Cork. The door frames and bookcases in the library (Fig. 19) and examination hall are decorated in bold relief with zigzag, dogtooth, and notched carving. The work is purposely simple in design and craftsmanlike in execution. Like the stone carving, it shows a dislike of smoothness and the clean, sharp edge and has its origins in Irish medieval work and Celtic design. These carved door frames also became identifying characteristics of all Deane and Woodward's later works, as did the decorative wrought-iron work used for functional purposes in the college gates, the gallery railings, and gas lamp fittings in the library and examination hall.[26]

Other precedents for Deane and Woodward's later work, besides the richness of the carved decoration in a variety of materials, were set at Queen's College. Like Pugin, the architects used only indigenous and locally available building materials. All the preparation of these materials, including the stone and wood-cutting and carving, was done by hand and on the construction site.[27] Consequently, every aspect of the work came under the supervision of the architects, and accounts for the quality of the workmanship, sense of coherence, and unity of thought and purpose which so fully underlie the complex.

In general, Queen's College surpasses Pugin's Irish work in quality of craftsmanship and variety of ornament. Pugin's convents and colleges have a bare, stripped quality—an austere simplicity which is appropriately conventual. Queen's College conveys a different spirit of generosity and joy in the diversity of the work.

As the first major work in the Gothic style of the newly formed association of Deane, Woodward and the O'Sheas, Queen's College Cork is an impressive achievement. With it, they established the principle of expressive functional design—as the true "spirit" of Gothic architecture—which was to become the basis for all their subsequent work.

THE KILLARNEY LUNATIC ASYLUM

The Killarney Lunatic Asylum, like Queen's College Cork, was one of a group of similar institutions built at the end of the 1840s in different parts of the country as a famine relief project.[28] Again the architects were given a specific and detailed brief. In 1848 a list of rules and guidelines based on newly reformed principles of medical care for mental patients was published by the Commissioners on Lunacy.[29] These specified that the asylums should be situated within easy access of the township or district for which they were erected, and on elevated sites away from disturbances such as railways, public thoroughfares, and offensive manufactures, with grounds ample enough to accommodate large airing and recreation areas.[30]

To facilitate management the asylum buildings were to be designed so that medical officers and attendants could pass through without having to retrace their steps. The rooms for attendants and supervisors were to be in immediate proximity to the dormitories and medical facilities, and to insure complete separation of the sexes, the building was to be divided into two equal parts for men and for women. Within these divisions, patients were to be further separated into three distinct classes and given separate accommodations: the old and infirm, the noisy and violent, the quiet and harmless.

In the interests of safety the buildings were to be only two storeys high, stone was to be used wherever possible instead of wood, and partition walls were to be insulated and provided with iron doors to seal off communication in case of fire.

For the comfort of the patients, exercise galleries and recreation rooms were to be provided indoors, with southern exposures, to obtain maximum light and air. One-third of the patients were to be accommodated in single rooms and the rest in dormitories for three to twelve patients. Suitable accommodation for the performance of divine service was also required for Protestant and Catholic worship.[31]

Like the colleges, the eight new district asylums in Ireland were to be carried out under the supervision of the Board of Public Works.[32]

The Board suggested, for practical reasons, that

> the style of architecture best suited to the general quality of the building materials in this country, and admitting also of additions being easily made to the asylums hereafter, is the "Gothic," the main walls being of uncoursed rubble masonry, with cut-stone quoins and dressings. It is open, however, to the architect to submit his views to the Commissioners respecting any other style that he may consider more suitable. Whatever style may be adopted, no external coating of stucco or other composition will be allowed.[33]

In fact, all of the architects followed the Board's suggestions and the Irish asylums were all nominally Gothic, displaying a minimal amount of Gothic detailing, and were built in stone quarried in the immediate area.

As regards internal arrangements, the Board's requirements for the new asylums called for greater differentiation in plan than had hitherto been necessary for such buildings.[34] A modified form of the "corridor plan"—a long gallery with rooms off it—was found most suitable. In its simplest form, this plan consisted of a long pavilion with wings at right angles on either end. The best had rooms on only one side of the corridors, which, in the daytime, could also be used as living areas. The administration and reception rooms were generally located in a central block projecting forward from the main pavilion. The service areas were usually situated to the rear of the main building.[35]

The Killarney Lunatic Asylum combines corridors with a system of pavilions. The result is a building of strong, clear outlines, and simple powerful masses. Of all the smaller Irish asylums it displays the greatest amount of High Victorian Gothic "realism" and explicit structural and functional expression.

Neither of the two sets of contract plans required by the Board of Works for the Killarney Asylum has survived. Consequently, we have very little information on the development of the design or Deane and Woodward's early conception of the building. However, a drawing in the National Library in Dublin (Fig. 20) of a building in plan and elevation could be an early design for the asylum.[36] The elevation shows a two-storey structure on a high base encompassed by a bounding wall about the same height as the base. The plan is typical of asylum plans of the 1840s—corridors with cells and dormitories on one side and day rooms at the ends. The basic form is an extended H with the administrative and service offices in a block at the center of the main front. Unusual features for this type of building and plan are the inordinately large Music Hall and Chapel (both called for in the Board of Works guidelines), which project forward from the front on either side of the main entrance. This idea of giving the large communal and ceremonial parts of the building prominence of place and treatment is carried over from Queen's College.

The drawing is obviously an early thinking-through of the design—the elevation being little more than a sketch. On the righthand side of the sheet one side wing of the building has been redrawn, eliminating the forward extension of the transverse range. The result is a more efficient consolidation of space which looks forward to the plan finally adopted. It is easy to see why this early design was rejected by the architects. The chapel and hall are, from a practical point of view, awkwardly situated, while the forward extensions of the side wings are a waste of space which unnecessarily increases the surface area of the building.

The final plans for the Killarney asylum were approved by the Commissioners and work began on the building in 1848. By 1849, as the Board of Works noted in its 17th Report to the Commissioners, construction was well underway and had been in progress for some time. Building continued into 1850 and was more or less completed by August of that year.[37]

Again, as at Queen's College, a commanding hill-top site was chosen. The main front (Figs. 21, 22) which faces south extends almost five hundred feet along the brow of the hill overlooking the town of Killarney, with a spectacular view of Pugin's Cathedral and the mountains and lakes of County Kerry behind. To the rear the grounds spread out in wide open spaces with pastures and fields beyond. The asylum is approached from the east and west past small gatehouses at the bottom of the hill.

Deane and Woodward's original building (which has been much altered since it was first built) was E-shaped in plan, consisting of a long central wing with a projecting central block and side wings extending back from the main front.[38] Pavilions of one or two bays projecting at cross axis from the principal spines are grouped at intervals along their lengths. These features again have a Puginian prototype in the illustration of "Ancient Residences for the Poor" in *Contrasts*, where there is a similar arrangement of two of these pavilions. To the left of the entrance block is a small Protestant chapel. At the back, separated by a narrow open courtyard, is another freestanding two-storey block which contains the Hall (now male dining room) on ground level and the Catholic chapel above (Fig. 23). Behind this, in a complex of smaller outbuildings, are the kitchens, laundry, scullery, and workshops.

Internally, following the Commissioners' prescriptions, the building was divided into equal halves with the female and male wards to either side of the entrance block. Within this division the patients were further classified and the building divided vertically by housing the "old and infirm" patients on the ground floor, the "refractory and violent" cases on the first floor, and the "quiet and harmless" patients on the second floor.

As regards sleeping accommodations, one-third of the patients of both sexes were in single bedrooms while the rest were in communal dormitories. These were placed along the north side and the corridors and day rooms with large bay windows on the south. The wards, connected by heavy wooden doors, were placed en suite with stairways linking the different floors on the corners and junctions of the wings.

The entrance hall in the forward extension of the central block has large reception rooms on either side and administrative offices behind. Above are the residences of the manager, matron, and chief physician; medical offices and surgery are located in the rear extension of the block. Directly behind this, on the far side of the narrow courtyard, are the hall, chapel, and outbuildings mentioned earlier.

The arrangement of the center block, and, indeed, the general plan of the asylum, suggest influence from a new source—the influential, widely publicized work of John Connolly, a doctor at the Derby Lunatic Asylum. Connolly's study was published in 1847, but the greater part of it had been presented in 1846.[39] Connolly listed the same requirements as those set down by the Commissioners, but he dealt in far greater detail with the specific form that mental hospitals and asylums should take. He particularly recommended the projecting central house with residential areas arranged in a series of galleries with bedrooms on one side. His suggestions and observations were based on practical experience and were spoken with professional authority.

Though not entirely original, Deane and Woodward's design is remarkably well suited to its purpose. All of the practical requirements specified by the authorities concerning supervision, medical care, communication, classification, security, lighting, and ventilation have been met with an economy of means. Unlike the design for Queen's College, the plan is kept tightly compact with the offices and the more private residential areas located in the wings but kept within easy access. Furthermore, the functions of the different parts of the building are all clearly expressed on the exterior in a variety of forms.

On the whole the Gothic detail on the exterior of the Killarney Asylum is sparse and restrained. Architectural decoration is kept to a minimum, perhaps as a result of the commonly held view expressed by Dr. Connolly that "much ornament or decoration, external or internal, is useless, and rather offends irritable patients than gives any satisfaction to the more contented," and is "more likely to rouse morbid associations than do any good."[40] Accordingly there is none of the naturalistic stone carving which characterizes most of Deane and Woodward's other work. Instead, much of the Gothic character of the building derives from the rough and natural quality of the materials used. These are two kinds of locally quarried Kerry granite. The first, because of its high chlorite content, has a bluish-green color and is called "greenstone." The second type of granite, with a high red oxide content, is called "brownstone" because of its reddish-brown color. The structural polychromy of the granite together with the cut limestone quoins and dressings (also quarried locally) create a rich variety of earth tones and organic textures. Occasionally, a more decorative effect is achieved by banding the stone in the voussoirs and relieving arches over several of the windows.

Consistent with the exterior, simplified Gothic forms and natural materials are also used inside. In the wards the walls were originally raw brick. The arched doors and windows placed flush with the exterior wall plane emphasize the extraordinary thickness of the walls. The floors and ceilings in the dormitories are constructed of heavy timber beams. In the more public areas of the center block there are arched-brace and collar-beam roofs (Fig. 24).

Like Queen's College, the Killarney Lunatic Asylum owes a considerable debt to Pugin. The system of bays projecting from a central spine, the expanses of plain rubble masonry walls with irregularly grouped windows, and more generally, the agglutinative grouping of individually articulated units, strong structural realism, and asymmetrical planning are all Puginian.

However, Woodward once again created a fresh synthesis from the Puginian prototype, which is essentially High Victorian Gothic in spirit. The earlier dependence on historicist forms has disappeared; instead, masses and volumes are freely formed and arranged in a functionally articulate composition. Characteristically High Victorian Gothic are the strong vertical accents, the sharp outlines, simplified forms, and the jagged profile of the gables and roof lines. The Puginian plane-positive quality has been replaced by a more volumetric sense. The shifting wall planes on the main front, the interpenetration of spaces and volumes, and the willful irregularity of the building are all features which were to become the hallmarks of High Victorian Gothic and appear again in G. E. Street's Cuddesdon College and Butterfield's Cumbrae College, both institutional structures of the early 1850s. (It is also interesting to note that the jerkin-headed bay window supported on a long buttress to the left of the entrance at Killarney was also used by Street several years later in a similar position at Cuddesdon). And, finally, the conscious use of structural polychromy for decorative purposes is characteristically High Victorian Gothic.

Queen's College and the Killarney Lunatic Asylum, the first Gothic works of the association of Sir Thomas Deane and Benjamin Woodward, were also the first ventures of the firm outside the provincial scene. The Board of Works' building projects themselves received a great deal of public and professional attention at the time. They were of special interest not only because they constituted the first large-scale public building undertaken in Ireland since the eighteenth century, but also, and more importantly, because they involved new *types* of public institutions—founded on newly reformed and experimental principles of education and medical care—which required fresh architectural solutions.

Deane and Woodward were well suited to the task. As provincial architects they were also experienced civil engineers, builders, and contractors. Thus, from a practical point of view they were well equipped for the challenge of meeting the new functional demands of the buildings. Their ability to deal with the more pragmatic aspects of design is reflected in both of these early works. It accounts for the structural realism, efficient planning, real understanding of the qualities of different materials, and the keen sense of economy and utility these works exhibit.

Queen's College and the Killarney Asylum also demonstrate Woodward's knowledge of the structural and organizational principles of medieval buildings. No doubt Woodward's early training as a civil engineer contributed to his understanding of Gothic architecture, and it may account for the fact that, though a self-taught Gothicist and architect, there are no signs of amateurishness in these works. On the contrary, it would seem that Woodward's lack of formal training gave him an enthusiasm and freshness of approach untainted by academicism.

There is also little doubt that he had read Pugin's published writings and not only understood his principles, but had taken them to heart. In each case Pugin's precepts in the *True Principles*:

> All ornament should consist of enrichment of the essential construction of the building. In pure architecture the smallest details should have a meaning or serve a purpose. Construction should vary with the material employed.[41] The external and internal appearance of an edifice should be illustrative of, and in accordance with, the purpose for which it is destined, . . .[42]

were all rigorously followed at Queen's College and the Killarney Lunatic Asylum.

Yet these buildings, particularly the Killarney Asylum, are considerably more advanced in terms of their planning and independence from specific medieval models than Pugin's executed buildings. Pugin himself did not follow his own principles to their logical conclusion. In practice a Gothic traditionalist, Pugin, like the Ecclesiologists, was primarily concerned with the revival of particular Gothic forms for their symbolic and religious meaning. By contrast, Deane and Woodward were modern and secular Gothicists. In practice they anticipated Ruskin by abstracting the lay principles of "convenience, construction, and propriety"[43] from Pugin's doctrine to create a fresh, "scientific" synthesis from the Gothic vocabulary of forms. In Deane and Woodward's later Ruskinian Gothic work of the 1850s, such general architectural principles, rather than doctrine or ritual, remained the inspirational root and mainspring of their forms.

II

THE MATURING OF THE STYLE:
TRINITY COLLEGE MUSEUM, DUBLIN

The year 1850 marked the beginning of a new episode in the firm's work. Queen's College had been opened with great ceremony on November 7, 1849, and the building was praised as a Gothic masterpiece. Work on the college was finally finished in 1850 by which time the Killarney Lunatic Asylum was also nearing completion. That building opened in 1851 to favorable reviews from the *Builder*.[1]

During this time Sir Thomas Deane began to play an increasingly active part in the local affairs of Cork and Dublin. In 1850 he was instrumental in establishing a branch of the Government School of Design in Cork.[2] A year later he was appointed vice-chairman of the executive committee of the National Exhibition which opened in Cork in June 1852.[3] And in 1853 he served on the executive committee of the Dublin International Exhibition.[4]

By the time this exhibition closed on October 31, 1853, Deane had become firmly entrenched in Dublin's social and professional life. He acquired the former premises of the exhibition offices at 3 Upper Merrion Street for the firm's Dublin offices in October 1853.[5] In the same year he was elected to the Council of the Royal Institute of the Architects of Ireland and in 1854 was listed as one of its vice-presidents.[6]

As Sir Thomas Deane's public and professional activities expanded, the responsibility for running the architectural practice devolved increasingly onto the two junior members of the firm, T. N. Deane and Benjamin Woodward.

Thomas Newenham Deane was Sir Thomas' only son by his second marriage. In contrast to his father, he was physically unprepossessing, shy, reserved in manner, and had a stammer. Born on June 15, 1828, he was sent to Rugby. Like the elder Deane he was an enthusiastic yachtsman and his earliest ambition had been to join the Navy. Instead, however, on the insistence of his father, he matriculated at Trinity College, Dublin, in 1846, and was graduated in 1849.[7] On January 29, 1850, he married Henrietta Manly of Ferney, County Cork, and after a brief stay in Dublin returned to Cork to join his father's firm. Thus he was involved in the work at the Killarney Lunatic Asylum and with Woodward supervised the completion of the building.

In spite of their difference in age, T. N. Deane and Woodward were good friends and Woodward often stayed with the younger Deane when he was in Cork. Both men were of a retiring nature and shared a keen interest in medieval art. Though T. N. Deane lacked Woodward's genius for architectural design, he was a talented and prolific draughtsman. His architectural training was supervised by his father who worried about his son's artistic interests outside the field of architecture. "First the Exhibition next the arts—I fear Thomas will turn over to painting. He raves about Maclise, Stanfield, etc," Sir Thomas wrote to Crofton Croker in 1851. Though he never did defect, T. N. Deane throughout his life painted watercolors for pleasure and in later years exhibited regularly at the Royal Hibernian Academy.[8]

In 1851 Woodward and T. N. Deane were made partners in the firm, and the name was changed to "Deane, Son, and Woodward" often abbreviated as "Messrs. Deane and Woodward." Though Sir Thomas did not officially retire from practice until much later, he played a considerably less active part in the work of the firm after the formation of this new partnership. T. N. Deane became increasingly responsible for management, and Woodward for design.[9]

In December 1851 they entered their first competition with a design for the new Town Hall in Cork (Fig. 25). The competition was won by Messrs. Atkins and Johnson, whose design, according to the *Builder*, had a hexastyle Corinthian portico with wings and a campanile at each end. Deane and Woodward's design, awarded third prize, is curiously clumsy and "roguish."[10] The *Builder* mentioned it in passing and remarked that it was "founded on the Belgic town-halls."[11] The style and arrangement of the main front—the square central tower, steeply pitched roof and stepped gable ends—are indeed characteristic of late medieval Franco-Flemish town or guild halls. The detail however is a strange confusion of Early English, castellated, and even Italian Gothic ornamental features.[12]

This eclecticism is difficult to explain and, in fact, much of it seems derivative of the firm's earlier work. The rear block with the large lantern on top, heavily buttressed wall, and large traceried terminal window resemble the examination hall at Queen's College, while the connecting block with its projecting chimney recalls the more domestic wings of the college. The grouping of self-contained masses, the irregular outlines, and powerful detail are similar to the Killarney Lunatic Asylum, but here the tight control and balance of the earlier design seem to be lost. Far more ornate than the college and asylum buildings, it incorporates full-figure sculpture and a great deal of applied ornament in a manner that comes remarkably close to G. G. Scott's Town Hall designs of the later 1850s.

The Cork Town Hall design is also significant for the firm's later work. As we will see Deane and Woodward were to return to the prototype of the north European town hall in their most famous building, the Oxford Museum, with quite different results.

In between these designs, however, came a commission that revolutionized the firm's work. In August 1852 Sir Thomas Deane was invited by the Board of Trinity College to enter designs in a limited competition to be held in that year for a proposed museum building to house the Lecky Science Library, various lecture rooms, geological and mineralogical collections and a series of engineering models. The other two architects invited were Decimus Burton (who declined) and Charles Lanyon. Deane accepted and assured the Provost of the College, "I shall lose no time in giving the subject my utmost consideration, and that I accede to the terms proposed."[13] In fact, the competition came at a time when Sir Thomas was most involved in the Cork and Dublin exhibitions and T. N. Deane was traveling on the Continent. Therefore it would seem that the major responsibility for the designs devolved to Woodward.

In April 1853, as the *Builder* reported, the Board "finally resolved to adopt the design of Sir Thomas Deane, Son and Woodward, for the extensive additional buildings—museums, drawing schools, and lecture-rooms—for the general plan of the interior arrangements."[14] In July the *Builder* gave a more detailed account, noting that "It will contain ten lecture-rooms, most of them about 38 feet by 30 feet. In the upper storey there will be two lofty museums, 84 feet by 38 feet, and a drawing-school 72 feet by 25 feet. The hall and staircase will display in their columns and fittings the marbles of the country."[15]

There was, however, some confusion as to who had actually won the competition. The idea for the museum had first been proposed in 1833. An international competition for a museum and lecture rooms was announced and adjudged in the following year. The competition was won by a Mr. Payne or Paine, who was asked to modify his plans, which were nevertheless abandoned shortly afterward. Then, in 1837, Frederick Darley, the College Architect who had not been a prizewinner in the competition, was given the commission. His scheme was also set aside while Darley proceeded with the design and building of the New Square at Trinity.[16] Finally, in 1849, Decimus Burton was called in to evaluate the site chosen by Darley between Parliament and Library Squares. He rejected this and proposed the site on the south side of the New Square on the edge of the College Parks, which was finally adopted (Fig. 26).[17] Following this decision, John McCurdy, Clerk of the College Works, made designs for a museum building. McCurdy's drawings show (what must have been intended as) a temporary pavilion-like structure with cast iron pillars and a glass roof.[18] These designs were also shelved, and some time later the Board requested McCurdy to draw up ground plans for a more permanent structure. This plan was subsequently modified by the Board, who proposed that Deane and Woodward collaborate with McCurdy on the design of the elevations.[19]

A long public debate ensued in the *Builder* between the two parties over who was ultimately responsible for the building as executed.[20] In the meantime, while these arguments raged on, the architects agreed to advertise for contracts for the foundations of the new building in April 1853.[21] In October 1853 Deane and Woodward submitted the working drawings and specifications for the building to the Board. And on January 14, 1854, the tender of Gilbert Cockburn and Sons, builders, for approximately £24,000 was accepted and their building schedule of three to four years for completion of the work was approved.[22] Construction began in February 1854. The exterior (Figs. 27, 28) was completed in 1855 and the interior in 1857.

The site, forming one side of the New Square in the third court on the University grounds, flanked by Darley's sombre granite buildings and in alignment with the Library, was no doubt an important consideration in determining the form of the building. Trinity College Museum (hereafter referred to as TCD) fits in well with the Palladian architecture of its surroundings, with its low roof, regular outline, and architectural ornament kept close to the wall surface. The materials used are also the local Dublin granite and Portland stone of the older buildings. Yet with all its conformity TCD is striking for its difference, and the *Ecclesiologist* (1854) recognized it as a "bold experiment to give life and variety to a mass of buildings now peculiarly sombre and heavy."[23]

TCD is also remarkably different from Deane and Woodward's earlier institutional buildings. Though not as large or complex as the college or asylum it also needed to incorporate various kinds of intellectual and physical activities.

Whereas at Cork and Killarney this variety of physical functions led to associationally expressive arrangements of contrasting masses and volumes, at TCD these activities are all gathered together into one block with symmetrical massing on the exterior and a nearly symmetrical plan (Fig. 29).[24] But TCD is associationally and functionally expressive nevertheless. The difference is conceptual. Rather than articulating the diversity of activities pursued in the building by a characteristically High Victorian Gothic variety of forms, TCD expresses the unity of intellectual endeavor and the idea of the teaching museum as a storehouse of practical knowledge by a single monumental block.[25]

Neither the source of these ideas nor the underlying rationale of the building were immediately apparent, however, and TCD received mixed reviews.[26] There was also considerable critical confusion concerning the style of the building. In July 1853 the *Builder* wrote, "The style which has been adopted by the architects, Messrs. Deane and Woodward, is the Venetian Cinque Cento. The design is founded, to a certain extent, on the front of the *Palazzo Dario* on the Grand Canal, Venice, given in our ninth volume . . . and that of the *Casa Visetti*, in the same volume. . . . It will be a novelty with us."[27] In August 1854 the *Builder* noted that "the general style of the building is the Venetian form of the Renaissance or Cinque Cento style. The mouldings and carved work are, however, intended by the architects to be of somewhat earlier character, that is to say, as far as is attainable Trecento or 'Giottesque.' "[28] In October 1854, significantly, the *Ecclesiologist* called it a "general classical type with a medieval variety of ornament."[29] The *Building News* called it "Romanesque."

And finally, in a fateful letter, William Allingham in May 1855 wrote to William Rossetti:

> Yesterday in Dublin I saw . . . the part-finished building in Trinity College, which is after Ruskin's heart. Style, early Venetian (I suppose), with numberless capitals delicately carved over with holly-leaves, shamrocks, various flowers, birds, and so on. There are also circular frames here and there on the wall, at present empty, to be filled no doubt with eyes of coloured stone. Ruskin has written to the architect, a young man, expressing his high approval of the plans, and so by-and-by all you cogniscenti will be rushing over to examine the Stones of Dublin.[30]

With this Deane and Woodward were ushered into their fate as the favorite architects of Ruskin and the Pre-Raphaelites. Meanwhile, however, Sir Thomas

Deane himself called the building "fifteenth century Byzantine Period," by which he probably also meant in the style of the early Venetian palazzi.[31]

TCD is all of these in part—and more. The exterior is eclectic; and we must look at the building in the light of these comments so as to come closer to the true nature of its style and individuality. The exercise will take us into the fascinating looking-glass world of Victorian architectural borrowing.

The similarity of TCD to the Italian palazzi published in the *Builder* in 1851 is one of details only. Nothing was borrowed without being modified and rearranged in its new context.[32] TCD bears little resemblance to the compact verticality of the three or four storey fifteenth and sixteenth century Venetian palazzi. However, a number of details are similar and may have been derived from the palazzi illustrated in the *Builder* in 1851. The discs of colored marble on the two main facades of TCD are prominent features of the Palazzo Dario (Fig. 30). The brack-eted cornice and richly carved window jambs also appear in the Casa Visetti. A more striking feature adopted from the Casa Visetti (Fig. 31) is the way the capitals of the windows flanking the main entrance rest on the imposts of the doorway capitals. Deane and Woodward's original design for the doorway, pub-lished in the *Builder* in 1854, was even more closely modeled on that of the Casa Visetti. The twisted colonettes on the corners and string course moldings of TCD are like those of the Palazzo dei Pergoli Intagliati (Fig. 32) which was also illustrated in the *Builder* in 1851. Here too we can recognize a carryover of the projecting balconies, though the form is different. In each case where a detail or ornamental feature was adopted from a Venetian example it was expanded and broadened—brought into scale with the massive and monumental proportions of the new building. Thus the ornamental relief becomes bolder and more striking as it is concentrated in certain areas of the exterior facade and set off against the restrained and austere lines of the building.[33]

The horizontal massing and the arrangement of the fenestration betray other sources of influence. TCD has neither the regularity of the northern and central Italian Gothic continuous arcading adopted by J. W. Wild in St. Martin's Northern Schools, which became a model for Victorian commercial architecture, nor the asymmetry of the Venetian Gothic prototypes.[34] In fact, the exterior massing of TCD, with the windows symmetrically grouped in varying combinations of double and triple arcades, is closer to that of the upper stories of the early-sixteenth-century Cornari Palace, also illustrated in the *Builder* in 1851.

The window arrangement and massing can also be related to the German

"Rundbogenstil" buildings of the 1830s and 1840s, as well as the garden facade of Charles Barry's Traveller's Club in London (Fig. 33) of 1829-1832, which was illustrated in W. H. Leeds' publication of 1839.[35] This is perhaps what the *Ecclesiologist* recognized as the "general classical type" of TCD, which also relates it to Tuscan Renaissance palazzi.[36]

Even more significant is the relationship between TCD and Henri Labrouste's Bibliothèque Ste. Geneviève in Paris, begun in 1843 and completed in 1850. A detail of the elevation of the library was illustrated in the *Builder* in 1853 and was no doubt familiar to Deane and Woodward.[37] Besides the similarity of building *type* there is a further strong formal resemblance to Labrouste's self-contained square block with its two-storey round-arched facade and heavy projecting cornice. At TCD ornament is also used to articulate and even dramatize structure, as for example in the distinctly marked floor divisions, the decorative discs that indicate the points at which the interior and exterior walls meet, and the strongly articulated supporting piers.

TCD also has a few possibly Irish characteristics. Its monumentality, heaviness, and the thickness of the walls are characteristic of Romanesque architecture in general; but the round-arched windows, decorated piers, recessed voussoirs, and the profusion of geometric ornament are more specifically Celtic, indeed Irish, in origin. There is little doubt that Woodward was familiar with such monuments as the Killeshin doorway (Fig. 34), which was in any case illustrated in the *Builder* in 1854. The Cork and Dublin exhibitions also helped to popularize Irish imagery, medieval workmanship, and indigenous building materials—and the Celtic references in TCD are without a doubt consciously and purposefully made.[38]

The interior of TCD is also eclectic. The plan, as executed with an arcaded vestibule leading into a large arcaded central hall, bears a certain similarity to Genoese palaces of the late sixteenth and seventeenth centuries. Douglas Richardson has related the T-shaped staircase in particular to that in the Palazzo Tursi-Doria (1564) by Rocco Lurago. In English work, the central stairhall with T-shaped staircase and high-domed skylit ceiling also appear in such Georgian work as Robert Adam's Home House in London of 1775-1777, a relation also noted by Richardson. More immediately apparent, however, is the influence of Charles Barry's Traveller's and Reform Club houses on the plan of TCD. These became the prototypes for many nineteenth century provincial libraries, small museums, and other cultural and corporate institutional buildings in England.

[33]

Their influence on TCD is therefore not surprising. The Traveller's Club, though ordered around an open courtyard rather than a central stairhall, is remarkably similar to the upper storey of TCD where the large museum rooms flank the central court. There is an even more striking resemblance to the Reform Club plan (Fig. 35) where a small entrance hall leads via a short flight of steps into a central skylit hall surrounded by a colonnade. Deane and Woodward were to draw from this plan again in their next museum building at Oxford.[39]

Individual features of the interior (Fig. 36) suggest other sources. The central domed space, though usually used in conjunction with a classical style of architecture, was the hallmark of the nineteenth century museum. Skylights illuminating museum rooms had also been a practical convention of museum architecture since the eighteenth century.

Stylistically the central hall is also a remarkable synthesis of Romanesque, Byzantine, and Moorish motifs. Sources for the round-arched arcade with red and white banded voussoirs can be found in early Italian medieval architecture and in the Moorish architecture of Spain, for which numerous well-illustrated books, published in the late 1840s and early 1850s, were available to the architects. Also by 1855 G. E. Street's *Brick and Marble in Spain and North Italy in the Middle Ages* had appeared. In addition Sir Thomas Deane had owned John Cavanagh Murphy's Batalha manuscript with his notes on Spanish medieval architecture.[40]

One of the most striking Byzantine features of the hall is the richly patterned double-domed ceiling constructed of blue, red, and yellow enameled bricks. Deane and Woodward would have been familiar with such work from Matthew Digby Wyatt's *Specimens of the Geometrical Mosaic of the Middle Ages* (1848), and Owen Jones' *The Grammar of Ornament* (1856) as well as from Ruskin's description of the mosaic domes of St. Mark's in the *Stones of Venice II* and his illustrations of what he called "incrustation."[41] Furthermore, zigzag-patterned brickwork and inlaid marble had also been recently used by William Butterfield in All Saints, Margaret Street, which Ruskin praised in the third volume of the *Stones of Venice*.[42]

A completely different mode is suggested by the open timber roofs and framed timber ceilings in the museums, lecture rooms, and offices in the building. As in Queen's College, Cork, and the Killarney Lunatic Asylum these timber structures are Early English in style.

Thus, it is difficult to identify a predominant stylistic influence in the highly eclectic design of TCD. Each of the contemporary commentators quoted above was partially correct in his attempt to classify the building within some context of historical styles.[43] But to read TCD as merely a surprisingly harmonious synthesis of a great number of stylistic characteristics is to miss the crucial importance of the building. To find the real source of influence on Deane and Woodward we must go beyond the search for purely visual precedents for TCD.

This real source, less specific than the others but more powerful and pervasive, was John Ruskin. The channel of Ruskinian influence was not so much through illustrated precedents (here the *Builder* was probably more influential in illustrating entire elevations whereas Ruskin illustrated only details) as through written description and theoretical reasoning. At the time of the competition for TCD in 1852 only the *Seven Lamps* and *Stones of Venice I* had been published. Here, more than in the later books, Ruskin used specific examples only to elaborate certain concepts he was trying to put forward and to illustrate the basic principles which he recognized as underlying all good architecture irrespective of style or building type. Ruskin's teaching at this point was philosophical and theoretical. It is true that in his choice of examples he inevitably expressed certain preferences, but taken together these hardly formed a consistent argument for any one style. His purpose in recommending the study of certain monuments was not to identify the styles but the principles underlying them which were to be followed by contemporary architects. Even when, at the end of the *Seven Lamps*, he suggests that "the choice [for contemporary architecture] would lie I think between four styles: 1. The Pisan Romanesque; 2. The early Gothic of the Western Italian Republics . . . ; 3. The Venetian Gothic in its purest development; 4. The English earliest decorated," Ruskin is only suggesting that they best embody the precepts he has endeavored to explain.[44]

We saw Deane and Woodward's ability to abstract the general architectural principles of "convenience, construction, and propriety" from Pugin's doctrine and to create from them a fresh synthesis in Queen's College and the Killarney Lunatic Asylum. It is, therefore, not surprising that they would be quick to grasp the real significance of Ruskin's "constant, general, and irrefragable laws of right" for architecture in the *Seven Lamps*.[45] Indeed, many of Ruskin's ideas in the *Seven Lamps* and the *Stones of Venice I* concerning the importance of sound and truthful construction, expressive architectural ornament, an honest use of materials that exploits their natural qualities of color and texture, close attention to detail and workmanship, and even concerning the proper employment of the

[35]

workmen, had already at least partially been realized in Deane and Woodward's earlier work. Thus, the firm was already in sympathy with Ruskin's ideology. In addition, while Deane and Woodward had used Pugin they did not have the same commitment to Puginian principles (codified by the Ecclesiologists) as Butterfield, Street, and other English Gothicists, all of whose early work was executed under the auspices and patronage of the Society. Furthermore, Ruskin's secularism and latitudinarian attitude to style would understandably have had more appeal for an Irish firm such as Deane and Woodward than the narrow nationalism and doctrinal purism of the Ecclesiologists. Thus Ruskin's writings struck a responsive chord and not only articulated ideas already nascent in the firm's work, but gave direction and form to these ideas.

The most important point of the *Seven Lamps* and *Stones of Venice I* which differentiates these books from Pugin's ideas and the *Ecclesiologist* as well as from Ruskin's later books on architecture, is that here Ruskin is not so much concerned with style as with form—and with discovering the general architectural principles that are the mainspring of form. Throughout the *Seven Lamps* broad aesthetic and moral principles are directly related to specific forms or "noble characters," which Ruskin summarizes and lists at the end of the fourth chapter. As we shall see, Deane and Woodward's TCD is a realization of this Ruskinian formal ideal.[46]

Indeed, if we read TCD as a practical application of Ruskinian principles, the underlying rationale for its eclecticism becomes apparent. In the *Seven Lamps* Ruskin stresses the importance of size and weight, balanced massing and strong profile, as essential attributes for a "noble" building—all of which are present in TCD. "It has often been observed that a building, in order to show its magnitude, must be seen all at once . . . it must have one visible bounding line from top to bottom, and from end to end."[47] Such is the case with TCD, whether viewed from across the court in the front or the park at the back, the entire building can be seen at once. This desire for clarity may have been a reason for Deane and Woodward's rejection of McCurdy's Greek cross plan in favor of a simple parallelogram.[48] It is also markedly different from the Puginian agglutinative massing of contrasting forms in the earlier college and asylum buildings. Ruskin continues: "What is needful in the setting forth of magnitude in height, is right also in the marking it in area—let it be gathered well together."[49] The outlines of TCD are clearly articulated within the restrained and regular contours.[50] The horizontal and vertical lines are given definition and emphasis by the three bands of carved

[36]

base moldings, the string course, and projecting cornice which are continuous around the building, and the quoins and twisted colonnettes on the corners. The true nobility of a building lies in its massiveness, and Ruskin asserts in *Seven Lamps* that "the relative majesty of buildings depends more on the weight and vigour of their masses than on any other attribute of their design: mass of everything, of bulk, of light, of darkness, or colour, not mere sum of any of these but breadth of them; not broken light, nor scattered darkness, nor divided weight, but solid stone, broad sunshine, starless shade."[51] As we have seen in the details taken from Venetian palazzi and other sources Deane and Woodward expanded and broadened their features. Everything about TCD is large and solid and strongly articulated—the flat planes of undecorated wall and the bold relief of the carving. This aspect of TCD is in marked contrast to St. Martin's Northern Schools, where the facade appears like a thin screen applied to the structure and gives little sense of weight and solidity. Very little of the wall surface of Wild's building is not pierced by window openings. This fenestral quality, this nonmassiveness, is also evident in Barry's Traveller's Club, also often (as above) compared to TCD. Here the wall is again a street facade, a curtain regularly punctuated by slightly recessed windows and low-relief ornament. As in All Saints, Margaret Street, the contrast between Butterfield's harsh intricate silhouette on the one hand and the Ruskinian "one visible bounding line" at TCD on the other could hardly be greater.[52]

Another of Ruskin's principles concerned truth to structure. "That building will generally be the noblest, which to an intelligent eye discovers the great secrets of its structure—so long as we see the stones and joints and are not deceived as to the points of support we may rather praise than regret the artifice."[53] We have seen how the ornamental discs of colored marble and string courses articulate the internal structure on the exterior of TCD. Inside, the same principle is followed. The round-arched arcades in the central hall support true groined vaults. As on the exterior, the decorative moldings are used to reveal and emphasize the structural elements and to articulate their parts, while the green marble pilasters resting on oversized corbels above the stairs and entrance dramatize the points of thrust from which the red and white banded arch springs to support the incrusted pendentives and domes overhead. Equally "truthful" are the exposed wooden-beam roof structures in the museum and lecture rooms.

Some of the most innovative functional features of this kind are the ornamental open tiles and pierced stonework around the walls, which are part of the ingenious ventilation system devised by Deane and Woodward. In an article in the *Builder* the architects described how the system works.[54] Similar round openings in the plinth of the east and west facades are connected to pipes which draw fresh air into the main hall and release it through large round openings under the main stairs. Thus the hall becomes a sort of reservoir of air for the other rooms, which are supplied by means of hollow bricks in the walls behind the stone and tile openings. Stale air is expelled from these rooms (Fig. 37) via small cone-like perforations between the joists on the lath and plaster of the ceiling into pipes which lead out to further ornamental openings on the exterior directly below the middle string course and the cornice on the east and west facades.

Ruskin had much to say concerning architectural ornament in *Seven Lamps*. To be beautiful and effective, he maintained, it is necessary that it also be well disposed. "Let, therefore, the architect who has not large resources, choose his point of attack first, and, if he choose size, let him abandon decoration; for, unless they are concentrated, and numerous enough to make their concentration conspicuous, all his ornaments together would not be worth one huge stone."[55] In TCD the carving was praised by contemporaries for its powerful and expressive appearance.[56] This ornament is also concentrated in specific areas: the horizontal bands and string courses, the marble discs, and around the apertures in the facade. Ruskin further recommended that the example of ancient monuments be followed in this respect and that the ornament should be "in greater effective quantity on the upper parts."[57] This may account for the addition of carved panels and archivolt moldings (not in the firm's original design) to the second storey windows which do not appear in the lower register.

This idea of concentrating carved ornament to give it emphasis ties in with Ruskin's ideas on proportion. "There is no proportion between equal things . . . to compose is to arrange unequal things . . . sometimes there may be a regular gradation, as between the heights of stories in good designs. . . ."[58] Deane and Woodward responded to this in the fenestration, grouped in arcades of two, three, and four windows which is similar to the massing of the Venetian Byzantine palazzi described by Ruskin in the second volume of the *Stones of Venice*.[59] This "well-balancing" of unequal elements and their rhythmical arrangement on the facade of a building was an important aspect of Ruskin's "Lamp of Life," "There is sensation in every inch of it, an accommodation to every architectural necessity, with a determined variation in arrangement, which is exactly like the related proportions and provisions in the structure of organic form."[60]

The interior spaces of TCD are also arranged to create the greatest possible variety of scale and proportion. The small entrance vestibule (Fig. 38) opens from a short flight of stairs into the large, colorful, and brightly lit central hall. This is the central focus of the interior spaces around which the lecture rooms (Fig. 37) and work spaces are arranged. Following Ruskin's dictum that the importance of the main space be emphasized by relatively larger size and a greater amount of decoration, these last are stark and bare, the only ornamental features being notched and molded wooden beams and braces, some of which were originally painted.[61]

Concerning materials Ruskin's ideas were very much in sympathy with Deane and Woodward's own. In the *Seven Lamps* he recommends the use of only natural materials, "that is to say, clay, wood, or stone."[62] This ties in with the architects' concern, expressed in a letter to the Board of Trinity regarding the use of the abundant Irish natural resources: "It is to be hoped that the good example now set by the college of largely using Native Marbles, may induce greater facility to be given and exertion made towards the proper development of the resources of the country."[63] And indeed all the marble used in TCD was quarried in Ireland. The stairhall gives a representative display of Killkenny and Galway black, Connemara green and blue, and Limerick and Cork red polished marbles.

Ruskin further maintained that whatever materials were used in different parts of the building—even those that are purely functional—there should be a consistency of style and workmanship.[64] Thus at TCD the carved timber-beamed roofs and wooden desks and work benches were designed to harmonize with the architecture, as were such minor fittings as the brass door handles obtained from the firm of Hart and Son, medievalizing metalworkers in London.

A further consideration in choosing materials, stipulated by Ruskin in the "Lamp of Sacrifice," was that whenever possible they should be of the highest quality. "If you cannot afford marble use Caen stone, but from the best bed; and if not stone, brick, but the best brick; preferring always what is good of a lower order of work or material, to what is bad of a higher."[65] Interestingly, the upper storey of the hall was first intended to be built of plaster covered rubble masonry and banded brick arches. In 1855, following the architects' suggestion, Caen stone was substituted for the rubble masonry and marble for the brick.[66]

Ruskin's ideas regarding materials were closely linked with those concerning color. "I cannot . . . consider architecture as in any wise perfect without color," he stated in the "Lamp of Beauty."[67] An early and insistent advocate of structural polychromy, Ruskin maintained the true colours of architecture are those of natural stone, and I would fain see these taken advantage to the full. Every variety of hue, from pale yellow to purple, passing through orange, red, and brown, is entirely at our command; nearly every kind of green and grey is also attainable; and with these, and pure white, what harmonies might we not achieve? Of stained and variegated stone, the quantity is unlimited, the kinds innumerable; where brighter colours are required, let glass, and gold protected by glass be used in mosaic—a kind of work as durable as the solid stone, and incapable of losing its lustre by time.[68]

The only notes of color on the exterior of TCD are the discs of red, green, and purple marble, which are in fact very similar to the chromolithographs of such ornament (Fig. 39) in the *Stones of Venice*.[69] But Ruskin's ideal was most completely realized in the interior, where the dressings and wall-lining of the outer and inner halls and the staircase itself are Caen stone. The hand-rail of the latter is polished green marble, further native marbles of different colors are used in the string courses, columns, and banded arches. Above and below the more brightly colored mosaic of the enameled soffit of the dome vaulting and the encaustic tile pavement contrast with the mellow natural hues of the stone.

Some of the most important passages in the *Seven Lamps* deal with architectural sculpture. "Ornament, as I have often before observed, has two entirely distinct sources of agreeableness: one, that of the abstract beauty of its forms . . . the other, the sense of human labour and care spent upon it."[70] Regarding the first, Ruskin further classified the forms of ornament, according to their uses in architecture, into four distinct types—all of which appear in TCD. In the first instance he specified that sculpture should be abstract in inferior ornaments and moldings.[71] Accordingly, geometric patterns of dogtooth notching, billet, nailhead, cable, chevron, and celtic interweave appear in the string courses, quoins, chimneys, window heads, and cornice and base moldings (Fig. 40). Other minor decorations of this kind are the pierced stone ventilation apertures—inside and out—cut in simple geometric shapes like the examples of such work from Lisieux, Bayeux, Verona, and Padua illustrated in the *Seven Lamps* (Fig. 41).[72] The second type of ornament involved color, which was to be introduced only in flat geometrical patterns (Fig. 42).[73] Deane and Woodward's use of this kind of decoration in the hall has already been described.

The third type was carved ornament where "organic form was subdominant" as, for example, in shallow decorative relief. This was what Ruskin called "Surface

Gothic" in the *Stones of Venice II* and by which he meant broad areas of relief sculptured on the surface of the building.[74] Examples of this sort of relief carving of slightly abstracted natural forms appear in the carved panels between the cornice brackets, some of the base and string course moldings, the upper storey piers, and voussiors.

The fourth type of ornament, most important because it was linked with Ruskin's second criterion for architectural sculpture, was the carving of living things, of plants, flowers, and animals, which were to appear in the most important features such as the capitals.[75] Here the ideal, as Ruskin stated in the third volume of the *Stones of Venice*, was to combine "the refinements of Italian art in the details with a deliberate resolution . . . to display the beauty of every flower and herb of the English fields."[76] He had illustrated examples of Italian carving from capitals in the Ducal Palace in Venice in the *Seven Lamps* and the *Stones of Venice*, and further illustrations of four capitals from the Ducal Palace were also published in the *Builder* in 1851.[77] The principal string courses, archivolts, and capitals on the exterior of TCD (Figs. 43, 44) are elaborately carved with flowers and plants. The *Builder* noted enthusiastically that "the ornature is for the most part wreathed in foliage—the oak, the ivy, acanthus, shamrock; lillies, lotuses, birds, and in fact, every variety of wreath—and these so diverse, so diffuse, so graceful, that the very diversity establishes its beauty."[78] Aside from foliage, the capitals especially abound in entirely naturalistic representations of squirrels, mice, cats, foxes, birds, and even monkeys.

In Ruskin's thinking this was inextricably linked with a moral or social principle which he felt was an essential part of good architecture and, more specifically, of true Gothic expression: that the workmen who carved the ornament should be active intelligences in the designing of their work and have a part in the creative planning.[79]

One of the most interesting aspects of TCD was the method of work employed for the first time by the firm. From information supplied by the architects the *Builder* reported that only verbal instructions were given to the workmen, who were left to determine the subject and design the details of the ornament themselves. "The architects are seeking to carry out views lately advocated [by Ruskin] by leaving the *design* of the ornament to the workmen themselves, in order to obtain variety; the only assistance afforded being verbal instructions from the architects as to the arrangement by geometrical forms, etc."[80] The truth of this account is borne out by sketches in one of Woodward's recently discovered notebooks (Fig. 45), where the ornament of the upper storey windows is roughly sketched in to show only the general arrangement of the areas to be carved.[81]

In 1856 the *Builder* illustrated some of the carved capitals in the interior of the Museum and listed the names of the workmen involved as "one Englishman, Mr. Roe, of Lambeth, assisted by the native talent of three [*sic*] brothers, workmen, the O'Sheas, of Ballyhooly, County Cork."[82] This is the first time that the names of the O'Sheas are firmly connected with the carved work on Deane and Woodward's buildings, and it was here that their full potential was to be realized under Woodward's liberal direction.

Ruskin maintained that if left to themselves to design their work the sculptors would naturally turn to nature for inspiration.[83] Indeed, there are stories of the O'Sheas bringing in plants each day to use as models for their work.[84] The *Building News* reported that nearly all the sculpture was executed "in situ," a fact substantiated again by a contemporary photograph of the building taken in the course of construction (Fig. 46) which shows the half-finished carving on the window heads already in place on the facade.[85] In Ruskinian terms this was an honest use of the workmen as well as the materials. The lively, bold, deeply undercut carving on the facades and the freestone capitals of the interior are a testimony to the rightness of this assumption. The O'Sheas and their work also accorded with Ruskin's ideas concerning the essential character of Gothic work and the workman. In the "Lamp of Life" he states of the carver:

> I believe the right question to ask, respecting all ornaments, is simply this: Was it done with enjoyment—was the carver happy while he was about it? It may be the hardest work possible, and the harder because so much pleasure was taken in it; but it must have been happy too, or it will not be living.[86]

Henry Acland wrote of the O'Sheas when they were working on the Oxford Museum in 1858: "The temper of the architect has reached the men. In their work they have had pleasure. The capitals are partly designed by the men themselves and especially by the family of O'Shea, who bring wit and alacrity from the Emerald Isle to their cheerful task."[87]

Of the carving Ruskin maintained that "*high* finish is the rendering of a well intended and vivid impression; and it is oftener got by rough than fine handling."[88] The sculpture must not only be faithful to its organic form but must also express its organic nature—it must be rough, uneven, and imperfect—only then will it come to life. This too is realized at TCD. The quality of the carving is unequal. Some plants are carved with greater delicacy than others. On the whole the bolder, rougher forms are more expressive and function better as ornamental designs. In all, however, there is variety and surprise—essential qualities of naturalism. Ruskin elaborated on this idea in his chapter on the "Nature of Gothic" in the second volume of the *Stones of Venice*. Here he lists the characteristic or moral elements of Gothic. The first three in order of importance are, in regard to the building, Savageness, Changefulness, and Naturalism; in regard to the workmen; Rudeness, Love of Change, and Love of Nature. These characteristics are the life-giving and life-sustaining elements of the architecture. In their absence the ornament becomes lifeless and sterile in its imitation of natural forms.[89] From contemporary reports of the O'Sheas colored by the popular English idea of the spirited and "clever" Irishman it is easy to see how they soon came to be seen as the epitome of Ruskin's ideal rude and imaginative workman taking only nature as his guide.[90]

The carved decoration in the interior of TCD is even more Ruskinian in this sense—more profuse, freer, and expressive than on the exterior (Figs. 47, 48). The capitals, carved almost entirely with floral motifs—and the occasional bird—are not so deeply undercut as those on the exterior. Individual flowers and sprigs, however, are not to be contained within the capital and creep upward into the abacus and outward along flanking walls. Closely observed realism is combined with abstract decorative design to create patterns which anticipate the floral designs of William Morris' wallpapers and fabric prints.

This lively and intricately carved ornament (Fig. 49) also appears in unusual places in the hall. Flowers and leaves are clustered in corners, in between the bases of the columns, and appear again at the terminations of the green marble balusters. Every crevice and joint has come to life with sprigs of holly, ivy, and oak which follow along the edge of the pendentives, cluster in bosses at the meeting of the architraves, and finally, in a dramatic gesture, spill out in a cascade of foliage on the staircase consoles. This profusion is in accordance with Ruskin's view that architectural decoration should be easily visible, and if it is to be intricately and carefully carved or colored, it should be protected from injury and sheltered from the weather.[91] The overall effect is that of the idyllic world of the ornamental backgrounds in Burne-Jones' and Morris and Company's late tapestry and stained glass designs where finely observed plants and flowers—irrepressible in their profusion—are likewise naturally arranged in accordance with their inherent qualities of growth, symmetry, and proportion, in infinitely variable "architectonic" decorative designs.

Once again the architects have signed their work—this time on a capital at the top of the stairs on which are carved two shields, one with a "W" and the other with an interwoven monogram of the partners' initials "DWD." These were designed by Woodward and there is a sketch of the capital and monograms in the notebook mentioned above.

In the decorative program of TCD another one of Ruskin's most important ideas concerning ornament is realized. Ornament, Ruskin argued in the *Seven Lamps*, must have meaning and a didactic purpose. "Better the rudest work that tells a story or records a fact, than the richest without meaning. There should not be a single ornament put upon great civic buildings, without some intellectual intention."[92] The decoration in TCD is meaningful in this directly didactic sense. The columns of colored marbles indigenous to Ireland, with their capitals of carved plants and animals, also mostly Irish, had significant associational references beyond the obvious nationalism. TCD was not only a national monument and a building in which science was taught, but, a natural history and geology lesson in itself.

Of all the traceable literary sources for TCD, none are so consistently manifest in all aspects of the building as Ruskin's architectural writings. In a letter read at the Architectural Congress in Oxford in 1858 Ruskin himself claimed that TCD was the first building in Britain in which the principle of the "liberty of the workmen" had been recognized.[93] And again, in a lecture delivered in Dublin in 1868, he declared that the museum building was "the first realization I had the joy to see, of the principles I had, until then, been endeavouring to teach."[94] Yet it is important to stress that TCD was the first example of a thoroughly Ruskinian building, not because Deane and Woodward had adopted Venetian Gothic motifs, but because it was the first practical attempt to follow Ruskin's theory and to apply his principles in the way in which he intended. Ruskin did not in the *Seven Lamps* and the *Stones of Venice I* advocate Venetian Gothic at the expense of all else. At the beginning of the *Seven Lamps* he states that his purpose is to uncover "those large principles of right which are applicable to every stage and style" of architecture.[95] Those principles are to be found in a wide variety of Gothic styles; in fact, he states, "I use the word Gothic in the most extended sense as broadly opposed to classical."[96] And the examples Ruskin chooses are accordingly eclectic. Similarly, to illustrate his text, Ruskin selected and drew details from Italian, French, and English Gothic monuments which best embodied his precepts. The physical presentation of these details on the page—overlapping and merging into each other—produced powerfully suggestive eclectic visual images.

[44]

At the end of the fourth chapter Ruskin brings these disparate formal characteristics together and lists the "noble characters" which constitute his formal ideal.

> Considerable size, exhibited by simple terminal lines. Projection towards the top. Breadth of flat surface. Square compartments of that surface. Varied and visible masonry. Vigorous depth of shadow, exhibited especially by pierced traceries. Varied proportion in ascent. Lateral symmetry. Sculpture abstract in inferior ornaments and mouldings, complete in animal forms. Both to be executed in white marble. Vivid color introduced in flat geometrical patterns, and obtained by the use of naturally colored stone.[97]

Deane and Woodward's Trinity College Museum is a realization of this richly decorated, monumental, symmetrical, and classicizing ideal.

Finally, TCD reflects another aspect of Ruskin's theory, which was gradually to become his primary concern with architecture: that is the ethical rather than the formal qualities of Gothic architecture. In the *Seven Lamps* Ruskin differentiated in this sense between a building's decorative features and its overall conception; "Sculpture is the representation of an idea, while architecture is itself a real thing."[98] In the final chapters of the *Seven Lamps* we can see the ideological shift in Ruskin's thinking from the thing to the idea, from the form to what he conceived as the spirit of Gothic work—that was to become the main theme of the *Stones of Venice*. In TCD this was manifest in every aspect of the work where the record of human labor and the metaphorical meaning of the building are carved and easily read on its surface.

In 1866 the *Dublin Builder* hailed TCD as a "great work, most important in its influence on the arts in this country . . . . To this remarkable building and this alone we trace the inauguration of the great revolution in public taste which has since taken place."[99] In fact, TCD had an almost immediate impact, particularly on commercial architecture in Dublin where it engendered a monumental commercial mode characterized by deeply recessed round-arched openings with "many bold and ornamental features being adopted in the detailed portions." The reasons for this are two-fold. The first are to be found in the comments of Sir Thomas Drew, who noted, "The novel building widely attracted popular favour by its charm of dignified palatial composition, and by its emancipation from all well-worn precedents of classic details."[100] Because of its essential classicism, its regular contours, and broad ranges of grouped arcades, it was both easily typified and ideally suited to modern commercial purposes. Also, while it departed from "well-worn" classical precedents the monumentality and palatial dignity of the design provided an equally appropriate image for great corporate houses. Furthermore, the Ruskinian ideal—plain massive building and concentrated sculptural ornament, in itself evocative of pre-Norman Conquest Irish architecture—could be easily translated into a national style.

The second reason, and one of the most important aspects of TCD for its contemporaries, was "its influence on the arts" in Ireland.[101] As Sir Thomas Drew noted, the "wealth of naturalistic and clever carving, and the introduction of hitherto unadmired Irish marbles, awakened local enthusiasm."[102] The sculpture which, as the *Dublin Builder* recorded, "we owe to 'native talent,' and in its style there has been little done since anywhere," was regarded at the time as having given the initial stimulus to a revival of "art-workmanship" in Ireland.[103] By 1866 the *Dublin Builder* could claim that "the state of architectural sculpture, of wood and stone carving generally . . . is perhaps the least backward of all our trades."[104] Yet some of Ruskin's most important ideas concerning workmanship and the liberty of the craftsman, followed at TCD, had to a certain extent already been put into practice in Deane and Woodward's earlier Irish buildings. The firm's old-fashioned methods of practice whereby all preparation of materials, including stone and wood cutting and carving, was done by hand continued well into the 1850s in Ireland. Consequently, there was still a sound tradition of craftsmanship in Irish building. Thus, for all its eclecticism and debt to Ruskin TCD owes an equal amount to "native talent."

The first attempt to give a distinctive form to Ruskin's theory, TCD embodies what will become the fundamental character of Ruskinian Gothic. As noted, many aspects of TCD—the expressive architectural ornament, the honest use of materials exploiting their natural qualities of color and texture, the close attention to detail and workmanship, and even to a certain extent the proper employment of the workmen—were already there in the firm's earlier work at Queen's College and Killarney. Yet the differences are great. Aside from the introduction of Italian Gothic forms, the new style of TCD also moves individualistically away from Puginian compositional and organizational principles. The contained contours, regular classicizing plan, compartmentation, balanced composition and elaborate sculptural ornament of TCD represent an aesthetic completely different from the irregularity, agglutinative planning, functional associationism, and use of inex-

[46]

pensive materials with a minimum of carved ornament which characterized the firm's Pre-Ruskinian style. In Queen's College and the Killarney Asylum, emphasis on the material purposes of the buildings had led to a clear differentiation of parts and functionally expressive massing. In TCD that emphasis has shifted. The latter's contained monumentality, simplified forms, and clarity of outline reflect a new preoccupation with surface articulation. The emphasis is now on the facade as a frame for an eclectic assembly of architectural details, richly associational story-telling sculpture, naturalistic relief carving, and constructive color.

III

THE OXFORD MUSEUM

Deane and Woodward's next commission was for the Oxford University Museum of Physical Sciences, their most famous building. The Oxford Museum also became for a time the focal point of the "Battle of the Styles" and the bulk of documentary material on the museum is a record of these polemical debates. The debates, like the building itself, remain unfinished today.[1] The Museum is also the most complex of Deane and Woodward's works, as so many different people with conflicting interests in the project were responsible for various aspects of its design and execution. Though the original designs were by Deane and Woodward, they were altered many times and for a variety of reasons, often by authorities beyond the jurisdiction of the architects.

Aside from the architects, the single most significant personality involved was Ruskin. His influence was both direct and indirect. Initially, as had been the case with TCD, the channel of Ruskinian influence on the firm's original design for the Museum was indirect—through his published writings and illustrations of Venetian Gothic details. Later, as the work progressed he became personally involved and was an active participant in the design and planning of the decorative scheme for the building. The Oxford Museum was, therefore, even less dependent than TCD on formal precedents and was in some ways an even more "theoretical," more consciously associational and didactic, building than the earlier museum.

For Deane and Woodward the Oxford Museum, hailed by the *Building News* as "the greatest civil building of our day," marked the turning point from provincial obscurity in Ireland to national prominence in England.[2] It was also the beginning of new professional and personal associations with the leading figures of the architectural and artistic avant-garde of the time.

But Deane and Woodward's success in the competition for the Museum was not just a personal achievement. It was also the most important victory won to date for the Gothic Revivalists as a whole. The Museum was the first major public building in England to be built in the Gothic style since the Houses of Parliament designed in 1835-1836 and begun in 1840. As such it was a major breakthrough for the Gothicists in the "Battle of the Styles," which raged with varying degrees of intensity throughout the mid-Victorian decades. The Oxford Museum became for a time the rallying point for Gothicists of all persuasions who were united for the first time in a common cause. The opposing factions of Classicists and Gothicists were thus once again polarized in a competition for the most important commission of the day.

The Museum as built was also a significant breakthrough within the Gothic Revival itself. As John Summerson has pointed out, the only secular Gothic Revival buildings of any note at this date were either domestic or collegiate— and the Palace of Westminster was by this time unanimously damned by Gothicists themselves. Thus, the Oxford Museum, as the first secular Gothic building of *public* character, established a new image of monumental secular Gothic architecture that was to influence the design of almost all major public buildings in England, whatever their purpose, in the second half of the nineteenth century.[3]

But the Oxford Museum was not only a major advance in secularizing the Gothic Revival and freeing it from historicism, ecclesiology, and antiquarianism. It also gave Gothic new associations with modern science, technology, and progress. Thus it provided both a contemporary prototype for secular public Gothic and an image of the "distinctive individuality" of modern Victorian Gothic that was "in harmony with existing sentiments and requirements and usages" at the same time as being "consistent with its own spirit and with [the architectural] profession"—"a really fresh and also a thoroughly Gothic expression of their style."[4]

Furthermore, largely because of Ruskin's involvement in the project and Woodward's personal friendships and professional associations with the major figures in the Pre-Raphaelite movement (who were also eventually enlisted in the work on the Museum), the Oxford Museum also became associated with the medievalist artistic avant-garde of the time.

The building has a long and complicated background which has never been dealt with completely in previous accounts. It is important to review it in the light of the new material presented here for a full understanding of the building's contemporary significance.

Dr. Henry Wentworth Acland, a life-long friend of Ruskin's since they had been undergraduates together at Christ Church, became the Lee's Reader in Anatomy at Oxford in 1845. It was he who first began agitating for a university museum and teaching facilities for the physical sciences at Oxford in a memorandum signed by himself and other science professors in 1847.[5] Nothing came of this initial effort. But again in 1848 Acland put out another pamphlet urging the creation of an Honour School in Natural Science.[6] This was finally established at Oxford in 1850. Acland and those who supported him continued to press the subject with letters and personal appeals to other members of the University. In May 1849 a committee was formed, with Acland as one of the secretaries, for promoting the establishment of a museum "with distinct departments under one roof, together with Lecture Rooms, and all such appliances as may be found necessary for teaching and studying the Natural History of the Earth and its inhabitants."[7] An architect was consulted who estimated the cost of the building at £25 = £30,000. It was hoped that this estimate could be met by private subscription, supplemented if necessary by the University.[8] Meanwhile, Acland and his colleagues continued to solicit funds and support until finally in 1852 a report of the University Commissioners strongly recommended the building of a "great Museum" for all departments of the physical sciences. However, there was still considerable opposition to the plan that once again delayed action on this decision.[9]

Finally, in February 1853, after lengthy debates concerning the site for the proposed building, it was decided that it should be somewhere in the University Parks, and a Delegacy was appointed to prepare a description of the required building and submit it to an architect for assessment.[10] The architect/builder consulted was Lewis Cubitt, who reported to the Delegates on April 4, 1853, that the cost would be approximately £48,000 with a further £2,000 for the Museum gallery and £5,000 for fittings. Cubitt appended a prophetic note to his report that "if a rich or highly decorative design be desired the cost will be correspondingly increased."[11] The Committee, however, chose to ignore Cubitt's estimate and adhered to the lower figure of £30,000 quoted four years earlier. Thus, when the Rev. Richard Greswell, a tutor of Worcester College, submitted plans in May 1853 which were to be "modified and brought into an architectural form by . . . Sir Charles Barry and Mr. G. G. Scott" with an estimate by Barry of £50,000, they were rejected by the Committee because they exceeded the £30,000 limit set by Convocation.[12] Greswell's plan (Fig. 50) was for a two-storey quadrangular building with an open court in the center for the Museum and teaching rooms around the perimeter. It was to be a castellated Gothic structure with octagonal stair turrets and corner blocks. The main drawback of Greswell's plan was that it did not allow for later extension—an important consideration in a teaching museum. This project triggered off new arguments as to whether the Museum was in fact necessary at all and the money might not be better spent for other purposes. By December, however, a site was selected and four acres of the Parks bought from Merton College, with an additional four acres acquired the following May.[13]

At last, in April 1854, a new Delegacy was appointed "for the purpose of obtaining Designs and Estimates from Architects, of examining and selecting from them, and of reporting thereon for the approval of the House." An open competition was decided on and architects were invited by public advertisement to compete for the commission and prizes for the three best designs. The requirements were for a building "two storeys high, three sides of a quadrangle with an area covered by a glass roof and the fourth side allowing for later expansion." The Museum's collections were to be displayed in the central court with teaching rooms and offices in three sides of the quad. The departments to be accommodated were Medicine, Anatomy, Zoology, Geology, Mineralogy, Chemistry, Experimental and Natural Philosophy, Astronomy, and Geometry. Further requirements were that "each plan must be distinguished by a motto—the author's name being sent under sealed cover . . . on or before Saturday, 14 October 1854 . . . [and] must be accompanied by an Estimate of the Cost—which must not exceed £30,000." And finally, "no limitations of the style of architecture will be imposed; but architects should bear in mind that excellence of interior arrangement will be judged more essential than exterior decoration."[14]

By the October deadline thirty-two designs had been received and were exhibited to the public in the Radcliffe Library. On November 11, 1854, the Delegacy met to select "those which appeared to them to be the most deserving of attention, with a view of submitting them to the scrutiny of professional judges."[15] The architects brought in were Philip Hardwick, S. P. Cockerell, and T. L. Donaldson. Six designs were selected by the Delegacy and the verdict of the judges was announced on November 28 that "not one of the Designs can be executed for the sum stated . . . [though] in respect to soundness of construction . . . no important difficulty presented itself."[16] The Delegacy did not feel justified in awarding prizes to designs which had not satisfied the conditions regarding cost laid down in the statement of requirements. The unsuccessful competitors

[51]

once again voiced their indignation in the architectural press, and the *Builder* noted editorially, "We shall be surprised if fitting buildings to the extent required by the University are obtained for the sum specified."[17] Nevertheless, from these six designs, four were chosen which were "best fitted with suitable and moderate changes to answer the intended purposes"—No. 6 "A. Z. (Italian)," No. 5 "Cross Compasses (Jacobean)," No. 11 "Fiat Justia ruat Coelum, design A (Palladian)," and No. 22 "Nisi Dominus aedificaverit domum (Rhenish)." Of these, the last two were considered "on the whole to be the most satisfactory and creditable to their authors and deserving of reward."[18] It was determined that the two designs, "F. J." by E. M. Barry and "N. D." by Deane and Woodward, were to be voted on by Convocation on December 12, 1854, as offers had been received from responsible contractors for their execution within the £30,000 limit.[19]

The competition released a deluge of pamphlets on the University—some directly attacking or supporting either of the two designs—and others from those opposed to the establishment of a science museum altogether who hoped to profit from the division of opinion on the two designs still in question. One of the most famous of these was written by G. E. Street, *An Urgent Plea for the Revival of True Principles of Architecture in the Public Buildings of the University of Oxford*, in which he advocated the revival of a fourteenth-century Gothic style in Oxford.[20] In fact Street's pamphlet had appeared in 1853, long before the actual competition took place. Its purpose was to prevent "the repetition of such a building as the Taylor Institute" in Oxford. In it he argued first that Gothic was the style of Oxford and second that "there seems to be a particular propriety in selecting the style which, above all others that have ever existed, took nature and natural forms for her guide and her ornaments, in a Museum intended mainly for the reception of a collection illustrative of Natural History." "Surely," he urged, "where nature is to be enshrined, there especially ought every carved stone and every ornamental device to bear her marks and to set forth her loveliness."[21] This reasoning—so in sympathy with Deane and Woodward's own—possibly had some influence on their design. It had perhaps an even greater influence on the governing bodies of the University, and may have been instrumental in weighing the balance in favor of Deane and Woodward's Gothic and "naturalistic" design. Though he did not enter the competition, Street also included a design of his own for the museum which will be considered later.

Street's pamphlet was answered by another, this time anonymous, urging the use of a thirteenth-century English prototype.[22] By the time of the final vote

[52]

this pamphleteering had reached a peak. And, on the eve of the poll Acland circulated an anonymous one advocating the Gothic design of Deane and Woodward. It was signed "ΕΡΤΑΤΗΣ" and was dated December 11, 1854. In it he argued that "N. D." required only minor alterations and otherwise furnished all that the University required for the practical purposes of a museum and moreover that the Gothic style was appropriate for Oxford; "new sciences with old associations."[23]

Finally, a vote was taken and Deane and Woodward's design (Figs. 51, 52) won by a slim margin of 68 to 64. In the following May 1855 the £29,041-tender of Messrs. Lucas and Son, Builders, of London was accepted by Convocation. On May 28, 1855, W.C.C. Bramwell, a local Oxford architect, was made Clerk of the Works with a contract terminating on October 13, 1856.[24]

The foundation stone was laid by the Earl of Derby on June 20, 1855, and work began immediately. In October 1858 the *Building News* reported that "the contractors . . . have finished their contracts for erecting the main buildings, and the workmen are now chiefly engaged upon the internal fittings."[25] The structure was substantially complete in 1857. In February of that year Woodward wrote to Acland from Dublin that "the work is stopped" for a time in Oxford.[26] The glass and iron roof of the central exhibition court, however, was not finished until 1859. Work on the interior fittings and the decoration both interior and exterior continued until 1861 and is still unfinished, though further furnishings and carved capitals were executed between 1905 and 1911.[27]

The building of the Museum did not proceed easily and was fraught with controversy. The professors and heads of the different departments to be housed in the building frequently changed their specifications. And each time an alteration was proposed a cumbersome academic and administrative bureaucracy of sub-committees, delegates from the OUM Committee, the Committee itself and finally Convocation—where a final vote was taken—had to be set in motion, which considerably delayed the progress and increased the expense of the work. Every decision taken by the architects had to be cleared with the academic board, who in turn often neglected to consult with the architects at all on decisions originating in their own circle.[28] As the *Building News* succinctly put it: "It is forgotten that as, according to the good old Proverb, 'too many cooks spoil the broth,' so too many masters are sure to spoil the estimates."[29] So it was with the Oxford Museum. The situation was further aggravated by the fact that Deane and Woodward, whose main office was still in Dublin, were also engaged in numerous other works in

Ireland, London, and even in North Wales during these years. The situation worsened and became even more confused when Ruskin appeared on the scene, and when at about the same time Woodward's health began rapidly to decline.

Even before construction began on the building Convocation proposed a series of alterations to Deane and Woodward's original design. On February 23, 1855, the firm submitted their modified plan to the committee. The building was re-sited closer to the western edge of the parks (Fig. 53). Further changes made at this time are documented in a private sketchbook of Woodward's and on some of the competition drawings which have survived. The alterations proposed by Convocation mostly involved the internal arrangements and are documented in rough sketches and handwritten notations in Woodward's sketchbook.[30] Major modifications were also made to the chemistry wing situated off the south side of the main block (Fig. 54). This was begun later than the main building. Additional rooms were built around the yard that do not appear in the original plan. The external shape of the laboratory also underwent a gradual transformation (Figs. 55, 56), again recorded in Woodward's notebook, from the original low, squat structure surmounted by a broad octagonal lantern-skylight which was illustrated in the *Builder* in 1855, to the taller and slimmer building with a much-reduced lantern and self-buttressing chimneys, which was finally executed.

To economize it was decided that the east or back elevation, from which point the building was later to be extended, should be left a blank windowless wall supported by a row of buttresses.[31] The original idea was to build another grand facade similar to the west front against this wall at some later date when the further expansion of the Museum should become necessary.[32] The *Building News* found this temporary facade "as ugly a piece of architecture as was ever designed," which it feared was "likely to be something more than temporary." In fact, a very plain extension designed by T. N. Deane was added in 1882-1885 to house the Pitt Rivers Anthropological Collections, which, though it is entered from the Museum, is a separate institution.[33]

A series of minor alterations documented in Woodward's notebook, were also made at this early stage to the main front of the building (Fig. 57). The low buttresses were eliminated, and the corner stair turrets were made symmetrical and later reduced in size, which in turn necessitated alterations to the south end of the front block (Figs. 58, 59). Further minor alterations were made to the decorative scheme of the west front.[34] But all in all, the exterior changed little from the original design and most of the alterations were due to restricted funds rather than to any real rethinking of the design.

THE OXFORD MUSEUM

The *Building News* declared the site of the Museum, on the southwest corner of the University Parks, "decidedly the best in Oxford. Though in effect quite in the country, it lies within five minutes' walk of the very heart of the University."[35] The west front on Parks Road originally faced the gardens of St. John's College before Keble was built in 1866. To the south were the gardens of Wadham College. To the north and east was open parkland extending at the east back to the river. In the 1850s all three fronts were visible from a distance and the architects took full advantage of their exposed site. Approached from the town the full view of the main front, with the chemistry buildings in the foreground and the Curator's house beyond, is seen to better effect than from any other vantage point.

At first glance the Oxford Museum seems very different from TCD. Instead of being tightly pulled together in one massive self-contained block it spreads out at the sides with irregular groupings of outbuildings and subsidiary courts. The *Building News* described the effect: "The main structure rises in glory and self-sufficient strength above them, and they cluster around it, varied and irregular, yet not ungraceful handmaids."[36] The reasons for this arrangement are, once again, as at Queen's College, and the Killarney Asylum, practical—due to functional considerations—and are, in fact, partly the result of lessons learned at Cork. At Queen's College the anatomical and dissecting rooms were originally situated in the main quad of the college complex. Shortly after the building opened, however, it was found necessary for health and safety reasons to move these away from the central pile into a separate structure with its own airing court.[37] Consequently in the Oxford Museum the anatomy department was from the beginning set apart from the main block and given a separate entrance and courtyard. The same rationale lies behind the location of the chemistry laboratory in a self-contained wing off the southwest corner of the main building so that students and visitors would not be exposed to harmful chemicals or the potentially dangerous effects of experiments.

However, the symmetry, containment, and monumentality of the main front are very different from the early works of the firm and much closer in spirit to TCD. So too is the organization of the interior spaces. In both buildings a small vestibule leads into a large skylit central hall (Fig. 60). The hall itself is surrounded by a two-storey arcade of banded arches, marble columns, carved capitals and string courses that follow around the entire court. The same variety of materials, patterns, and colors is displayed. Even the arrangement of workrooms (Fig. 61), offices, and lecture rooms around the periphery of the court has been carried over. The peripheral circulation pattern in the Oxford Museum is, however,

[55]

a great improvement over the central axis pattern used at TCD, where it was necessary to use the upper wings of the grand T-shaped staircase to cross from one side of the building to the other. So is the provision of natural lighting from the glass roof and tall windows in the corner stairwells. Otherwise the window sizes vary with the dimensions of the rooms—small and narrow on the first floor containing mostly offices, considerably larger on the upper floor for the lecture theaters, library, and museums, which also have additional overhead lighting from dormers in the roof.

It appears that the architects had a problem providing sufficient natural light for the chemistry laboratory, however. Woodward's sketches show that after reducing the size of the lantern gallery he first considered putting in dormers. His final solution was ingenious: he inserted bands of thick green glass around the roof, which—from the exterior—were indistinguishable from the banded slates of the rest of the roof.[38]

As with TCD, there was considerable critical confusion among contemporaries concerning the style of the building. Professor Hort, Acland's biographer, dubbed it "Veronese Gothic of the best and manliest type, in a new and striking combination."[39] The *Building News* called it "Early Decorated, with a very strong tinge of Southern-Gothic, and somewhat more than a tinge of Southern-Gothic detail."[40] These comments are true in part. The tower (except for the roof) and the brown and gray banded voussoirs of the second-storey windows are north Italian, while the lower windows, all of which were intended to be richly carved, are more specifically Venetian. The original design, before the squat buttresses and canopied entrance porch were eliminated, was more English in character, though some "Early Decorated" features remain—the most striking of which are the side stair tourelles. The chemistry laboratory was directly modeled on the Abbot's kitchen at Glastonbury and at Stanton Harcourt, which were illustrated in T. Hudson Turner's *Some Account of the Domestic Architecture of the Middle Ages* (1853). The associational references of this last feature were intentional. The laboratory, like the medieval kitchen was set apart, as Acland wrote in *The Oxford Museum*, so that "all noxious operations are removed from the principal pile."[41]

But the most obvious stylistic sources for the main front of the Oxford Museum (as has often been pointed out) are northern medieval cloth and town halls. These, with their steep gabled roofs, central towers, dormers, and regular fenestration are clearly reflected in the Oxford building. (The Museum is especially close to the Brussels Town Hall and Ypres Cloth Hall.) Though the Museum, unlike its medieval prototypes, was neither a municipal nor a strictly urban building, the town hall type makes a fitting associational reference to its public nature. George Hersey has also suggested the possible influence of T. Penson Jr.'s project for Shrewsbury Station which dates from before 1848, but this is a "phantom prototype," and except for the central tower, gabled roof, and regular fenestration the buildings are hardly similar in spirit or character.[42]

The interior is also eclectic. The arcaded central court recalls the open courtyards of north Italian Gothic palaces. The bright natural light from the glass roof heightens the illusion of openness and gives the brick walls and stone pavement of the court a bleached and sunbaked exterior quality. The exposed timber roofs in the lecture rooms, offices and library around the court are Early English. The plan of the building is a typical palazzo arrangement. The scheme is also related to the classical plan of Barry's Reform Club—another palazzo. At the same time it can also be assimilated to the Oxford college quadrangle tradition.

The source of much of this eclecticism is once again Ruskin. His influence on the architects was this time immediately recognized by contemporaries. The *Building News* reported:

> We have been told that they stared so long and so steadily upon Mr. Ruskin's "Seven Lamps," that they have quite destroyed their eyesight for everything that is not reflected in Mr. Ruskin's mirror, and that he has availed himself of their pitiable condition to overwhelm and bury them in his "Stones of Venice."[43]

Like TCD the Oxford Museum reflects Ruskin's ideas concerning monumentality, proportion, and bounding lines. The rhythmically arranged windows, distribution of the ornament, clearly marked verticality of the tower, and the strong horizontality of the string courses, contained within the bounding lines of the corner moldings, cornice, and roof line of the main front are all reflections of Ruskin's prescriptions in the *Seven Lamps*. Furthermore, Ruskin's illustrations of north Italian and Venetian windows and palace facades in the *Stones of Venice* and *Examples of the Architecture of Venice* supplied the architects with numerous models for the exterior windows and the inner arcades.

In sum, however, the Oxford Museum is closest to the spirit of the *Stones of Venice III* where Ruskin recommends that nineteenth-century English Gothic buildings should be "designed in the forms of English and French thirteenth-century surface Gothic and wrought out with the refinement of Italian art in the details."[44] By taking the basic form of the northern Gothic town hall and combining this with Italian decorative motifs, Deane and Woodward were following Ruskin's counsel to "adopt the pure and perfect forms of Northern Gothic, and work them out with Italian refinement" to the letter.[45]

But there are other recognizable contemporary sources of influence on the Oxford Museum design. G. G. Scott, in a lecture "On the Pointed Architecture of Italy" published in the *Ecclesiologist* in 1855, and G. E. Street, in *Brick and Marble in the Middle Ages* (1855), gave detailed accounts of north Italian Gothic architecture. Street's book was especially valuable for its visual documentation, in numerous illustrations, of banded brick and stone decoration. The aesthetic principles Street iterated in this book had already been propounded in his earlier writings. In *The True Principles of Architecture and the Possibilities of Development* of 1852, he advocated the study and use of Continental Gothic motifs by English architects and stressed the importance of structural color, unbroken roof lines, and horizontality in Gothic architecture.[46] These and other ideas expressed by Street in the *True Principles* and elsewhere are not unrelated to Ruskin's and no doubt owed something to the *Seven Lamps*. Street also employed a similar vocabulary to describe his ideal—"harmonious combination of horizontals and verticals," "repose," "grandeur," and "regularity of parts."[47] In 1853 he too advocated the use of Gothic in secular architecture and supported his argument with archaeological evidence culled from Parker.[48]

The most directly influential of Street's contributions was naturally his proposed design for the Oxford Museum in the *Urgent Plea* (1853) (Fig. 62). This was his first design for an entirely secular building, and the large scale and quantity of elaborate French Gothic detailing are unusual. It is a monumental, practically symmetrical, U-shaped structure with a long center block and wings projecting forward at either end and joined at the front by a low arched screen. The only irregular features are the tower and circular turret. The same monumentality and regularity have been noted in Woodward's design for the Museum, also the tower and turrets. The tower is in fact even closer to Street's tower for All Saints' Boyne Hill, begun in 1854.

Generally, the Oxford Museum is closer to the mainstream of High Victorian Gothic architecture than is TCD. The constructive color, flat planes, angularity, steep roof, asymmetrical features at the sides, and the exposed iron in the interior all bear this out. The smooth surfaces and structural color in particular suggest the direct influence of Butterfield's All Saints, Margaret Street. But if so, this was filtered through Ruskin's thinking as well as coming directly to Woodward.[49] Furthermore, the building materials—Bath stone, Hornton stone dressings, and red Bristol sandstone—(instead of the characteristic brick of High Victorian Gothic) and the wealth of "surface Gothic" relief carving are decidely Ruskinian rather than Butterfieldian.

For its contemporaries, however, the Oxford Museum signified far more than the sum of its parts. In spite of its eclecticism the *Building News* hailed it as "a living witness to the revived energy and unquenched vitality of our own Old English Style."[50] In their next edition they went even further:

> We venture to say that it is a thoroughly English building, conceived in the thoroughly English spirit of "Live and Learn;" that the basis of the style adopted is fully-developed Early English or . . . very early "Decorated," and that the accomplished architects deserve the highest praise for their liberal and enlightened treatment of their style, and for the judicious manner in which they have worked into it the excellencies and convenient arrangements of the style of other countries.[51]

These comments reflect an important change in the attitude of Gothic Revivalists at this time to the question of style. By the mid-1850s the Gothic Revival as a movement was no longer dominated as it had been in the 1840s by antiquarian and ecclesiological concerns for reviving traditional types and forms of English medieval architecture. Instead, as travel became easier, following the French Alliance in 1854, and an increasing number of thoroughly documented and well-illustrated books on Continental Gothic architecture were published in English, foreign influence on British architecture became acceptable.[52] This change in attitude is reflected in the comments of the *Building News* in January 1859:

> It is the bounden duty of the architect who would really study his art, to avail himself of those facilities of visiting the greatest architectural monuments in Europe, which our ancestors never dreamed of, but which they should have used to the best advantage, without a doubt, had they possessed them. He may go anywhere now, wherever there is anything worthy of a visit. . . . Architects, we are thankful to say, have broken loose from the old thraldom; they *will* go abroad, and, what is worse they will take 'unnatural lines,' and visit and study all manner of naughty

buildings; and all the Architectural Conservatives in the land cannot hold them in. This then, is accomplished—the practical recognition of the fact that it is no degradation to learn from others what we can not know ourselves.[53]

Thus architects in the mid-fifties were less concerned with the question of style as a national and historical expression than with the development of a *modern* Gothic style—expressive of its time and suited to contemporary needs. The *Building News*, the mouthpiece of the architectural avant-garde during these years, raised the cry in an article titled, "What are the Gothic Leaders Doing?"

We do not want to know whether our Gothic architects have decided which is the nobler or more admirable Gothic—that of the thirteenth century or that of the fourteenth; neither is it a matter that excites our present interest to be informed whether these gentlemen have determined, in their practical study of the style, to extend their researches beyond the Gothic of our own country. We ask them, on the contrary, what are they doing to render the Gothic of the present as great, by rendering it as definite, as the Gothic of any one of the grand eras of the past? We know what the Gothic of the Plantagenets was, and the Gothic of the Edwards. What is the Victorian Gothic? The early expressions of the style became great in their distinctive individuality. Is our own Gothic becoming great through the same eminent quality?[54]

By logical extension, if Gothic was to be a modern style then it had to be adaptable to modern needs and to a broad range of building types. The "absurd theory that Gothic architecture is unfit for civil and domestic purposes"[55] had been eloquently attacked by Ruskin and from within the Ecclesiological Society by Street—who received enthusiastic support from other Gothicists who were also by this time eager to extend the range of their work beyond the traditional Gothic building types. The Oxford Museum seemed to prove their point.

Contemporary critics of the Museum were far more concerned with its "modernity" than with the eclecticism of its style. And reports in the architectural journals repeatedly stress the pioneering and experimental nature of the enterprise. The architects, the *Building News* claimed, "had to set out upon hitherto untrodden ground, and were obliged, as they went on, to learn many things which were not known before, and which could not be suggested by theory, but only in the course of practice."[56]

[60]

The feature which attracted most attention and interest was the glass and iron roof of the central exhibition court. Here something entirely new was being attempted—to combine Gothic with modern building materials and techniques. Thus the Museum was seen by the medievalizing avant-garde as the testing ground not only for modern Gothic in large-scale public building but also for the "applicability of Crystal Palace architecture Gothicised."[57]

The glass and iron roof is indeed one of the most remarkable features of the Oxford Museum. The glazed roof *was* included in the commissioners' list of requirements; however, no specifications were made concerning the form or support structure to be used. The execution of the roof was from the beginning contracted to F. A. Skidmore of Coventry, an ironmaster interested in ecclesiology. Skidmore had carried out numerous church furnishing commissions for ecclesiological architects, and between 1854 and 1856 gave several lectures on the use of iron in Gothic architecture to the Ecclesiological Society and the Oxford Architectural Society.[58] In a paper of 1854 "On the Use of Metals in Church Building and Decoration," Skidmore had argued that metal should not be used merely as a cheap expedient but should be exploited for its inherent and unique qualities, which permit it to be hammered, reformed, and remodeled into finer and more delicate forms than stone. Iron could cover a wide span, impossible in other materials, and yet remain pliable into delicate plant and animal forms. Thus, in view of his experience and the compatibility of his ideas with Woodward's own, Skidmore seemed ideally suited to the task.

The original design for the roof was, however, made by Woodward. And though the firm's competition drawing for it has not survived, a sketch by Woodward for the proposed ironwork to be made by Skidmore accompanied the firm's list of minor modifications submitted to the University in February 1855.[59] This design (Fig. 63) was very different from the earlier more purely functional iron structures of the Crystal Palace and Kings Cross Station. The entire structure was to be of wrought iron. The roof itself supported on rows of wrought iron shafts arranged in groups, with each shaft approximately the width of a gas pipe and resting on a small stone base. The spandrils, wrought into leafy branches, formed five arcades from east to west across the quadrangle. This method Skidmore believed "held . . . out the possibility of uniting artistic ironwork with the present tubular construction, and a prospect of a new feature in the application of iron to Gothic architecture."[60] Indeed, this first design for the roof was extremely light and elegant.[61] However, the *Building News* had warned against following Ruskin's "pernicious heresy . . . to copy nature" in structural ironwork.

The unfortunate who, by the meretricious glitter of that empty lyricism which flows from Denmark Hill may be led astray from the true and wholesome teachings of art under the pretense of "going to nature" will find at the end of their downward course, not nature—but confusion, disappointment, and grief.[62]

And even before it was completed the roof had to be taken down. The failure was blamed on Woodward for making the glass, wood, and clay external roof too heavy, whereas the fault lay in the support construction itself. For though Skidmore had spoken with seeming authority on the spanning of large areas with wrought-iron structures, he had in fact never actually undertaken anything on such a large scale. The real problem was that the structure could not support its own weight. Though the shafts and spandrils appeared light and graceful, they were heavy and structurally weak. Thus, even before completion they began to bend under their own weight.[63]

The second roof, designed by Skidmore for an additional £5,000 and fitted up in his works in Staffordshire, was finished in March 1859. Though it lacked the lightness and elegance of the first design, it was more pleasing to the "scientific eye." The narrow bases were replaced by larger stone ones, the groups of wrought iron tubular pillars were changed to large cast iron shafts and the arched piping was replaced by solid cast iron arches. Only the spandrils remained the same. Even this structure was found to be unsound in parts and had to be subsequently reinforced with extra struts and more substantial shafts.[64]

As it now stands, the roof is supported by clusters of cast iron shafts (Fig. 64). Then, at less than half the total height of the court, wrought iron spandrils spring from the caps to form pointed arches. The iron pillars divide the court into three main aisles somewhat like the nave and aisles of a church. This suggests, as has been shown by others, that Woodward was familiar with the unexecuted design by William Slater for an Iron Church begun in 1855 by R. C. Carpenter and published in *Instrumenta Ecclesiastica*[65] in 1856 before work began on the roof in Oxford. To be sure, this glass and iron roof seems a particularly un-Ruskinian feature. Ruskin objected to the use of iron as a visible support because of the formal aspects of the material. In the *Seven Lamps*, however, he did admit that "abstractedly there can be no doubt that iron will have to be used as well as wood; and the time is probably near when a new system of architectural laws will be developed, adapted entirely to metallic construction."[66] Furthermore, it was necessary somehow to support the glass roof of the inner court, and the most practical way was to use iron.

It was also necessary for Ruskin and Acland to rationalize this use and to bring it into the general iconographic scheme of the building. Acland in *The Oxford Museum* explained it thus:

> The rigid (cast) material supports the vertical pressure; the malleable (wrought) iron is employed for the ornament, and chiefly hand-wrought.
> . . . The wrought iron ornaments represent in the large spandrils that occupy the interspaces between the arches of the principal aisles, large interwoven branches, with leaf and flower, of lime, chestnut, sycamore, walnut, palm, and other trees and shrubs, of native or of exotic growth; and in various parts of the lesser decorations, in the capitals, and nestled in the trefoils of the girders, leaves of elm, briar, water-lily, passion-flower, ivy, holly, and many others.[67]

The wrought iron capitals (Figs. 65, 66) are remarkable for their naturalism and delicacy. The bells of the capitals themselves are plain and unmolded. The wrought iron plants and leaves are not in fact a part of the support structure of the capital at all. Instead, they have been applied to it and are attached to the necks of the capitals by a narrow ornamental band at the base of their stems. This method of construction allowed for the fineness of detail and free-flowing naturalism of these capitals which, it is true, would be impossible in any other material.[68]

Thus an attempt was made both to Gothicize the ironwork and to bring it into harmony with the carved foliate decoration of the interior. But more than that, the leafy branches of the spandrils create a literal forest of the Gothic arches (Figs. 67, 68). The reference here to the naturalism of Gothic, even perhaps to the mythic origin of the Gothic arch, is clear. This was certainly one way in which the "principle of diversity in unity" was carried out in the building's overall scheme.[69] Indeed, the ironwork was painted white, buff, and a dark brownish purple to harmonize with the colors of the surrounding stone and brick in the inner court. Ruskin approved of its execution. Though he did not think it "an absolutely good design" he himself drew patterns for some of the wrought iron leafage for one of the spandrils.[70]

Ruskin took an active interest in many other aspects of the design of the

Museum. And it is important here to determine the full extent of his involvement in the work and his responsibility for decisions made concerning the design.

He had supported Acland from the beginning in the idea of a science museum at Oxford, and when the question of style arose, he realized that it was a good opportunity to take a stand for Gothic in an important building for a number of reasons. He felt strongly that the museum building should be Gothic in a university whose architecture was predominantly Gothic. Furthermore, Gothic architecture lent itself easily to later expansion which would probably be necessary in a teaching museum. The naturalism which he recognized as the basic character of Gothic architecture made it appropriate to a museum of natural history and a place where science was to be taught. Finally, by this time he was already familiar with the Irish work of Deane and Woodward and no doubt he approved of their practice of allowing the active creative participation of the workmen.

It is possible that Ruskin, as Allingham wrote to Rossetti, may have written to Woodward to express his approval of TCD, but probably not before the competition was held for the Oxford Museum. Furthermore, it seems very unlikely that he had anything to do with the architects' invitation to enter the competition, which was in any case open, with architects invited by public advertisement. In fact, there was a far closer personal connection between Acland and the Deanes. Sir Thomas Deane and Sir Thomas Dyke Acland, a politician and philanthropist and the father of Henry Acland, were both keen yachtsmen and old friends. In 1842 Henry Acland had visited Cork as the guest of the Deanes, on which occasion he also met Woodward and wrote enthusiastically to his parents of his hosts; I "have done more and heard more strange things in six hours than heretofore. I cannot sufficiently admire the apparent harmony, and well conducted and elegant accomplishments of every member of the family."[71] There is, however, no evidence of collusion between Acland and Deane in the Oxford Museum competition. In December, 1854, Deane wrote to Sir Thomas Acland,

> My collegiate course in Architecture progresses—my early debut, the Queen's College Cork (how well I recollect your anxiety for me). Next, time honoured Trinity College Dublin, the plans of which you saw, the building now a storey high, developing much beauty and making not a little stir in Architectural observation. And now we are about to leave behind our footprints on the sands of time in beautiful Oxford. To be in the field of fame with my professional Brethren of England was our

ambition, and after an honourable and well fought competition by thirty-three [sic] architects for the museum, "Sir Thomas Deane, Son and Woodward have been successful." "Nisi Dominus aedificaverit domum suum" was our motto. God prospering his own word. Your high-minded, energetic and talented son Doctor Acland of course, knew not who were the architects of Nisi Dominus. I am thus doubly proud that he was one of its anxious supporters, merit alone leading him in his opinion.[72]

Ruskin, however, was initially less interested in the actual design which Deane and Woodward submitted than in the Gothic *cause*. At the end of the *Stones of Venice III* he had written:

The effort to introduce the [Gothic] style exclusively for ecclesiastical purposes, excites against it the strong prejudices of many persons who might otherwise be easily enlisted among its most ardent advocates . . . let us use it for our civil and domestic buildings . . . churches are not the proper scenes for experiments in untried architecture, nor for exhibitions of unaccustomed beauty.[73]

But he did not have high hopes of success in Oxford and was in any case otherwise occupied at the time, as he wrote in October 1854 to Mrs. Acland:

As for the plans, it is no use troubling myself about them, because they certainly won't build a Gothic Museum and if they would—I haven't the workmen yet to do it, and I mean to give my whole strength, which is not more than I want, to teaching the workmen, and when I have got people who can build, I will ask for employment for them.[74]

Nevertheless, he was strongly opposed to E. M. Barry's Palladian design, "Fiat Justitia," which he considered "one of the most commonplace and contemptible imitations of those masters [Sansovino, Palladio, San Michele] I have ever seen."[75] But at this point Ruskin was also not very enthusiastic about Deane and Woodward's design. He wrote to Acland: "I think N. D. though by no means a first-rate design, yet quite as good as is likely to be got in these days, and on the whole good."[76] Yet when Deane and Woodward's design was successful he felt it as a personal victory. As he wrote to Acland, "I have just received your telegraphic message from Woodward, and am going to thank God for it, and lie down to sleep. . . . To me this is as a kind of first fruits for sowing of which 'I knew not whether should prosper.' I am glad after all, it is at Oxford."[77] Ruskin's interest in the project grew after he met Woodward and realized the opportunity which the Museum seemed to offer for testing his aesthetic and moral theories directly. Again he wrote to Acland:

> Now then—indeed. The great good of this matter is that Mr. Woodward is evidently a person who will allow of suggestion and is glad of help— though better able himself to do without either than most. But there seems to be something quite providential . . . in the way my work is being laid out for me at present . . . here is this college [*sic*] with you and Woodward both ready to do anything possible with money.[78]

It is not known exactly when and under what circumstances Ruskin and Woodward first met. However, they were probably introduced by Acland when Woodward came to Oxford to begin work in December 1854.[79] From the accounts of Acland, Tuckwell, Cook, and Ruskin himself, he and Woodward were in constant communication during the building of the Museum.[80] Ruskin expressed his high estimation of Woodward and described the nature of their interaction in a letter to F. J. Furnivall in 1855:

> Sir Charles [*sic*] Deane and Mr. Woodward are, I believe, partners. Mr. Woodward is, as far as I am concerned, the acting man. I see Woodward, and tell him what I want—and if Sir Charles Deane does it, I am much obliged to Sir Charles Deane. . . . If I want Gothic, I must for the present go to Mr. Woodward or Mr. Scott.[81]

Tuckwell gives perhaps a more accurate account of their interaction: "Ruskin himself hovered about to bless the Museum work and to suggest improvements, which silent Woodward sometimes smilingly put by."[82] Even when Ruskin, years later, relinquished his championship of the Gothic Revival, he remained constant in his praise of both Woodward's work and character. In 1865 he spoke of Woodward as "one of the most earnest souls that ever gave itself to the arts, and one of my truest and most loving friends."[83] Tuckwell described Woodward in Oxford:

> Then into our midst came Woodward, architect of the museum, a man of rare genius and deep artistic knowledge, beautiful in face and char- acter, but with the shadow of an early death already stealing over him.

> He was a grave and curiously silent man: of his partners, men greatly
> his inferiors, the elder, Sir Thomas Deane was a ceaseless chatterbox,
> the younger, son to Sir Thomas, stammered . . .

and gave a rather satirical characterization of the three partners in congregation, "One won't talk, one can't talk, one never stops talking."[84]

During the building, Woodward spent half of the year in England, dividing his time between Oxford and London, where he opened an office and established residence in 1857, and the other half in Ireland. When in Oxford, both he and Ruskin stayed with the Aclands in Broad Street. According to Ruskin, he took charge of the Oxford work when Woodward was absent.[85] It is from Ruskin and Rossetti that we get the impression that during this period Woodward was the principal designer and superintendent of the firm's work in England while Deane managed the Dublin offices.

It is clear that Ruskin was not directly responsible for any aspects of the firm's original design for the Museum. He only became involved when construction was substantially completed and work had begun on the decorative scheme and fittings. But even here his direct participation was limited. He had very little to do with the design for the interior or the didactic decorative scheme for the central court, which was a part of Deane and Woodward's original plan for the Museum.

Acland and John Phillips (Professor of Geology) were more involved with the interior arrangements than was Ruskin. In 1858 Phillips drew up a plan for the distribution of the marble columns and the plants to be carved in the capitals. All the natural orders of botany were to be displayed in the capitals and the geological epochs in the columns, where igneous rocks were employed in the ground floor and sedentary rocks in the upper corridor. Each column and pier was inscribed with a number and a label giving the geological name of the stone and the botanical name of the plant.[86] There were 126 columns, 64 piers, and 192 capitals and corbels in all. The carving was to be paid for by public subscription. Of these only the 30 capitals of the lower level and 16 in the west corridor of the upper level were executed in 1858-1860 before funds ran out and work was abandoned. The remaining capitals were done at various times in the following years. By 1905 all the capitals in the lower corridors had been carved. The remaining 80 capitals in the upper corridors were completed following Phillips' original plan, between 1905 and 1910 by Mr. Mills and Louis Holt of the firm of Messrs. Farmer and Brindley of Westminister Bridge Road, London.[87]

[67]

The original 46 capitals were carved by the O'Sheas, their nephew Edward Whellan, and others.[88] Again, the O'Sheas were given a free hand in the decoration and they brought in plants to carve from the botanical gardens, which had been specially selected by John Phillips. The stone for the capitals was left in block, "to allow as much liberty as possible to the carver . . . in some cases the foliage might run up on [the abacus]—covering some of the moulding here and there . . . the upper half . . . [of the necking] is left in block because the foliage springs out of it in some cases, or may do so."[89]

The quality of the carving varies partly because there were a far greater number of capitals and corbels to do than in TCD and partly because it was not just the work of the O'Sheas. The capitals of the lower and upper levels also differ considerably in handling. The upper ones are much less elaborate than those in the lower ranges. This is due mainly to a difference in materials. Caen stone was used in the lower ones and Taynton stone, which does not lend itself to such fine work, in the upper capitals.

The lower capitals are bolder and more deeply undercut than at TCD and again display the O'Sheas' remarkable talent for rendering plant and animal forms. The designs are also more varied and unconventionalized. The capitals themselves are larger and it is perhaps due to Ruskin's influence that those in the lower arcade are more closely based on the loggia capitals in the Ducal Palace in Venice, engravings of which were published in the *Builder* in 1851 and illustrated in the *Seven Lamps*, the *Stones of Venice* and the *Examples*.[90] The O'Sheas adopted the octagonal shape of these capitals in their carvings and one in particular of foxes and ferns is very much like one of the Ducal Palace capitals illustrated by Ruskin in the *Examples* (Figs. 69, 70). It is also possible that some of the more abstract designs were influenced by Ruskin's schematic drawings of Venetian carved leafage in the *Stones of Venice II*.[91] In any case, the general shape of the capitals, as Woodward explained in a letter to William Bell Scott, followed the "form which Ruskin so much likes" (Fig. 71).

Again, the O'Sheas' work is characterized by a controlled balance of naturalism and abstract design where each capital is different according to the natural qualities of growth and structure of the individual plants represented (Figs. 72-76). In one, spiky grasses, forget-me-nots, and small birds and insects are depicted in a random cluster as they would be found on any wayside. In others, delicate lilies and crocuses have an almost transparent fragility against the solid mass of the capital bell and show every vein and cicatrice in their folded petals and leaves. A most remarkable sense of stored energy and potential growth is expressed in one capital where young shoots and ferns furled like tightly coiled springs twist with rhythmic tension around the bell. Even more than in TCD these capitals have the consummate sense of design that was to distinguish William Morris' wallpapers and chintzes.

The originality of the work cannot be overstressed and is unparalleled in contemporary architectural sculpture. It was not so much unique in manner as in excellence. Similar naturalistic carving was being done in other buildings at the time; but if we compare the work of Thomas Earp, the sculptor who worked with Street—say at St. James the Less, Westminster, or Thomas Nicholls, Burges' sculptor—with any one of the Oxford capitals by the O'Sheas, the former appears stiff, repetitive, and conventionalized. It is perhaps because Street and Burges designed the ornament for their buildings themselves that the sculpture lacks freedom, daring, and exuberance.[92] But this is not the whole reason, as we can see from another example in University Church, Dublin begun in 1855. John Hungerford Pollen allowed his untrained Irish workmen the same freedom Woodward had given to O'Sheas.[93] The result, though competent, is awkward and uninspired by comparison. It would seem that Ruskin's admonition that one could not "secure a great national monument of art by letting loose the first lively Irishman you could get hold of," was true.[94] The inventiveness and excellence of the Oxford Museum carving is due largely to the remarkable and original talent of the O'Sheas. The supposition that it influenced William Morris is conjectural. However, he and Burne-Jones had recently matriculated at Oxford and there is no doubt that they were familiar with the Museum work in progress during their most impressionable undergraduate years. Furthermore, they had already made the acquaintance of Woodward, with whom they were soon to collaborate on the Union Society building.

The capitals of the upper corridor of the Museum are carved in shallower relief without the depth and undercutting of the lower ones (Figs. 77, 78). The arrangement of the plants themselves is more schematic. Some of them seem almost like botanists' samples—laid out for study, which in a sense they are. A good example is one of sweet peas where the roots and the plant in bud and in flower are shown.

Other foliate stone carving is to be found in the lower string course of the Exhibition Hall, in the spurs of the column bases, the large corbels in the exhibition court and the corbel-capitals in the entrance hall, which are as vigorously representational and deeply undercut as the lower range of capitals (Figs. 79, 80). Here the work is not as tightly composed as in the freestanding capitals. It spills out at the sides along the walls, giving the same sense of irrepressible and exuberant natural growth as the carved consoles in the hall of TCD. The corbels, like clumps of teeming plant and animal life, are nestled under the springing of the arches with the occasional monkey or sprig in angles and corners around the pier. The foliage sprouts from small pointed bases, sometimes shaped like pots or stylized roots and stems. It would seem that the O'Sheas were given an even freer hand in choosing subjects for the capitals in the entrance vestibule (Fig. 81). They are carved with rabbits, birds, owls, and snakes rather than the carefully selected botanical specimens in the exhibition court. Another example of the O'Sheas' work is a carved fireplace in the Hope Entomology Department, where insects of all kinds are depicted crawling among the leaves and creepers carved on the mantelpiece.

The general decorative scheme of the exhibition court changed somewhat after 1855. Columns were attached to the sides of the upper piers and the lower string course of foliate carving was added. Relief carving in the voussoirs of the lower arches and large roundels in the wall above, which appear in the diagram by Woodward of 1855 (Fig. 63), were left out in the final execution.[95] It is possible that the last features were replaced by the unexecuted idea for a large painted mural on these walls. An anonymous colored drawing for the mural (Fig. 82) shows heroic and chivalric medieval scenes, and probably dates from about the time that Rossetti and other Pre-Raphaelites began on the Oxford Union murals in 1857. Indeed, the *Art Journal* noted, "It is proposed to adorn the new Museum with similar decorations." The romantic medievalism of this design seems somewhat incongruous in a science museum and out of place with the iconographic scheme of the building. It is not surprising, therefore, that it was not executed.[96]

There was, however, one instance of large-scale mural painting in the Museum, in the Geology Department. Here, The Reverend Richard St. John Tyrwhitt, a writer on art and a friend and disciple of Ruskin's as well as a friend of John Hungerford Pollen's had painted the *Mer de Glace* across one whole wall.

There was also a small amount of painted decoration in other parts of the building. The walls of a number of the offices and side rooms were painted a dark olive green and some of them had ornamental friezes just beneath the cornice line done in mellow earthy colors—greens, browns, dark purple, yellows, and reds. The designs in these friezes are always abstract, often geometric and Celtic

[70]

in inspiration. A well preserved example is in the rooms of the Hope Entomology Department (Fig. 83) where the top third of the wall is painted like a tapestry of repeated geometric and stylized plant forms. The colors are browns, greens, and blues with the occasional red and yellow highlight. The wooden rafters are also painted, as in TCD, in lively purples and reds and marked with black stripes and chevrons. The effect is highly successful. Much of this stenciled work was reportedly done by Swan, a friend of William Morris, who also worked on the Union roof.[97]

It is also possible that John Hungerford Pollen was involved, as he too was in Oxford at the time working on the Union murals. The style is similar to some of his decorative painting at Blickling Hall and Kilkenny Castle in the same years. Throughout the 1850s, until Woodward's death in 1861, Pollen's name is closely linked with the firm's, and the instances of their collaboration are many. Thus it is possible that he also had a hand in painting the beams and rafters in TCD, since he was in Dublin at the same time. He had, in any case, done similar work before—notably, on Butterfield's restored roof of Merton Chapel in 1849.[98]

The woodwork in the Museum is decorated with Deane and Woodward's distinctive zigzag and dog-tooth "transition Norman" style notching on the roof beams and around the door frames. These last were designed by Woodward, who made several sketches for them in his notebook.

The furniture and wooden fittings designed by the architects, including chairs, tables, desks, book- and show-cases, are notable for their structural realism. Construction is not only revealed but dramatized. Joints, hinges, and chamfered corners become decorative features in themselves. Fret-cut foliage and pierced geometric patterns are incised into the furniture and heavy oak doors (Fig. 84). These are very different from Butterfield's Gothicized furniture of the same period with its tracery forms and other Gothic motifs. Instead, Woodward used simple vernacular construction and ornamentation to medievalize his work. There is nothing like it in English furniture until the Morris circle began designing their own arts and crafts furniture in the early 1860s along the same lines of honest construction and independence from period precedent. Such "purpose built" furniture designed by Woodward became a characteristic of all the firm's future buildings.[99]

The hand-wrought metal work fittings were also designed under the architects' direction. Often, as in the brass lock on the front door, these were decorated with leaf patterns—sometimes picked out in colored enamel. Wrought-iron door hinges and firedogs were shaped, following the principle of "diversity in unity," into graceful plant and flower forms like the spandrils of the roof structure.

While all of the carved and painted decoration in the Oxford Museum follows Ruskin's hierarchy of ornament, elaborated in the *Seven Lamps*, he had little to do with the interior of the building directly. His only recorded designs were made for some of the wrought-iron spandrils. Otherwise, he is reported to have raised one of the brick piers, but this is largely legend.[100]

Instead Ruskin concentrated his efforts on the exterior of the Museum. His interest in the external decoration, almost to the exclusion of all else, was the source of a considerable difference of opinion with Woodward. In October 1855 Ruskin wrote to the Rev. George Butler, Secretary of the Museum Delegacy: "If Mr. Woodward will undertake that the capitals in the inside shall be decorated with floral sculpture, I wish all my contribution to be spent in decorating the external windows of the facade—or porch of the same as Mr. Woodward thinks best."[101] Woodward objected to Ruskin's attitude which, in any case, ran contrary to the conditions of the commission that "interior arrangement" was to be considered "more essential than exterior decoration,"[102] and must have tried to change his mind, but as the latter wrote to Acland,

> I would not on any account change the destination of what I can give you . . . I press on people the duty of decorating outside rather than in—my main principle being simple life, and richly besowed public joy—nor do I think the inside of a museum in much *need* of decoration and hence my obstinate answer to Woodward.[103]

Ruskin described his actual participation in the work to Mrs. Carlyle in 1855, "I have also designed and drawn a window for the Museum at Oxford and have every now and then had to look over a parcel of five or six new designs for fronts and backs to the said Museum."[104] In fact, he made designs for a number of windows for the main front, at least one of which was carved, as he recorded in *Sesame and Lilies*.[105] He also proposed modifications to the lower range of windows on the principal facade and published a design for one in *The Oxford Museum*. He prepared other drawings for a series of windows in the upper range, but none of these have survived.[106] Ruskin's design for a canopied balcony, published in *The Oxford Museum*, was never executed, even though he made a special donation for it.[107]

Ruskin was also responsible in a more general way for the fact that a greater amount of ornament was ultimately designed for the exterior than had originally been planned. The most noticeable additions were made to the tower and second-storey windows. These were worked out by Woodward in a series of sketches of relief carving for the jambs, archivolts, capitals, and the tracery in his notebook (Fig. 85). Ruskin offered his advice on these windows, which Woodward seemingly did not follow.

> I have been thinking that if it came to a question of expense, the ornament might be better spared in the capitals than anywhere, as the flower work down the shafts and mouldings is nearly enough, and you might have plain bell capitals.[108]

The decoration of the windows, like so much else, was never completed. In fact, only one was entirely finished. The carving here was also done by the O'Sheas, to their own designs except for the general guidelines provided by Woodward. In a letter to Acland of 1859, James O'Shea included a sketch for a window he was working on (Figs. 86, 87), and added,

> I wish I had three or four more like myself and would carve every jamb in the Place from time to time and Bob [sic] all the cost of them—I would not desire better sport than putting monkeys, cats, dogs, rabbits, and hares, and so on in different attitudes on those jambs.[109]

The most significant alterations were made to the entrance portal. Woodward's original idea, for which he made many studies, was for a recessed and richly carved porch.[110] Thomas Woolner, at the request of Ruskin and Woodward, prepared a drawing for it. He wrote to Woodward concerning his design:

> As to subject, the most poetical and appropriate seems to me the "Tree of Knowledge" as exhibited in the "Temptation" and "Expulsion" . . . there would be in one [spandril], two figures, a tree and serpent, and in the other three figures and a serpent—perhaps a tree.[111]

Convocation, however, refused to sanction the expenditure for a porch and an alternative design for a carved portal was prepared by John Hungerford Pollen (Fig. 88).[112] Acland described the new design and explained its iconographic significance:

> The idea contained in the bas-relief is that of evolution, spiritual and

[73]

material; it takes the received origin of Man as the basis of the thought. On the left-hand side is the first man, Adam, in a state of innocence, holding back the bloodhound, emblem of suffering and death. At the base on the right, Eve is attentively listening to the voice of the tempter, still undecided. From these two ascend flowers and thorns and fruit. These reach to the top of the arch, on which rest the Angel of Life, bearing in one hand an open book, the emblem of intellectual and spiritual life, in the other the dividing nucleated cell, the type of all material function, growth, and decay.[113]

The iconography of this portal is significant. In 1859, the year in which it was designed, Charles Darwin published his *Origin of Species*. Woodward and Acland's goal in the Museum was to bring art and science into a relationship of mutual service using the metaphor of the building as the Book of Nature.[114] Pollen's portal extends this metaphor to include the Book of God. It is somehow fitting that the famous debate between Thomas Huxley and Bishop Wilberforce in 1860 took place in the Museum.[115]

Pollen's drawing was exhibited in the offices of the Clerk of the Works in Oxford, and a pamphlet soliciting subscriptions to pay for its execution was circulated by Acland. Though it was begun, the carving was never completed.[116]

It had been Ruskin's desire, and a realization of his principles, that eminent artists should design decoration for the Museum. He wrote concerning this to Acland:

> I hope to be able to get Millais and Rossetti to design flower and beast borders—crocodiles and various vermin—such as you are particularly fond of . . . and we will carve them and inlay them with Cornish serpentine all about your windows, I will pay for a good deal myself, and I doubt not to find funds. Such capitals as we will have![117]

Though Millais never did any work for the Museum, Rossetti and Munro were consulted on some of the designs for the lower windows.[118]

Ruskin was also instrumental in introducing Woodward and Rossetti. The two met late in 1854 and rapidly became friends. Rossetti recorded, "Many were the plans for work to be done between us and our friends."[119] Yet when Woodward asked Rossetti and Elizabeth Siddal to undertake some designs for the decoration in July 1855, both refused, though apparently Elizabeth Siddal made some drawings which Ruskin found exquisite, but thought too delicate to be carved by Woodward's carvers.[120] Rossetti had been commissioned to paint "Newton gathering pebbles on the shores of the Ocean of Truth" for the Museum. The subject had understandably little appeal for him, and he abandoned it in favor of painting the *Morte D'Arthur* murals at the Union. Georgiana Burne-Jones further records that Rossetti and Morris carved one capital each at the Museum. Rossetti's reportedly had "ivy and bryony on it" and Morris' had "foliage and birds, done with great spirit and life." Neither capital has been identified—from their descriptions, they could be any one of a number of carvings.

Generally, however, Rossetti was more active in helping to enlist his friends. He wrote to John Tupper, Woolner, and Munro—all members of the Medieval Society, whose aim was to promote the study of thirteenth century art and architecture—recommending Woodward as "a friend of mine, and a thorough 13th century Gothic man," requesting them to execute some of the statues for the Museum court for hardly any pay.[121] Rossetti also introduced Woodward to Morris, Burne-Jones, and others who frequently assembled in Oxford during these years. In 1859 Woodward became a member of the shortlived Hogarth Club to which Ruskin, Street, Webb, Bodley, Pollen, Halliday, the entire Pre-Raphaelite Brotherhood (except Millais), and many others belonged.[122]

Through Ruskin and Acland, Woodward also met Sir Walter Calverley and Lady Trevelyan. Sir Walter, a well-known philanthropist, geologist, antiquarian, and botanist, had long been a keen supporter of the new science museum in Oxford. His wife, Pauline, was a writer, critic, artist, friend of Ruskin's, and patroness of the Pre-Raphaelites. She and Woodward became firm friends while he was working in Oxford and the Trevelyans too were drawn into the project.[123] In June 1859 the *Builder* reported that "in arranging two or three of the capitals, Mrs. Brodie [the wife of Sir Benjamin Brodie, Professor of Chemistry at Oxford] and Lady Trevelyan had lent their aid with good result."[124] In September 1859, Lady Trevelyan sent Woodward a lily to be carved by the O'Sheas and in the same year a capital was carved "from a design by Lady Trevelyan from a plant or plants and animals named by Sir Walter."[125]

Ruskin was perhaps most effective in soliciting funds for the Museum. He contributed a considerable amount of money himself and managed to gather support from many private sources for the decoration when the University cut off its funds in 1858. He gave £300 from his own pocket and another large sum was donated by his father.[126] He also launched appeals and prepared pamphlets soliciting subscriptions for the columns, capitals, and the freestanding statues of "the Great Founders and Improvers of Natural Knowledge" which were placed along the arcade of the court (Fig. 89). Donors could give a statue for £70, a marble shaft for £5, and a capital for a gift of £5. The Queen donated five statues, and her example was followed by a number of other eminent and wealthy benefactors. When Woodward was away Ruskin also handled subscriptions for carving the external windows and paid for a set of them himself.[127]

In 1859 he and Acland published their booklet *The Oxford Museum*. Intended as both a guide and fundraiser, it is also the most important contemporary document relating to the building. In it they stated their ambition for the Museum, "All the building was intended to teach some great lesson, not only in art and architecture, but also in the illustrations afforded by the several parts of the purposes to which the whole is devoted."[128]

Ruskin and Acland's goal; to bring art and science into a relationship of mutual service, was expressed at Oxford as at TCD, but with more conscious intent. Acland explained it thus:

> In this building every facility would be offered to the student of the world and of man. The very pillars around the corridors would teach geology; the iron foliage of the spandrils of the roof would teach botany; and . . . the capitals and corbels . . . would one day exhibit a complete series of our Flora and our Fauna.[129]

Statues of eminent men of science and philosophy—Euclid, Archimedes, Aristotle, Hippocrates, Pliny, Bacon, Gallileo, Newton, Leibnitz, and others—lined the walls. The didactic purpose and symbolic meaning were clear: the Oxford Museum was to be a center for the ongoing study of science and a monument to the scientific heroes of the past.

Ruskin contributed a statement of the guiding principles of the Gothic Revival which he saw at least partially realized in the Oxford Museum:

> to make art large and publicly beneficial, instead of small and privately engrossed or secluded; to make art fixed instead of portable, associating it with local character and historical memory; to make art expressive instead of curious, valuable for its suggestions and teachings, more than for the mode of its manufacture. . . . The second great principle of the Gothic Revivalists, is that all art employed in decoration should

be informative, conveying truthful statements about natural facts, if it conveys *any* statement . . . with as much resemblance to nature as the necessary treatment of the piece of ornament in question will admit of. . . . The third great principle of the Gothic Revival is that all architectural ornamentation should be executed by the men who design it, and should be of various degrees of excellence, admitting, and therefore exciting, the intelligent co-operation of various classes of workmen. . . . The Museum at Oxford was, I know, intended by its designer to exhibit in its decoration the working of these three principles.[130]

Ruskin's statement is revealing. He was primarily concerned at this time with the ethical and social responsibilities of public art, decoration, and the moral conditions of the workmen who execute it. And it was these aspects of the work at the Oxford Museum, rather than the particulars of its design, that interested him most. Essentially, he cared far more about the principles themselves than about their embodiment. The Oxford Museum interested him directly only so far as it was a vindication of these principles. He was pleased to learn from Sir Thomas Deane that if the workmen are allowed to "vary their designs and thus interest their heads and hearts in what they are doing . . . the moral energy thus brought to bear on the matter quickens, and therefore cheapens, the production in a most important degree."[131]

He also gave personal encouragement to the carvers. Acland had secured a building of the Radcliffe Institute with reading rooms and other facilities for the workmen. In 1856 Ruskin delivered a lecture there enlarging on the scope for originality afforded by the principles Woodward was following. In 1858 he offered a prize for a sculpture of "an historical subject," which was won by James O'Shea.[132] These efforts seem to have made an impression on the workmen. As O'Shea wrote to Acland in 1859: "If I was to doo [sic] all the upper windows I would carve every jamb for nothing for the sake of art alone—."[133] Indeed, O'Shea would seem to have become the very embodiment of the Ruskinian workman.

The publication of *The Oxford Museum* marked a turning point in work at the site. From this time on Ruskin began gradually to take over from Woodward. The latter's declining health forced him to spend the last three winters of his life in Madeira, Algiers, and the south of France. During this time Ruskin assumed much of the responsibility for handling the subscriptions and managing the work. In January 1860 he wrote of his activities to Miss Heaton,

You will be glad to know that [your donation] will enable another window to be carved in the front of the building, under my immediate direction, as the architect, Mr. Woodward, is ill and had to go to Madeira for the winter, and I was obliged to take the conduct of the decoration while he was away.[134]

Ruskin also played a perhaps unknowing part in the dismissal of the O'Sheas. A decision had been taken (in the interests of economy) that the jambs of the upper windows were to be left uncarved. O'Shea, however, proceeded with the work and appealed without success to both Acland and Ruskin for money and authorization to continue: "I hope you will do all you can to have those carved. It will give me more work for the money, but I never carved anything in my life that I will be so proud of if I do these."[135] Subsequently a member of Convocation ordered him to stop and complained about his refusal to do so. In fury, O'Shea began blocking out parrots and owls on the portal arch, which were taken to be a parody of the members of Convocation, and as a result he was dismissed.[136]

When Woodward died in May 1861, Ruskin lost interest in the project and work ground to a complete halt. To Acland he wrote, "I don't know where I am . . . I'm very sorry for Woodward. There is nothing whatever to criticise in the Oxford Museum. . . . Nothing bad and nothing good. Your wife's regret is the reasonablest."[137]

Ruskin later changed his mind. Rather than seeing it as an exciting but not wholly successful experiment, he decided it was a failure. In a lecture of 1877 he declared that he had never meant that "a handsome building could be built of common brickbats" or that "you could secure a great national monument of art by letting loose the first lively Irishman you could get hold of."[138]

Though he was ultimately critical of the execution of the Oxford Museum, he still never openly criticized Woodward's design. His disillusionment grew gradually with the frustrations of insufficient funds and the constant interference of University officials. In 1858 he had warned Acland, "*Entirely* satisfactory very few issues are or can be; and when the enterprise, as in this instance, involves the development of many new and progressive principles, we must always be prepared for a due measure of disappointment."[139] By this time his enthusiasm was already fading and he realized that rather than being a great testimony to the rightness of his ideals, and a glorification of science, the Oxford Museum "will have the look of a place, not where a revered system of instruction is

[78]

established, but where an unadvised experiment is being disadvantageously attempted."[140]

Later, Ruskin even tried to dissociate the theory from its embodiment entirely. The failure of the Oxford Museum, he claimed, was due to "the general conditions of the time," not to the deficiency of the principles which guided it.[141] In 1877 he declared, "I was virtually answerable and will answer, so far as either my old friend, Mr. Woodward, or I myself, had our way with [the Museum], or were permitted by fate to follow our way through."[142] Rossetti, too, asserted,

> I know how much there is in this building with which he himself [Woodward] was greatly dissatisfied—the influences at work in its direction being in great measure unartistic not only to the extent of indifference but of antagonism—carping and opposition had wearied him partially of a work on which he entered with the warmest enthusiasm but still it is in the main a very noble one and worthy of its purpose. Many faults in it—were things traced to their sources—are not his at all, but committed in his absence by the presumptuous (stupid) interference of Oxford Dons to suit each man's fancies for his own department.[143]

Rossetti drew an allegory of Woodward's martyrdom at the hands of the University in which he depicted Alma Mater pressing a Judas-kiss on the brow of a knight with Woodward's features, while unobtrusively disarming him.[144]

The Oxford Museum was one of the most important and influential English buildings in the second half of the nineteenth century. It laid the groundwork for Gothic in monumental public building and pioneered the integration of Gothic with modern engineering. Furthermore, it was one of the first instances in architecture of the successful collaboration between architects, artists, and craftsmen. These last innovations were slower to catch on than the first. But the formal type of the Oxford Museum had an immediate and decisive impact on public architecture even before construction on the building was completed.

The Museum became the prime object in a series of replications. Because of its formal clarity, symmetry, axiality, and regular compartmentation, in other words, its essential classicism, the Oxford Museum, unlike most High Victorian Gothic buildings, was easily typified.[145] As the type itself was historically associated with medieval municipal structures, it is not surprising that the earliest replications of the Museum were Government buildings and town halls. The first

[79]

of these was G. G. Scott's nearly contemporary project for the Hamburg Rathaus of 1855-1856, which is, in fact, even closer than the Oxford Museum to the Ypres Cloth Hall. Scott did two more designs in 1857 along these lines, with two or three storeys of regular Gothic arcades and a central tower. The *Building News* immediately recognized the source of Scott's first competition design for the Foreign Office (Fig. 90) which, it claimed, "recalls at a glance the Oxford New Museum," and added, "We have heard him [Scott] speak with a warm admiration of the distinguished merits of the latter building, and he has proved the sincerity of his admiration by casting his own plan in the same mould."[146] But it is interesting that Scott's design for the War Office in the same competition recalls just as strongly Street's design for the Oxford Museum of 1853 in the *Urgent Plea*. In 1857 Scott produced another unexecuted design, for the Halifax Town Hall, in which the same format of regular two-storey facade, high-pitched roof and dormers is used. Only here the tower is brought forward and placed above a projecting porch. Another design, in the Government Offices competition for the War Office by Pritchard and Seddon, also followed the Oxford Museum in the massing of the main front. Pritchard and Seddon even reproduced a variant of the tangential chemistry laboratory to the side. These replications provided, in turn, a monumentalized and diversified Oxonian prototype for the next major competition of the following decade, the Law Courts. The influence of the Oxford Museum even ranged as far afield as North America and is evident in Fuller and Jones' Canadian Parliament building in Ottawa begun in 1859.

In England the type reappears in E. W. Godwin's provincial town halls in Northhampton, 1861, and Congleton, Cheshire, in 1864, which have a profusion of Ruskinian detailing. On a much larger scale are Alfred Waterhouse's Assize Courts, 1859-1864, and Town Hall, 1868, in Manchester. Here, however, the influence of the Oxford Museum was probably filtered through Scott's work. Finally, Waterhouse's Natural History Museum in South Kensington begun in 1871—though in style it owes more to Scott's Law Courts design of 1866—is the natural offspring of Deane and Woodward's Oxford Museum. It was the next major museum in England to be built in the Gothic style and was, like the Oxford Museum, a science museum. Following Woodward's lead Waterhouse similarly exploited the functional expressiveness and decorative symbolism of the Style to create a richly associative and instructive "informational appliance"—a science museum building which was itself a microcosm of natural facts.[147]

Thus the formal type of the Museum established an image of monumental secular Gothic architecture which persisted for more than two decades. Equally decisive was the impact of the naturalistic stone carving in the Museum. The example of the O'Sheas' work was not only a convincing vindication of Ruskin's principles concerning the liberty of the workman and the representational aspects of sculpture, but also had the effect of encouraging a more general use of plants and other natural forms rather than historicist motifs for ornament in Gothic buildings in the late 1850s and early 1860s.

However, nothing like the Gothicized iron and glass roof of the Oxford Museum was attempted again. It was generally felt that the roof was not entirely successful. And the *Building News* was correct in its judgment that it would "not convert the world to a belief in the universal applicability of Crystal Palace architecture Gothicised."[148] The prejudice that iron construction falls "within the province of engineering rather than architecture" had not been overcome.[149] Though iron structures in the 1860s became more elaborate, few other attempts were made to integrate iron into architecture as Woodward and Skidmore had done at Oxford until the 1890s. Instead, perhaps picking up the cue from Ruskin, and following the example of Woodward's collaboration with the Pre-Raphaelites in the Museum and at the Oxford Union, the medievalist avant-garde in the early 1860s—Street, Burges, and to a lesser extent Scott—began advocating "art-architecture" rather than "engineering-architecture" as pointing the way of the future.

IV

"ART ARCHITECTURE": THE OXFORD UNION

Woodward was responsible for a number of other buildings and small projects executed in Oxford while work on the Museum progressed. The earliest of these was the house for the curator of the Oxford Museum. Though it was a part of the same building program as the Museum, the curator's house was more importantly the first in a series of houses designed and built by the firm in the second half of the 1850s (see Chapter VI).

The remaining commissions are also closely connected with the Museum and resulted from Woodward's new associations and friendships with members of the Oxford community who were either involved with the Museum or were personally acquainted with Ruskin and Acland. Like the Museum these works were executed in an experimental and collaborative spirit and in particular provided Woodward with additional opportunities for trying out the new ideas concerning architectural ornament being developed in the Museum. (Smaller projects—additions or alterations to existing buildings—are discussed in the Appendix along with the firm's other minor works.)

The Oxford Union Society debating hall (now library), is the only complete building of the group. Famous as the site of the Pre-Raphaelite mural paintings of scenes from Mallory's *Morte D'Arthur*, the Union was important in fostering a new notion of "art-architecture" in the 1860s involving richly associational decorative sculpture and painting.

Founded in 1823 as an undergraduate debating society, the Union had, by the 1850s, become something of a school of "practical rhetoric," "political oratory," and a training ground for England's political and judicial leaders.[1] Weekly debates were held in various rooms in the town until the Society, "having grown in fame, a chance room was thought no longer a suitable arena."[2] Thus in 1856 it was decided that a hall specifically for debates should be built. In the same year Woodward was appointed as the architect.[3]

THE OXFORD UNION

The commission was a direct result of Woodward's work at the Museum. Several members of the Society were friends of Acland's and some of them had also served on various Oxford University Museum committees. Furthermore, the president of the Union at the time, John Oakley of Brasenose, was an enthusiastic supporter of the Pre-Raphaelite movement and the "religious aesthetes."[4]

Neither the minutes of the Union building committee nor Woodward's plans for the debating hall have survived. Consequently there is no contemporary record of the development of the design or progress of the work on the building. However, details of the contracts were published in the *Illustrated London News*.[5] Construction began in 1856 and the building was completed by the summer of 1857 when Rossetti and his friends began work on the murals.

The Union building (Figs. 91, 92) is essentially one large room (measuring 62 x 33 x 48 feet) with a small projecting entrance porch on the east side and a tall chimney on the west. In the form of an elongated octagon, the two long sides are twice the length of the other six, which form trilateral aspidal ends on the north and south extremities. A low wall enclosing the Union grounds runs along the south and west sides of the building adjoining the buttressed walls.

The original entrance porch is now obscured by later additions to the building. The first of these, the brick building with stone dressings adjoining the debating hall, was designed by T. N. Deane in 1864. In 1878 a new debating hall by Waterhouse was built on the Union grounds just northwest of Woodward's original hall.[6] Further extensions to Deane's wing were made in 1891, when a new smoking room was added, and in 1910-1911, when a north wing including a new library, rooms, and the steward's house were erected to the designs of Messrs. Mills and Thorpe of Oxford.[7]

The *Ecclesiologist* condemned Woodward's building: "It seems to us to be singularly devoid of any feature, either in detail or proportion; no doubt it was built with very little money. But we have often seen great effects produced with small resources,—there the effect is none at all."[8] Indeed, the Union design was plainly functional and executed within a very limited budget. Practicality was a primary consideration.

The hall had a double purpose, first as an arena for debates and second as a library and reading room. The elliptical form was well suited to the room's dual purpose in providing both the centrality necessary for the debates and a maximum of wall space for the library. These functions were also kept separate, with the debates taking place on the floor of the hall and the library on the gallery which was reached via a staircase outside the room itself. Thus, the public and more private activities could be conveniently accommodated in one room. The gallery also provided additional space for members not taking part in the discussions to observe the debates without causing any interference. Furthermore, the arrangement of the hall was acoustically sound. The apsidal ends and elliptical vault of the roof ensured that speakers' voices would carry throughout the room, while the booklined gallery muffled incidental and otherwise disturbing noises.

The most ingenious practical feature of the hall is the central fireplace. Open on two sides, it projects heat from the middle of the room toward the two far ends of the hall. The design is both unusual and original in having neither a visible flue nor chimney within the room. The flue in fact was constructed underneath the floor to connect with the chimney on the west side of the building. It was calculated that the great height of the shaft would create a sufficient draft to draw the smoke out through the sunken flue.[9]

As in all of his buildings, Woodward made a great display of structure in the Union. The *Illustrated London News* published "an internal perspective view" of the hall (Fig. 93) where "the features of its constructive characteristics" are clearly shown.[10] Indeed, the revealed wooden beams, braces, and wall posts of the gallery and roof constitute the sole "features" of the interior, and form an entirely rational endomorphic support system. The interlocking of this internal skeleton with the epidermal brick shell of the outer walls is also clearly shown. The outward thrust of the wooden wall posts and braces is taken up by the buttresses on the exterior corners of the building. These are further strengthened at points on the south and west sides of the building where they adjoin the low bounding wall of the Union enclosure and their surfaces merge in a fluid interpenetration of their masses. The thinning of the clerestory walls can also be read as a rational expression of the decreased load at this level, and the stone course beneath as a girdle binding the building together.

No medieval precedents for this type of building existed, and Woodward's design is an amalgam of several different but nevertheless related types. The *Building News* gives a clue as to the first: "We should judge that this is not an inconvenient form for such a room, where the members rise to speak from their seats in the body of the hall."[11] Indeed, the most obvious formal prototype for the hall is the English Parliamentary house—a model which is also fitting from an associational point of view. The elongated shape of the room and the arrangement of the benches facing inward from opposite sides of the hall immediately recall the House of Commons. The seat for the Union president chairing the debates is placed like that of the speaker of the House at one end of the chamber. Likewise, the observers' gallery performs a function similar to that of the Strangers' Gallery in the Commons.

The secondary purpose of the hall as a library has been mentioned, and it is not unlikely that Woodward drew on his earlier design for the library at Queen's College Cork, with its long hall and book-lined gallery. Once again, the collegiate type is as fitting here as the parliamentary. The open timber roof—by long tradition a feature of collegiate architecture—was also used, both in the library and in the examination hall at Queen's College. Finally the apsidal ends, clerestory, and ranges of benches suggest a church choir and apse. Indeed, the shape of the building in many ways resembles a large chapel, and though it is a far less elaborate structure, it exhibits several of the same formal qualities as G. E. Street's contemporary design for the Constantinople Memorial Church of 1856-1857, which was likewise a contained apsidal block with buttressed corners, expanses of plain wall surface, and unbroken roof line.

Stefan Muthesius' comment that the Union is "little more than a big school-room" is also telling.[12] The large unified space and rustic timber roof are identifying characteristics of the Victorian Gothic village or parish schoolhouses—a type established by Butterfield, Street, and White in the early 1850s.[13] The matrix of this type involved, aside from rustic cottage features, the articulation of each room as an independent volume from the ground up. Within this context the Union hall can be seen as one large schoolroom. Woodward also assimilated the formal qualities of these simple structures, particularly the simple contours, plain brick walls, volumetric hollowness of space, and coherent mass offset by tall chimneys.

Woodward was not only familiar with the constructed schoolhouses and published designs of Butterfield, Street, and White, but the firm was itself engaged in building a series of small schoolhouses in the Dublin area at this time (see Appendix). Economy and the desired formal qualities of these simple structures led Woodward to use brick or rubble masonry for the schoolhouses as for the Union.

As for style, the building was dubbed a "Venetian Gothic modification" by contemporary reviewers.[14] Indeed, the red and white banded voussoirs of the clerestory openings and the lower windows are Italianate, though the detached window colonnettes are a French convention, and the form of the building is not

[85]

southern but northern Gothic, even Early English—an expansion of the Glaston-bury Kitchen-Stanton Harcourt prototype used by Woodward for the chemistry laboratory at the Museum.

In short, the Union building can be regarded as a variant of Ruskin's ideal—"designed in the forms of English and French thirteenth-century Surface Gothic" (characterized by large and simple mass and closed profile), and "wrought out with the refinement of Italian art in the details."[15]

However, particularly un-Ruskinian are the materials used and the resulting absence of "broad sculptured surfaces."[16] The brick walls did not allow for great expanses of cut stone decoration. Instead Woodward exploited the polychromatic and textural qualities of the red brick. He chose the best and thinnest handmade bricks available which though equal in size are uneven in color and bonded them together with fine mortar joints. The bricks are laid in English bond—rows of headers alternating with rows of stretchers—to create a fine, dense texture. The wall surface ranges in color from yellowish-orange to bluish-purple. In strong sunlight the juxtaposition of these complementary colors creates a vibrant lu-minosity. The warm mottled surface coloration, following Ruskin's "first great principle of architectural color," is here "visibly independent of form."[17] It softens the linearity of the evenly bonded bricks and contrasts pleasantly with the sharp outlines of the building's angular form. Thus a rich surface texture is created without Ruskin's desired broad sculptured ornament. Yet Woodward did stick closely to Ruskin's principles concerning architectural coloration. While Ruskin maintained that color "never follows form, but is arranged on an entirely separate system," he also noted that "in certain places you may run your two systems closer, and here and there let them be parallel for a note or two."[18] Thus the brick is banded in the voussoirs of the lower windows and around the circular clerestory lights. But these areas of ordered pattern are clearly delineated from the accidental variegation on the broad flat wall, and here the color defines rather than dissolves form.

The areas of three-dimensional ornamentation are also strictly regulated. The brick architraves are cut into zigzag and saw-tooth moldings. Here, following Ruskin's dictum that molded material should be uniform in color, Woodward used evenly colored bricks instead of the variegated ones used for the broad expanses of flat wall.

Representational carving, where in Ruskin's terms "organic form is domi-nant," is again confined to specifically restricted areas in the capitals, bosses, and circular window surrounds.[19] Here the material used is stone. This carving is probably by the O'Sheas and displays their characteristic vivid naturalism and decorative control. A stone tympanum above the main entrance carved in low relief with the figures of King Arthur and his knights is by Alexander Munro after Rossetti's design.

The only piece of stone carving in the interior is on the central mantelpiece. The rather conventional stylization of this carving is unusual for Woodward and suggests that it was not the work of the O'Sheas. Even more unusual is the applied color on the mantelpiece, where the carved portions are somewhat garishly painted and gilt. Since this feature was noted by the *Building News*, it would seem that the carving and the color are original. In the absence of documentation it is difficult to account for this strange aberration from Ruskinian principles and the obvious "surface deceit" of this feature.[20]

Otherwise the hall is rich in ornament of a subsidiary type. The wooden structural supports, bookcases, door and window frames, are variously notched and hatched in the firm's characteristic medievalizing manner. The original wooden furniture, probably also made to Woodward's designs, displays the same constructive realism found in the Museum furnishings. Bench and table legs are cut into simple Gothicizing cusped arches and trefoil shapes.

Some of the most successful functional ornament in the hall is the metalwork done by Skidmore. The original gasoliers suspended from the ceiling were "medievalized" in keeping with the general character of the room. So too were the iron railings and attached book rests on the gallery (Fig. 94). These are exquisitely simple in design, the book rests repeating the rustic notchings of the wooden beams in their decoration. Most striking are the different pairs of finely wrought leaves affixed like spandrils to each post of the railing.

All of these styles and forms of ornament, many of which are recognizable hallmarks of Deane and Woodward's individual style, appear in the Oxford Museum and elsewhere. Yet the most novel features of the Union decorations are its murals. The story has often been told and is perhaps one of the most famous in the history of Pre-Raphaelitism. Though the murals have been assigned a somewhat inglorious place in the history of painting, their significance for the history of architecture has not been fully appreciated.[21] They were not a part of Woodward's original design for the hall but were suggested to him by Rossetti.

In the summer of 1857 Woodward took the latter and William Morris to see his recently finished building. Rossetti described the event and its outcome.

Thinking of it only as his beautiful work and without taking into consideration the purpose it was intended for—indeed hardly knowing of the latter—I offered to paint figures of some kind in the blank spaces of one of the gallery window bays; and another friend who was with us—William Morris—offered to do the same for a second bay. Woodward was greatly delighted with the idea; as his principle was that of the medieval builder to avail himself in any building of as much decoration as circumstances permitted at the time, and not prefer uniform bareness to partial beauty. He had never before had a decided opportunity of introducing picture work in a building, and grasped at the idea.[22]

The Union building committee authorized the painting and offered to defray the cost of materials, scaffolding, lodging, travel, and provisions for the team of eight artists assembled by Rossetti, who all offered their services free of charge. Rossetti continues, "In the course of the Long Vacation, six other friends of ours Edward Burne-Jones, Val Prinsep, Arthur Hughes, John Pollen . . . R. S. Stanhope, and Alex Munro joined in the project."[23] Each of the seven painters took one bay and the sculptor the stone shield above the entrance porch. The subjects were all taken from Malory's *Morte D'Arthur*, a legend close to their hearts. Indeed, Rossetti had just completed a series of illustrations with Hunt and Millais for Moxon's edition of Tennyson's *Morte D'Arthur*.

The original work was intended to take six weeks, but in fact continued for five months. Even then Rossetti, Pollen, Prinsep, and Stanhope's murals were left uncompleted.[24] Morris was the first to finish his panel and began painting the roof of the hall. Both he and Burne-Jones had been great admirers of Pollen's painted roof in Merton Chapel and Morris was no doubt inspired here by Pollen's example. He was assisted by Faulkner, Webb, Tyrwhitt, and Swan. The last two had also worked on the painted decoration in the Museum. Rossetti described Morris' design as a "vast pattern work of grotesque creatures."[25] This is no longer visible as Morris repainted it in 1875 with a simpler foliate design which is even closer to Pollen's Merton roof decoration.[26]

Shortly after work on the paintings began they were enthusiastically reviewed in the press and descriptions appeared in the *Times, Morning Chronicle, Le Moniteur,* the *Art Journal,* and elsewhere. In the *Saturday Review,* Coventry Patmore noted that "Oxford . . . is at this moment making some remarkable experiments in architecture and architectural painting. . . . The paintings, which are in distemper, not fresco, promise to turn out novelties, and quite successful novelties, in art."[27] Their completion was eagerly awaited. However, the murals almost immediately began to fade and today are almost invisible. Neither the painters nor Woodward had any previous experience in mural painting. The distemper was applied without undercoating directly onto the whitewashed brick walls before the mortar had even dried.[28] In addition, smoke and heat from the gasoliers and fireplace contributed to a general blackening of the walls. By June 1858, William Bell Scott reported that the murals were already "much defaced" by the grime and damp.[29] Furthermore, when the circular windows, which had been whitewashed during the painting, were uncovered it was noticed that the entering sunlight had the effect of making the murals almost invisible. Woodward was severely criticized for this oversight by the *Ecclesiologist*, "Of course the position of the paintings renders it almost impossible for them to be seen, owing to the cross lights between and upon them";[30] however, this was not entirely Woodward's fault, since the walls were not originally intended for painted decoration. No doubt Woodward, carried away by the enthusiasm of Rossetti and friends (Ruskin said of them, "They're all the least bit crazy and it is very difficult to manage them"), had chosen to disregard the obvious unsuitability of the spaces for mural painting.[31]

Nevertheless, the novelty of the experiment and the significance of the murals in the history of architectural decoration should not be overlooked. After the relatively unsuccessful attempt in the 1840s to revive fresco painting in the Houses of Parliament, very little large-scale wall painting had been undertaken in English building outside the domestic sphere.[32] This was particularly the case in Gothic Revival architecture. The Ecclesiologists' concern for color in architecture had led them to concentrate on the structural polychromy of different building materials. Ruskin also had counseled in the *Seven Lamps* against the use of figurative painting in architecture on the grounds that "pictorial subject, without . . . abstraction, becomes necessarily principal, or at all events, ceases to be the architect's concern."[33]

Yet, as Coventry Patmore noted, the Pre-Raphaelites' paintings differed in an important way from the earlier types of fresco and mural painting. His description is revealing.

We have not seen any mural painting which at all resembles, or in certain respects equals them. The characteristic in which they strike us as differing most remarkably from preceding architectural painting is their entire abandonment of the subdued tone of colour and the simplicity and severity of form hitherto thought essential in such kinds of decoration, and the adoption of a style of colouring so brilliant as to make the walls look like the margin of a highly illuminated manuscript. The eye, even when not directed to any of the pictures, is thus pleased with a voluptuous radiance of variegated tints, instead of being made dimly aware of something or other disturbing the uniformity of the wall surfaces. . . . Architecture, being itself characterised in all its leading features by the strongest definiteness of outline, ought to be relieved—not, as hitherto, emulated—in this respect, by mural painting. Mr. Rossetti and his associates have observed the true conditions and limitations of architectural painting with a degree of skill scarcely to have been expected from their inexperience in this kind of work.[34]

The Pre-Raphaelites had brought their previous experience in decorative illustration, stained glass design, and furniture painting to bear on the Union murals. The problem in all decorative painting of this kind is to establish the proper balance between pictorial representation and two-dimensional abstract design. To achieve this balance the painters of the Union murals emulated the formal principles of the medieval stained glass windows and illuminated manuscripts they admired. The emphasis is on color, broad simplified forms, dense architectonic composition involving a sometimes arbitrary treatment of formal space and volume, and a richness of surface detail. Thus, while remaining concretely representational the paintings also fulfill their abstract decorative function. These were the qualities that Ruskin recognized as suitable to architectural painting, but which he claimed owed "their architectural applicability to their archaic manner." He objected to what he called "a voluntary condescension" to primitivism in painting on the same grounds that he had used to condemn antiquarianism in architecture—as imitation and base copyism.[35] "No painter has any business to be an antiquarian," he asserted in the Stones of Venice.[36] Yet, Ruskin made an important distinction between antiquarianism and historicism.

The best art either represents the facts of its own day, or, if facts of the past, expresses them with accessories of the time in which the work was done. All good art, representing past events, is therefore full of the most frank anachronism, and always *ought* to be.[37]

This then is the essence of Rossetti and the younger Pre-Raphaelite generation's medievalism. It was neither antiquarian nor reconstructive. The formal qualities of medieval work attracted them as much as the intellectual and poetic content. And in their work medieval motifs and details are employed as much for their visual richness as for their symbolic value. It is these formal qualities of their painting: rich surface pattern, luminous color, and dense composition—that made them particularly well suited to architectural decoration and appropriate in a Gothic building.

Another important characteristic of the Pre-Raphaelite murals is their architectonic sense of composition which corresponds closely to Woodward's own intensely visual sense of architectural composition. Again the painters drew on their previous experience in designing frames for their easel paintings. These frames, like the architectural setting of the murals, both define the spatial limits of the picture plane and are part of the formal structure of the composition itself. Within this boundary, broad areas of color and finely observed naturalistic detail are woven together in a composition that is at once abstractly decorative and concretely representational.

A similar visual sense of composition is apparent in Woodward's architectural designs. Here the broad, simplified, and essentially regular form of the building provides the frame within which the architectural features are arranged in a rhythmically balanced composition. This sense of closure, of composing within a frame, is repeated in every part and feature of the building down to the smallest detail. Each element, be it a carved capital, window, or entire facade, contains within it the abstractions of order, proportion, and rhythm of the whole. The compartmentation and balanced proportion of Woodward's designs represents a completely different aesthetic from the truncation, compression, slicing, irregularity, and harsh outlines which characterize High Victorian Gothic. The inspiration for this visual sense of composing within a frame—shared by Woodward and the Pre-Raphaelites—is Ruskin. In fact it is the identifying characteristic of what we can call Ruskinian Gothic.

The importance of the Union was not just that it was one of the first instances where mural painting and Gothic architecture were combined, but rather that it embodied a new way in which pictorial representation could be integrated into an architectural frame.

Though Street and Scott had occasionally used figurative fresco painting in works of the late 1840s and early 1850s these were of comparatively little significance.[38] On the other hand the example of the Oxford Union murals was decisive in giving impetus to the development in the late 1850s and 1860s of the new concept of "art-architecture."[39] In 1858, Street gave a lecture, "On the Future of Art in England," in which he suggested "that we should be better artists and greater men if we did a little less in architecture and a little more in painting." In the same talk he referred to the Union and, repeatedly, to the Pre-Raphaelite Brotherhood. Finally, he claimed that "the Pre-Raphaelite Movement is identical with our own."[40] During the same years William Burges also echoed Ruskin's earlier plea that architects should "turn painters" and began to design large-scale medievalizing painted decoration.[41]

However, a valid criticism of the Union murals was also voiced by the *Building News.*

> Mr. Woodward is a man of mind burning to excel, and we should have thought he would have so dealt with the task offered to him by the Oxford Union as to have lost no vantage ground. Thus he adopts a novel treatment of style; the plan of his room shows some fancy, he introduces mural decoration, he countenances the artists in novel effects, he restores distemper painting, and adopts coloring for a carving in stone. There is no doubt the Union hall is so striking in its appearance as to gain great applause for its author, yet, having done all this, he has perversely gone out of his way to miss the very purpose and object of the building. The room having a purpose, the architect was not driven to adopt a chance decoration, as he might have been in a room having no such settled subjects for decoration. Had this been a hall in a mansion or palace, the Arthur Room, with the romance so displayed, would have been a distinguishing feature. . . . The Mort Arthur might have given poetry to some structure, which had neither poetry nor other intellectual association; but it would betoken poverty of thought to lug it into the Union room. . . .[42]

Praising the effect of the mural painting but noting that it was more appropriate to domestic work, the *Building News*, foretold the realm into which it was about to move. While Woodward never attempted anything on the same scale again, together with John Hungerford Pollen, he made further experiments with narrative decorative painting in some domestic works of the late 1850s.

V

LONDON: RUSKINIAN GOTHIC, PUBLIC AND COMMERCIAL

In 1857 Deane and Woodward opened an office in London at 88 St. James's Street.[1] The firm's work in London was not extensive—three projects in all, of which only two were built, and both of which were destroyed within a few years of their completion. And yet the two civil projects, the competition design for the Government Offices in Whitehall and the Crown Life Assurance Company Office, New Bridge Street, Blackfriars, were among the most influential designs ever made by the firm.

THE GOVERNMENT OFFICES COMPETITION DESIGN

The architectural competition for a new building to house the Foreign and War Offices has become one of the most famous serio-comic episodes in the history of Victorian architecture. It was the scene of the bitterest skirmish in the endless "Battle of the Styles." The story of the confrontation between Lord Palmerston (the Prime Minister), Ruskin, and G. G. Scott, the architect who obtained the commission without winning the competition, and who then was not permitted to build his original Gothic design, is well known. It is best told (though not without bias) by Scott himself.[2]

Though in the end Scott lost the battle to Palmerston, the competition was ultimately an indirect but nevertheless decisive victory for the Gothic cause. Never before had public interest in architectural designs been so keen. Crowds in unprecedented numbers flocked to Westminster Hall and the Royal Academy where the projects were exhibited. "Four days a week are already devoted to the admission of the public, and neither the building nor the time is found too great, for as yet the Hall has been thronged, and by all classes, from the senator to the artisan, from the artist and scholar to the schoolboy . . . ," the *Building News* reported.[3] Several of the designs were also published in the building-industry press where their relative merits were discussed in detail. The publicity surrounding the competition, the first major Government competition since the Houses of Parliament in 1835, and the ensuing struggle between Scott and Palmerston over the style of the buildings, brought the "battle" into the public arena and served to focus attention on the Gothic designs.[4]

Interest and discussion of the issues extended beyond the closed circle of professionals and connoisseurs to a far wider public than ever before. And here, where the persuasive teachings of Ruskin held the greatest sway, popular opinion, voiced in pamphlets, articles, and letters to the press, was overwhelmingly in favor of Gothic. Thus Palmerston and the classical party represented a minority, and an outmoded attitude. In fact, the Government Offices competition had the side effect of politicizing the "distinctly political art of Architecture."[5] Classical became associated with the reactionary, the antiquated, and the autocratic, while Gothic was newly identified with the progressive, the modern, and the democratic.[6] The *Building News* noted in 1858, "We have already professed our inability to comprehend true freshness and originality in the Classic, without its proving to be the Gothic, somewhat modified and in some degree tinged with the direct influences of the antique."[7] (It is ironic that this is what Scott's final and executed design for the Government Offices turned out to be.) The *Art Journal* also proclaimed the "absolute superiority of these [Gothic] designs over all their fellow competitors" and warned, "the opponents of the Gothic have put forth their strength, and in so doing they have both unmasked their resources, and declared their standards of excellence; as the contest proceeds they will learn the nature and the capacity of the Gothic reserve, which has not yet been brought into action."[8]

Though Scott was the chief Gothic protagonist in the battle of 1857, Ruskin, as the most popular purveyor of architectural knowledge to the mid-Victorian generations, and the avowed champion of Gothic, was looked to as the spokesman and leader of the Gothic cause. His writings were quoted in Parliament. His every opinion was faithfully reported in the press. In actual fact, however, Ruskin took little interest in Scott's design or the struggle between the architect and the Prime Minister. Instead, as always, he singlemindedly pursued his own interests, which at the time centered around Deane and Woodward's design for the building. It is not surprising that Ruskin should take a particular interest in the firm's design, for the architects had already shown their willingness to comply with his wishes at the Oxford Museum, and Ruskin recognized the Government Offices as providing a further opportunity for testing his principles and possibly even for realizing his ideal in a major public building. Thus he lent his full support to their efforts and took advantage of his position to direct public attention to the design. Ruskin's consistent championship of the firm, and his well-known association with Woodward at Oxford led to rumors that he was responsible for the firm's entry or had at least collaborated with the architects. The *Illustrated London News* and the *Builder* claimed that the firm's design "both from the evidence which is on the face of it, and from report, owes much to Mr. Ruskin. Mr. Woodward alone, or in conjunction with Sir Thomas Deane, has, however, some of the credit of the architecture."[9] Thus, Ruskin was pressed into making a public denial of the report which "had gone abroad . . . that he had sent in one or two drawings himself . . . he was quite unable to design a building of the kind, and he never dreamed of interfering in any way."[10] As Henry-Russell Hitchcock has pointed out, the planning alone for such a complicated building would have been beyond Ruskin's capabilities or interests.[11] However, though he was not connected with the design on a practical level, there is no doubt that he was closely involved in an advisory capacity. As a result, though Deane and Woodward's project was awarded only the fourth premium in the competition, because of Ruskin's personal interest it received a great deal more publicity than most of the other premiated entries.[12]

There were other Ruskinian projects besides Deane and Woodward's.[13] Scott's and Pritchard & Seddon's designs were greatly elaborated replications of the Oxford Museum. Symmetrical and classicizing in plan they both also made use of the regular towered northern town hall prototype for the St. James's Park front of their buildings. Indeed, G. E. Street's was the only Gothic design which did not follow Deane and Woodward's Oxonian model. The only deeply committed Ecclesiological architect of the group, Street chose a more traditional composition. As George Hersey has pointed out, the agglutinative planning, irregular grouping of individual blocks, and picturesque profile of Street's design relate it to the traditional ecclesiastical collegiate program—here on a monumental scale.[14] At the same time, however, the project can also be seen as an elaboration of Street's own, non-Ruskinian design, for the Oxford Museum. As in the earlier project the enclosed forecourt is fronted by an arcaded screen, large areas of blank wall alternate with different sized openings, and the complex is dominated by a tall tower, with the corners accented by spired turrets.

Deane and Woodward's design, number 35, with the motto: Thou hast covered my head in the day of battle, departs from both their own Oxford Museum type and from the High Victorian Gothic functional expressiveness of Street's project. Though entered in the Foreign Office list, the firm's design incorporated both the government departments involved.

None of the five sheets of plans and drawings submitted by Deane and Woodward has survived, though a recently discovered, and very important, private notebook of Woodward's contains many sketches of details.[15] The design of the building itself, however, is only known from a wood-engraved perspective view published in the *Illustrated London News* which shows the War Office facade fronting onto Parliament Street (Fig. 95).[16]

The *Builder* described the plan: "The War Office portion . . . forms three sides of an internal quadrangle" with further "open courts at the angles, and internal corridors . . . along the other (inner) sides."[17] The Foreign Office, which included the residence of the Foreign Secretary, likewise formed "an oblong block, with internal courts, and a staircase in the center."[18] This portion of the complex, fronting onto St. James's Park, comprised the fourth side of the inner quadrangle. Thus, the entire building was almost perfectly square in plan, According to the *Builder* the Park front was very similar to the Parliament street facade shown in the *Illustrated London News* engraving with the exception of a mezzanine floor introduced in the Foreign Secretary's residence and the substitution of square windows with shafts for the circular openings at basement level on the opposite facade.[19] The side facades continue the massing of the fronts. The center pieces of these ranges were also broad archways here forming a carriageway into the central inner courtyard. Drawings in Woodward's notebook show that grand staircases were intended for both the Foreign and War Office block, which connected the external street entrances with those in the center court. Other drawings in the notebook of canopied porches are probably for these courtyard entryways.

It would seem that here, as in the firm's two other large multi-functional buildings, practical considerations led the architects to adopt a regular classicizing plan. Like TCD the various different parts of the complex are gathered together into a contained monumental block with a high base, strongly marked corner accents, rhythmically grouped ranges of windows, heavily bracketed cornice, low hipped roof, tall chimneys, and a profusion of carved ornament kept close to the surface of the wall. At the same time, the massing of the principal facades can also be read as a compressed version of the west front of the Oxford Museum;

[96]

integrating the arcaded principle with the Gothic arch which was to have such crucial significance for the development, in the 1860s, of commercial street architecture along medievalizing lines.[20] As in the museum buildings, these arcades are structurally integrated and a rational expression of the interior arrangement that reflects the different sizes and functions of the rooms behind.

With regard to style, the *Building News* called the design "Lombardo or Byzantine Gothic" and remarked that "the whole smacks of the *Stones of Venice* and the *Seven Lamps* more than is suitable to an edifice which is not to be a department of the Doge and Senate of Venice, but of the English commonwealth."[21] Indeed, the Government Offices design has none of the Northern Gothic features such as gabled roofs, dormers, and spired tourelles which characterized the Oxford Museum. Instead, as the *Building News* concluded, "to enumerate the several details of this design would be to go over the repertory of Adriatic architecture."[22] Only the roof strikes a different note, and this is in fact more French Second Empire than Northern Gothic. Essentially, Deane and Woodward adopted the regular classicizing plan and form of a traditional palazzo block, and overlaid its facades with Venetian Gothic detail.

While the Government Offices are the most Venetian of Deane and Woodward's designs, they are also the most Ruskinian in spirit.[23] Here as at Oxford, Ruskin had a direct influence on the design. Though, as noted, it is unlikely that he had a hand in the preparation of the firm's competition drawings, he was without doubt closely involved with the project. And the Government Offices design clearly reflects Ruskin's increasingly dominant concern at this time with ornament and the subject matter and execution of architectural sculpture.

While in 1849 Ruskin had maintained that architectural sculpture, as ornament, must always be subordinate to the architecture, by the mid-fifties his attitude had changed.[24] And in the preface to the second edition of the *Seven Lamps*, he asserted:

> It gradually became manifest to me that the sculpture and painting were, in fact, the all in all of the thing to be done; that these, which I had long been in the careless habit of thinking subordinate to the architecture, were in fact the entire masters of the architecture; and that the architect who was not a sculptor or a painter, was nothing better than a framemaker on a large scale.[25]

Ruskin regarded the Government Offices competition as furnishing "a fine opportunity for bringing forward, and popularizing, as it were, the art of sculpture—an art so intimately and beautifully allied to that of architecture."[26] The principle to be followed in the new public buildings he asserted was "that they would be well-lighted and well-decked within, and that they would have gorgeous and noble facades."[27]

It needs to be pointed out here, in discussing the important and vexed question of "Ruskinian architecture," that Ruskin himself was almost completely unconcerned with space and structure. As he explained in the first volume of the *Stones of Venice*, since the form of a building "depends on its special fitness for its own purposes . . . [and since] there were never, probably, two edifices erected in which some accidental difference of condition did not require some difference of plan or of structure . . . respecting plan and distribution of parts, I do not hope to collect any universal law of right."[28] Planning belonged in his view to the craft of building, not to the art of architecture. "What we call architecture," he asserted again in *Seven Lamps*, "is only the association of [sculpture and painting] in noble masses, or the placing of them in fit places. All architecture other than this is, in fact mere *building*; and though it may sometimes be graceful . . . or sublime . . . there is in . . . it no more exertion of the powers of high art, than in the gracefulness of a well-ordered chamber or the nobleness of a well-built ship."[29]

It is this attitude which the Government Offices design so clearly reflects. Deane and Woodward's projected building was clearly designed as an architectural frame for the elaborate sculptural embellishment which Ruskin desired. Indeed, the architects made use of every type of ornamentation recommended in the *Seven Lamps*.[30] There is structural polychromy in horizontal courses across the facades, in the alternating bands of the voussoirs, and the inlaid marble discs. Geometrical shapes are pierced into the stone tracery of the corner staircase windows and balustrades and carved in the string courses. Foliate relief carving is concentrated in the architrave moldings and capitals and spreads across the walls in broad friezes. Much of this program was worked out by Woodward in a series of loose freehand sketches contained in the notebook mentioned earlier. These sketches are private notations or ideas—in fact working drawings for a variety of architectural and sculptural details for the building (Figs. 96-98). Except for a few plans of staircases, they are almost exclusively of external and decorative features and clearly show the architect's preoccupation with surface detail and ornament. Most of Woodward's drawings are for the windows of the principal facades. There are plans of the arcades showing the arrangement of shafts and piers coupled within the thickness of the walls. Elsewhere the form and decoration of individual windows are studied in sketches of ornamental details and sectional drawings of moldings. Thus, in these loose sketches individual features of the exterior were worked out in detail by Woodward to be assembled, grouped, and arranged on the facades.

Woodward also responded to Ruskin's call for associational, story-telling sculptural ornament.[31] Public buildings especially should be "animated by a metaphorical or historical meaning."[32] As an example, Ruskin proposed,

> let us imagine our own India House adorned . . . by historical or symbolic sculpture: massively built in the first place; then chased with bas-reliefs of our Indian battles, and fretted with carvings of Oriental foliage, or inlaid with Oriental stones; and the more important members of its decoration composed of groups of Indian life and landscape.[33]

Woodward's program also included figural relief sculpture of this type to be carved on the piers and spandrils of the first and second storey arcades. It was designed by John Hungerford Pollen, though the idea was probably Woodward's, and there are a few rough sketches for the design in Woodward's notebook.[34]

A drawing by Pollen of a segment of the Foreign Office facade, exhibited with the firm's competition drawings in Westminster Hall and later published in the *Builder* in October 1857 (Fig. 99) shows a broad band of foliate carving at basement level where multi-foil openings alternate with circular discs carved with a variety of heraldic emblems.[35] Above this the spandrils of the first-floor arcades were to be decorated with battle scenes. On the piers below are pairs of soldiers and medieval yeomen, here having put down the plow and taken up the sword in defence of their country. On the second-floor piers the crowned defenders of the realm and protectors of the faith are depicted on horseback gloriously decked in full armor towering over their vanquished foes. In the spandrils above are inlaid roundels carved with the heraldic lion of the Royal Arms. Thus, the associations of war, and hence of a War Office, are vividly expressed in the full richness of a sculptural pageant.[36]

A reviewer in the *Builder* found the sculpture "good in itself" but justly criticized it for being "scattered about, so that there is a deficiency of the special architectonic character,—the framework of lines, and the order in masses,—

which most conduces to the effect of sculpture itself."[37] A reviewer in the *Building News* found fault with the design on practical grounds.

> The figures are cut partly into the wall, not as in Italian bas-reliefs, on the wall, so that, perhaps, the upper portion of a group would stand in full relief, leaving a space behind for the accumulation of dust, dirt, and smoke. . . . There is no instance of such sculpture in Venice, or anywhere else, except on some cathedral porches, and they are well canopied, and in clear climates.[38]

It was perhaps for these reasons and the no doubt prohibitive cost of executing the vast sculptural program that Deane and Woodward's project was not selected. It is of course also possible that the building was less conveniently planned than some of the other projects. Woodward himself was dissatisfied with the design, as he wrote to Acland in February 1857:

> What has been occupying me so much for some time is the planning of the New Government Offices. I think they will be the death of me and the worst of all is we are very backward indeed with the drawings— the arrangement is so difficult. I know there is no chance of our getting them. I don't like speaking of it, but we feel impelled to go on, and I think it as bad to hold back, as to go in and lose.[39]

Aside from being pressed for time, Woodward may also have been hindered by Ruskin's interference from carrying out his own ideas for the building. Nevertheless, the Government Offices project is significant as the most complete realization, at least on paper, of Ruskin's ideal for monumental public architecture.

THE CROWN LIFE ASSURANCE COMPANY OFFICE

At the same time that Deane and Woodward were preparing their design for the Government Offices competition, they were also engaged in rebuilding the business premises of the Crown Life Assurance Company at 33 New Bridge Street in Blackfriars. The two projects are closely related. Together they extended Ruskinian influence beyond the universities to London and established a Ruskinian urban mode, with monumental Italianate details and maximum window space, for public and commercial architecture.

The Crown Life building (Fig. 100) was immediately recognized as an important innovation in commercial street architecture. The *Building News* noted that "the structure has a novelty of design about it quite new to London; and it is quite possible that some of our architectural brethren may object to it as being essentially exotic in its characteristics. Let this be as it may, we consider it a step in the right direction, and [it] certainly commands attention as an advance out of the beaten track of stereotyped monotony in our street architecture."[40] It received an honorable mention in *Hansard* and a lengthy review in the *Building News*.[41] Yet, in spite of the considerable notice it attracted, the building was demolished in 1865, less than ten years after its erection, to make way for the London, Chatham, and Dover railway. The Crown Life Company itself fared little better. After a succession of amalgamations with larger companies, it was finally dissolved in 1959. Thus, very little information on the building and none of the architects' drawings have survived. The whereabouts of the Company records have also been for many years unknown and were only recently located. This explains various errors that have been made regarding the date of the firm's work and the nature of the commission in accounts of the building.

In *The Gothic Revival*, Eastlake recorded that the building was begun in 1855 and completed in 1857.[42] It would seem, however, from the Crown Life Board and Committee Minutes that Deane and Woodward received the commission on August 8, 1856, at the same time that the competition for the Government Offices was announced.[43] This marked the beginning of a long association with the Crown Life, for whom T. N. Deane designed two more offices after Woodward's death. The source of the first contract and the initial connection between the firm and the Company was probably through Joseph Manly, Jr., Deane's brother-in-law, who had recently been appointed the Company's Head Agent for Ireland in 1855.[44]

The commission was not for an entirely new building but for alterations to the Company's existing premises. Deane and Woodward were responsible for the designs, Cubitts of Grey's-Inn-Road were the general contractors, and the O'Shea brothers and their nephew, under separate contract, were entrusted with the various carvings under the direction of the architects. The work consisted of extensive alterations to the exterior street front, the interior, and the addition of a waiting room at the back of the building.[45]

The Board Minutes contain numerous, though tantalizingly uninformative, references to a succession of designs for the front elevation which were reviewed by the Company. It seems that the firm's first design was rejected as too elaborate

and the architects were requested to send in "a plainer plan for the exterior."
Finally, it was decided that three schemes for the street facade should be submitted: "two designs for the front Elevation such as they can recommend after the form of the Rounded Arch, one to be ornamented and the other to be plain, and also a third design preserving the windows of their present shape to be executed with white brick and stone." In the end, after considerable debate, one of these designs was selected—presumably the ornamented round-arched one.[46]

Final authorization to proceed was given on November 28, 1856, but work did not begin until the spring of 1857. Construction progressed rapidly, and the building was substantially complete—except for the stone carving—by May 1858.[47]

Deane and Woodward's Crown Life building is now only known from contemporary engravings and descriptions. The *Building News* published a view of the street facade in 1858.[48] Tall and narrow, it was four stories high with another level of attic dormers in the gabled roof. Three bays wide, the size of the windows decreased as they rose.

The *Building News* remarked on the materials used and the general effect of varied color and pattern. "In the principal facade are red and grey granite, Portland stone, red brick, and Sicilian and other marbles; it will be seen that there is no sham about it, the various materials having been allowed to show their own natural faces without the aid of compo embellishments."[49] The effect of the structural polychromy must have been unusual indeed in that sombre street of Georgian terraces. The *Building News* later gave a fuller description, noting that the banded voussoirs were of blue and red granite, the second-storey pointed archivolts of white marble, while long horizontal bands across the walls consisted of "deep courses of a bluish colour, divided by thin black ones."[50]

An early engraving of the Crown Life building before Deane and Woodward's alterations (Fig. 101) shows that the original building was a four-storey town house set in a terrace of uniform Georgian houses.[51] Deane and Woodward retained the vertical proportions and massing of the original facade and the two adjoining buildings, which reflect the different purposes and functions of the interior spaces. The first two storeys containing the main business offices and the board room are greater in proportion and have larger windows than the upper storeys. The Crown Life was an old-fashioned business, and the top floors were used for residential purposes, thus their scale was reduced to more domestic and private proportions.

At the time that the Crown Life Company was incorporated in 1825 the commercial office as a distinct building type did not really exist. Small insurance companies which did not require specialized interior spaces were easily accommodated in the existing Georgian town houses. But, as Henry-Russell Hitchcock has shown, with the increase of industry and commerce in the following decades businesses expanded and a new need arose for buildings more specially suited to commercial purposes.[52] With this came a demand for appropriate architectural symbolism to express the new affluence and status of private business. In the 1840s the Renaissance palazzo type of Barry's club houses was generally adopted as the fitting commercial paradigm. The fifteenth-century palace form seemed to answer both the symbolic and practical needs of mid-Victorian business. Historically associated with the commercial aristocracy of Renaissance Italy, its regular rows of large windows also seemed well suited to the new office purposes. Features of the style were even grafted onto earlier town houses to "monumentalize" them, as we can see from the Mutual Life Insurance Co. flanking the Crown Life to the right.

However, the type also had distinct limitations. The massing and proportions of the original palazzo paradigm were rigidly inflexible—allowing for only three stories of widely spaced windows. Thus, by the 1850s the classical formula had to be stretched to accommodate the increasing need for greater height, brought about by a scarcity of good urban sites, rising property values in commercial districts, and the need for more windows to light large offices. To meet these needs and the desire for formal diversity and ornamental richness, the commercial palazzo went through a series of modifications. By the late 1850s several variants had appeared. "Mannerist" modulations gave way to round-arched "Sansovinesque" efflorescence and "Veronese" continuous arcades introduced in conjunction with trabeated systems.[53] The elaborate Neo-Renaissance facades were often "regular mongrel affairs"[54] that hardly met the functional requirements of the new commercial office more successfully than the plainer original palazzo model. It was necessary to find a new multi-storey commercial formula that could accommodate more continuous windows and increased height without the uneasy mannerisms of the Renaissance palazzo hybrids.

The Government Offices competition was decisive in turning commercial design away from the classical palazzo toward more flexible "Gothic" solutions. The competition itself had finally freed Gothic from its traditional religious and feudal associations and endowed it with new associations in tune with the increasing wealth and status of Victorian businessmen. Gothic came to be seen as an acceptable mode for monumental public building. Furthermore, the design problems for the Government and commercial buildings were essentially the same—the former being little more than large office buildings. The Gothic designs, especially Deane and Woodward's, characterized by superposed ranges of grouped arcades, disproved the old argument that Gothic windows were necessarily narrow and dark.[55] Even more than this, the flexible massing and vertical proportions of the style seemed to provide an alternative that was eminently more suitable than the palazzo formula to modern commercial purposes. Thus, the multi-storey facades with structurally integrated Italianate arcades, which had characterized Deane and Woodward's Government Offices design in particular, turned the attention of commercial architects toward alternative Venetian Gothic modes for urban office buildings.[56]

Of course, this whole development had already been hinted at much earlier in the decade by Ruskin and by Street. In the preface to the first edition of the *Stones of Venice*, Ruskin made clear the analogy between mercantile Venice and nineteenth-century commercial London. Venice, he claimed, "should be interesting to the men of London, as affording the richest existing examples of architecture raised by a mercantile community, for civil uses, and domestic magnificence."[57] Throughout his books he advocated Italian Gothic for all forms of secular architecture. G. E. Street also included many examples of Italian civil buildings in his *Brick and Marble*. In 1852 he noted that Gothic styles had as yet made few inroads into urban street architecture, and called attention to J. W. Wild's recently completed St. Martin's Northern Schools in Soho, suggesting that architects might well look to this building with its continuous ranges of Italian Gothic arcades as a model to be adapted to commercial architecture. Street also noted that for the purposes of urban street architecture the Gothic style would have to be altered and assimilated with forms from other periods.[58] This theme was taken up by G. G. Scott, who, writing at the same time that Deane and Woodward were building the Crown Life office, argued against the palazzo and the more elaborated round-arched Sansovinesque styles for the evident structural deceits involved in the conjunction of decorative non-load-bearing arcades with structural columnar systems.[59] He advocated a simpler and more structurally expressive mode and, like Street, recommended combining styles of different periods. In his *Remarks* Scott noted the basic formal similarity between Venetian Gothic and Renaissance palaces: "the block form of these varieties does not very essentially differ, all having a horizontal cornice, . . . the stories clearly marked, and the ranges of windows forming the chief architectural feature."[60] The difference was essentially one of details and these in Scott's view should be Gothic. The solution was simple: "the construction upon a Gothic basis of a new palatial style."[61] And its possibilities for monumental office building had already been demonstrated in the Government Office competition designs.

Deane and Woodward's Crown Life building was just such a compromise. The *Building News* noted that "it shows how much of the Gothic element may be retained even after the rejection of many common Gothic features. Without any studied irregularity, without gables, turrets, buttresses, or window tracery, it has a beauty which differs little from that of the medieval buildings possessing them all."[62] Thus the Crown Life facade is historically important as the first commercial building in which the arcaded principle was synthesized with Gothic. As we now know, the rounded arches were a stipulation of the Crown Life Board of Directors which Deane and Woodward "Gothicized" with carved ornament and slightly pointed voussoirs. Of course, the architects had already used a round-arched "Gothic" mode some years before in TCD, and the Crown Life owes a great deal to this earlier essay. Like TCD everything about the building is large, solid, and strongly articulated. This aspect of the Crown Life is in marked contrast to St. Martin's Northern Schools, where the facade as noted appears like a thin screen applied to the structure.

The second significance of the Crown Life office is its extension of Ruskinian influence. The materials, color, and eclectic Italian details all have Ruskinian sources. Ruskin's principles concerning the distribution of external ornament are also carried out by Woodward with great effect. By concentrating the more delicate carved decoration in the lower portion of the facade and the bolder surface polychromy in the upper areas, where relief carving would be virtually invisible, he was following Ruskin's oft-repeated counsel to distinguish in form and execution between ornament which was to be seen from a distance and that which was to be seen from close by.[63]

Some of the sculpture was designed by John Hungerford Pollen and a drawing by the artist of a band of relief carving for the left side of the entrance gable showing dogs has survived.[64] These features of the facade were praised by Rossetti who had a studio across the street: "It seems to me the most perfect piece of civil architecture of the new school that I have seen in London. I never cease to look at it with delight, and the decoration, designed by Pollen and executed by Wood-ward's excellently trained workmen the brothers Shea, is worthy of the building."[65] The lyrical, wanly poetic, beauty of Oxford seemed to have taken root in the heart of commercial London. Finally, said Ruskin, "our buildings generally" were to be carved with "the birds and flowers which are singing and budding in the [English] fields."[66] The Ruskinian rural idyll which the Crown Life seemed to embody was appreciated by Thomas Woolner, who wrote to Woodward: "If London streets were often treated in this manner they would be worth walking in, and would reconcile poor devils to not being able to dwell in the country, where everything is beautiful."[67]

Even more important is the way in which the Ruskinian formal ideal was so easily adaptable to commercial purposes. The typical Ruskinian facade composition, involving an eclectic assembly of details disposed into separate ranges across the facade gave just the flexibility needed for this type of building. In fact, it is interesting that this is also the way in which the Crown Life building was presented in the building press. The *Building News* described the facade storey by storey, taking each level as an independent compositional feature, and illustrating one window from each of the principal floors as representative of the whole (Fig. 102).[68] More than any other of Deane and Woodward's buildings, the Crown Life was truly a composition of independent details.

Perhaps because of the narrow lot, the Crown Life building seems to resemble more closely, in massing and proportion, the constricted verticality of Venetian Gothic palazzi. In fact, Deane and Woodward had actually retained the arrangement and vertical proportions of the original Georgian facade that lay within their Ruskinian wreathings. Though the new facade was hailed as "the complete fulfillment of modern requirements with a strikingly medieval spirit," the window area of the new front had not been increased at all from the original.[69] Instead, an illusion of openness was created by carrying the voussoirs across the facade in a continuous arcade and by transforming the blank wall space between the windows into capped piers. Ironically, given the acclaim they were receiving for opening up the wall, Deane and Woodward had actually done little more than graft an Italian facade onto a Georgian town house, thus reframing a fully traditional set of window proportions.

For an account of the interior, we must rely on the description in the *Building News*.

Internally, the building is very simple in its arrangements. The ground floor is occupied by the business offices of the Company, and comprises an area of 33 feet by 22 feet 6 inches, and are fitted up in admirable style, the counters, desks, partitions, and other conveniences for the particular business being in mahogany. From the area which we have given a width of 6 feet must be deducted as an entrance corridor, having immediate access to the general counter. This corridor is separated from the main office by a series of arches, supported by shafts of British marble, highly polished. These arches have enriched capitals and moulded arch volts of Caen stone, and the floor is paved with Minton's tiles in lozenge pattern . . . the painted works of the interior, including the roof of the staircase and the friezes under the ceilings, composed of foliage, birds and animals (there being no moulded cornices), are extremely peculiar, and have been painted with great skill . . . by J. H. Pollen, Esq., artist.[70]

From this account it would appear that the interior was characterized by the same variety of materials, forms, colors, and handcrafted fittings as the firm's earlier buildings, though here greatly enriched by Pollen's painted friezes, which pick up the naturalistic themes of the carved ornament on the exterior.

The influence of the Crown Life building was enormous—on other architects and on the later work of the firm itself. T. N. Deane's next office building for the Crown Life Company (Fig. 103) is essentially an expansion of the earlier design. This commission, unlike the first, was for an entirely new structure for the Company's new premises at 188 Fleet Street in London (built to replace the soon-to-be demolished Bridge Street building) and was completed in 1865.[71] The similarities between this building, which has also disappeared, and the earlier one are striking. The corner lot was considerably larger than the earlier one, but the system of arcades, decoration, and vertical proportions is retained. The arcaded windows run continuously around the two exposed sides of the building and are unbroken at the chamfered corner.[72]

But there are a number of subtle changes. The ornamental voussoirs and marginal archivolts have been generally raised and expanded. On the fourth-floor a blind arcade is carried across the blank wall between the grouped windows. Certain ornamental features have also been added, such as the quoin moldings and the gratuitous Italianate balconies.

The materials used were as varied and colorful as in the earlier building for the Company, "Portland stone in the piers and caps; Forest of Dean, red Mansfield, and blue Warwick in the other portions of the front, and over the arches Sicilian marble."[73] The carved decoration was here done only by Edward Whellan, the nephew of the O'Sheas who also had a hand in the carving on some of the firm's earlier buildings.[74] In general, however, the exterior ornament of this building tends to be less bold and expressive, more stylized and flatter, than in the earlier building.

An explanation for both the similarities and the differences of the two buildings may be found in the fact that the second was designed after Woodward's death and executed without the assistance of the O'Sheas. This accounts for much of the direct copying and for the less imaginative carving. The *Building News* was forthright in its judgment;

> The architectural genius of the celebrated Dublin firm took wing when its junior partner died. No one who has carefully looked at the Crown Life Assurance Office, Bridge Street, Blackfriars . . . and at the Crown Life Assurance Office in Fleet Street, just completed, can fail to recognize the enormous loss Mr. T. N. Deane has sustained in the loss of his partner.[75]

But by this time the Ruskinian commercial type established in the first Crown Life building had taken firm root and several off-shoots from the original mode had appeared.[76] These buildings in the later 1850s tended to be combinations of arcaded and palazzo types—that is, characterized by Italian detail and medieval treatment of the broad round arches, such as J. K. Colling's Albany building in Liverpool of 1858 and J. A. Picton's Richmond Buildings, Liverpool, of 1857. In the 1860s, following the example of the Government Offices designs, a few architects tried Italianate pointed arches. The second-storey windows of George Somers Clarke's Auction Mart Co. building in London of 1866 are directly copied from Ruskin's illustrations of Venetian windows in the *Stones of Venice*. William Wilkinson's Crosby House, London, of 1860 owes more to Deane and Woodward's competition design. The best examples of the round-arched mode are Waterhouse's Royal Insurance building in Manchester of 1861 and George Aitchison's offices in Mark Lane, London, 1864, which advance the development begun in the Crown Life building toward a screen of open loggia-like ranges.

In Dublin an Irish variant of the round-arched "Byzantine" style, which owes as much to Deane and Woodward's TCD as to the Crown Life building, appeared in the commercial work of M. D. Wyatt, W. G. Murray, and T. N. Deane in the 1860s.[77] Wyatt's 24-25 Grafton Street building, 1862-1863, the earliest of these, established the mode. Here the inspiration for the deeply recessed round-arched windows is as much Irish Romanesque as Early Italian.[78] Wyatt also made much use of Celtic motifs in the carved ornament. A similar use of Celtic designs was made by the unknown architect of the Caledonian Insurance Co., 31 Dame Street, of 1865. The best examples of the mode, which Douglas Richardson has dubbed "Hibernian Monumental," are T. N. Deane's Munster Bank on Dame Street, 1872-1874, and G. W. Murray's Hibernian Bank on College Green of 1871, which also show the influence of Deane and Woodward's TCD in the massiveness of scale, plasticity, and profusion of rich naturalistic carving[79]—here executed by Charles Harrison who had also worked for Deane and Woodward in the 1850s.[80]

T. N. Deane's third Crown Life Office on Dame Street in Dublin (Fig. 104) was also designed and built at this time. The building was begun shortly after the completion of the Fleet Street Office and was finished in 1871.[81] Here Deane seems to have returned with even more dependence to the form of TCD. The upper storeys are like a miniature of the main front of TCD, though the urban height and the dormers have been retained from the earlier office designs, and the stepped windows of the side staircase adapted from the firm's Government Offices design. Deane built a number of other commercial office buildings in Dublin in the late 1870s and 1880s in conjunction with his son, Thomas Manly Deane, but these are unrelated to the firm's innovations in the 1850s.

The Government Offices design and the Crown Life Assurance Office are products of the "happiest days" of the association between Woodward and Ruskin.[82] Of all the firm's work, these buildings most closely express the ideas, explicit and implicit, of the *Seven Lamps* and *Stones of Venice*. More than anything else by the firm, they embody, in the most positive sense, Ruskin's teachings on the question of facadism—the notion that the "art" of architecture lies almost exclusively in external decoration. Their contributions to the London architectural scene, direct and indirect, brought about a powerful change not only in the appearance of the Victorian street, but in the very notion of the role and significance of the street facade itself.

VI

DOMESTIC WORK

Though domestic work remained a sideline in the firm's practice, it was never-theless a considerable one. Taken together, Deane and Woodward's houses built in England and Ireland between 1856 and 1861 far outnumber the firm's pro-duction in other areas during this period. The reasons for this are twofold. On the one hand, by the mid-1850s Woodward's Irish pupils (in particular J. E. Rodgers, who had accompanied him to Oxford), having served their apprenticeship with the firm, had gained sufficient experience to take over the supervision of buildings in progress as clerks of the works, leaving the senior partners free to devote themselves fully to producing new designs.[1] Furthermore, dealing with single clients rather than official building committees, the architects were able to carry through their original plans and to proceed rapidly with the work un-hampered by the lengthy and often frustrating negotiations with corporate bodies which considerably delayed the progress and increased the expense of so many of their other buildings.

On the whole, the clients who sought the firm's services were inclined to give the architects a free hand in the design and execution of their work. Thus, work of this kind provided a unique opportunity for experimenting with different materials, types of decoration, and modes of construction and planning. As a result, in the period between the Oxford Museum competition and Woodward's death, they produced some of their most individual and distinctive domestic architecture.

Nevertheless, these houses remain the least well known of Deane and Wood-ward's works. This is largely due to the remoteness of many of the Irish buildings and the fact that as generally small private commissions they received little notice in the press. Furthermore, the buildings themselves, and their documentation, have fared badly over the years.

[110]

DOMESTIC WORK

As moderate-sized, freestanding gentlemen's residences set in their own grounds, these houses form a coherent architectural group. All built for middle-class rather than landowning clients, the houses are correspondingly modest in size but spacious and commodious inside. As a building type, they owe much to Pugin's smaller houses of the 1840s and Butterfield's, White's, and Street's country vicarages executed under the auspices of the Ecclesiological Society in the early 1850s.[2] But there are important differences between Deane and Woodward's houses and the Ecclesiologists'. First, the former were never as plain as the country parsonages built for the early Tractarian clergymen, which for economical and doctrinal reasons were as a rule unornamented and built with inexpensive materials. Deane and Woodward's houses reflect a more secular aesthetic, partly of course because they were not built for the clergy, but more important because here, as elsewhere, they adhered to Ruskin's premise that unadorned buildings are not architecture and that even the most humble edifice deserves that name. Second, there is a similar tendency in these houses toward the contained monumental forms and play with windows which characterized the firm's large public buildings and sets them further apart from the Ecclesiologists'. Thus, in these modest houses Deane and Woodward developed an independent Ruskinian domestic mode characterized by regular unified volumes and elaborate decoration inside and out in which the primary emphasis is on materials and craftsmanship.

EARLY HOUSES IN BRITAIN

Curator's House, Oxford

The first project of this group was the house for the Curator of the Oxford Museum. (Not strictly a private commission, the building was included in the official program.) The firm's plans for the house were submitted along with their competition drawings for the Museum complex in December 1854, and the building was executed under the same contract. Construction began alongside that of the Museum and was completed in October 1858 when Professor Philips, the Museum's first Curator, and his family took up residence.[3]

The firm's original (unexecuted) competition design (Fig. 105) was for a detached house, very modest in dimensions, little more than a cottage.[4] It shows the same clear differentiation of parts into separately roofed blocks of different heights and sizes as Pugin's smaller houses of the 1840s. Thus, the reception rooms, with the dining room on the ground floor and the drawing room above (a disposition also frequently used by Butterfield and White in their country vicarages of the early 1850s), are contained in the tall narrow front block.[5] Behind this, the kitchen, main stairs, and master bedroom form another independently roofed block with a separate gable over the stairs leading up to the attic rooms. The scullery, pantry, and other service areas giving onto the kitchen yard, and two back bedrooms on the second floor, are gathered into a third low block at the rear. Here, as in Pugin's work, irregular massing and planning are contingent on the convenient disposition of the rooms. Also like Pugin, Deane and Woodward used a variety of vernacular domestic forms—gables, dormers, porches, bay windows—to decidedly picturesque effect on the exterior.

It is interesting that Deane and Woodward's design—even for such a small and unpretentious building—included a considerable amount of decorative detail in the form of banded voussoirs, string courses, and marble shafts for some of the windows and the porch, as well as carved capitals, hood moldings, and label stops.

This house was never built. In October 1856 the Museum delegates decided that designs for a larger house should be prepared,[6] and in early February 1857 new plans were approved and construction begun.[7]

The original plans for the built house have not survived, but floor plans drawn in 1921 by Alfred Robinson, the University architect at the time, have been preserved and are now in the University archives.[8] The building itself was demolished in 1955 to make way for new science buildings on the site.

In the new design the ground plan (Fig. 106) was enlarged and simplified into an almost perfect square with an L-shaped service wing extending back from the main body of the house to enclose a kitchen yard to the north. Inside, the rooms are ordered around a long hall extending from the entrance on the south front to the center of the house at which point two staircases, east and west of the hall, effectively divide the house across the middle, separating the front and back portions of the interior.

The arrangement is articulated on the exterior (Figs. 107, 108). The reception rooms are located in the principal front block. Behind this, the west staircase is separately housed in a tower while the east staircase is marked by a window breaking through the divisions of the storeys on the opposite facade. The smaller north block containing the kitchen and bedrooms has a simple saddleback roof and the service wing is contained in a low single-storey range.

[112]

Once again this irregular grouping of individually articulated units is Puginian in origin and characteristic of the Ecclesiologists' vicarages, as are the tangential service wing, the external expression of the staircases, and the irregular massing of the facades. In particular, the parallel arrangement of the two main blocks is characteristic of a number of Butterfield's small country parsonages such as those at West Lavington in Sussex of 1850 and Pollington in Yorkshire of 1853-1854.[9]

Yet while retaining the clear separation of parts from the first design, Deane and Woodward strove for greater coherence in the second. The regularity of the plan has already been noted. The exterior also shows the same tendency toward a more unified composition with neater contours and outline. Except for the balconies the external features are all kept close to the wall plane without any gratuitous irregularity or bold projection from the surface. The porch was added after the building was completed and was not a feature of the original design. The original doorway was a simple pointed arch, chamfered, and with a relieving arch of colored stones flush with the wall.[10] In Ruskin's terms, the building was "gathered well together."[11] In this respect Deane and Woodward could have been influenced as much by G. E. Street as by Ruskin. In his lecture "On the Revival of the Ancient Style of Domestic Architecture" delivered to the Ecclesiological Society in 1853, Street recommended that "it would be a great advantage to see our various parochial buildings, as, Eg., schools and parsonages, brought together, that so they might form a more imposing mass."[12] This, he argued, was more consistent with medieval practice where "builders always . . . strove as much as they could to simplify their plans. . . . The consequence is, that in old designs one sees long lines of roofing and no attempt at a display of gables, except where they are positively necessary."[13] Street's vicarages at All Saints, Boyne Hill, Maidenhead, and St. Ebbes in Oxford, both of 1854-1855, display the same tendencies of massiveness, strong horizontal emphasis, unbroken rooflines, and broad expanses of blank wall offset by grouped openings (though not, significantly, the squared blockiness and monumental facadism) which characterize the Curator's House. In these buildings Street also used a considerable amount of structural polychromy and cottage features (hipped gables, hooded dormers, and tall chimneys) and, unlike Butterfield, was prepared to introduce "foreign elements," that is, Italian and French Gothic features, in these modest parochial structures.[14]

But in comparison to contemporary British architecture Deane and Woodward's house is unusually eclectic for a building of its size and type. The broad simple forms, the "muscular" mural quality, and features such as the detached cylindrical shafts and the tall hip roof of the front block, are essentially French Gothic, while the tower roof and dormers are German.[15] The upper-storey windows are north Italian or Veronese Gothic, while those on the lower range are Venetian. Much of the carved ornament is Early English in manner, though the plate tracery of the balconies is once again Italian.

Much of this eclecticism as indeed also the general massing of the building and the materials used—creamy Bath stone, white marble, red and brown sandstone dressings, and polished marble window shafts—can be explained by the auxiliary position of the Curator's House as an adjunct to the Museum.

Like the Museum, the most striking feature was the "depth and richness" of the O'Sheas' carving.[16] Following Ruskin's dictum, this work is not just decorative but has "subject and meaning."[17] Thus, there is a great deal of playful story-telling carving, including scenes from Aesop's fables such as the fox and the goose on the impost of a second-floor window on the east facade.[18]

In sum, the Curator's House represents the concurrence of the organizational principles of the Ecclesiologists' modest parochial works, involving an asymmetrical and functionally expressive disposition of parts, and Ruskin's aesthetic principles calling for contained monumental forms, elaborate fenestration, a variety of materials, and rich and finely executed ornament.

Llys Dulas, Anglesey

Deane and Woodward's next domestic commission was for an addition to a house in a remote corner of North Anglesey near Dulas Bay. Llys Dulas, the name of the property on which the house was built and after which it was named, belonged to Lady Gertrude Dinorben, the second wife of William Lewis Hughes who had built the original house on the site in the 1830s in the popular Tudorbethan style of the day.[19] In 1856 she decided to enlarge the house and commissioned Deane and Woodward to design a "grand addition."[20] Her choice of architects is not surprising, as Lady Dinorben was Irish-born and came from Ballynatray, County Waterford, and may well have known the firm in Ireland.

Construction began in 1856 by the Dublin firm of Gilbert Cockburn and Sons and was completed in 1858. None of the original plans or drawings for the house have survived. The building itself, after having stood derelict for many years, was then used for storage and was finally demolished in 1975.

Deane and Woodward's design involved an extensive addition to the front of the house (Fig. 109), the central feature of which was a great skylit hall rising the entire height of the building. The hall, entered directly from the doorway beneath the arched porch, was surrounded on all four sides by a double arcade of pointed arches springing from squat, square pillars with carved free-stone capitals and massive stone bases. The arcades formed cloister-like vaulted passages around the hall from which the reception rooms on the ground floor and the bedrooms on the second floor were reached. Directly opposite the entrance on the other side of the hall were the principle stairs connecting the two levels within the hall and leading back into the original rear portion of the house.

This arrangement followed well-established domestic traditions. The glass-roofed two-storey hall with a gallery underwent something of a revival in both classical and Gothic domestic architecture in the 1830s and 1840s. Barry used it in his Pall Mall clubhouses and Pugin in Scarisbrick Hall (1837-1852).[21] In the first instance the source is the cortile of the Renaissance palazzo. Pugin's hall at Scarisbrick, which appears again on a smaller scale in The Grange, is clearly an adaptation of the medieval Great Hall. Goodhart-Rendel suggested that the popularity of the formula in grander Victorian houses had practical reasons "inspired by its capability of keeping the whole house warm," enabling "the planner to dispense with long outlying passages, which in Victorian winters seem always to have been icily cold."[22] In any case the feature was not new in Deane and Woodward's work, having been used earlier in TCD and the Oxford Museum.

On the exterior some effort was made to harmonize with the style of the earlier structure. Thus the idea (if not the form) of the towered entrance porch, the shape of the chimneys, the stepped gable ends, and the white stone quoins gave the exterior a vaguely Elizabethan or Tudor character. The detail, however, was Italian. The window shapes, plate-tracery balconies, and the enclosed loggia in the upper level of the tower were all Venetian in character.

The most notable feature of the building was the O'Sheas' carving (Fig. 110). In September 1858 the *Building News* noted that they were "engaged in carving every sort of natural object in the capitals, strings, etc. . . ."[23] The quality came very close in design and execution to the carving in the Museum. The hard stone, which in both cases allowed for deep undercutting, also weathered well.

Carved ornament of a lower order—that is nonrepresentational geometric designs—appeared in the moldings and pierced stonework. Inside, the capitals and imposts of the hall arcade were also richly carved with foliage, birds, and other small animals.[24] The wooden beams supporting the glass roof of the court were notched and scalloped while the timbers were decorated with a stencil-cut frieze of leaves and quatrefoils like the wooden furniture in the Oxford Museum.

In both the Curator's House and Llys Dulas, Deane and Woodward followed the same principles of design and composition involving monumental, balanced frontages, axiality and compartmentation of plan and elevation, and disposition of ornament and cut-stone detail as they did in their larger buildings. In their Irish houses of the late fifties, these qualities are developed into a more distinctive individualistic domestic mode.

Houses of the "Parti-Ruskin" in Ireland

Following completion of Llys Dulas and the Curator's House, Deane and Woodward embarked on a series of houses in Ireland, begun in 1858 and nearly complete at the time of Woodward's death in 1861. The series forms an interesting group of what the *Building News* called the "Parti-Ruskin."[25] Though each one is different according to the particular requirements of site, the individual desires of the clients, and the natural resources of the districts in which they are built, they share certain general characteristics. As in all of the firm's Irish work there are strong local associations in the emphasis on site and landscape, the use of indigenous building materials, vernacular forms and modes of construction, and Celtic ornamental motifs. In addition they all have basically square house plans with loosely attached service wings, windows set behind stonework frames, and generally simpler outlines and features than the earlier houses. Unlike these, the Irish houses have a limited amount of representational carving, partly due to the fact that the O'Sheas were not involved in any of these works, but also because the hard Irish granite and limestone did not lend itself to finely detailed carving.[26] As a result the exterior surfaces tend to be plainer and the emphasis on the windows greater than in the English houses. The interiors, on the other hand, are more richly detailed with ornament executed in a variety of materials.[27]

Brownsbarn, County Kilkenny

Brownsbarn (Figs. 111, 112), now the property of Lord Teignmouth, was built for a client named Mcdougal just outside Thomastown on the road to Inistioge. The house faces west and takes full advantage of the broad prospects afforded by the hilltop site of the Nore and Barrow river valleys and the Wexford hills beyond.

Unlike the Curator's House and Llys Dulas, Brownsbarn has a fully excavated basement, around which the ground has been cut away to form a moat-like ditch to drain off water and to increase the amount of daylight entering the sunken storey. Where the ground slopes down at the back, the basement, in which the kitchen and storerooms were originally located, opens out onto the kitchen yard bordered on the west by the low range of servants' quarters and additional service areas.

Above this monumental base the ground-floor rooms are ordered around a large central hall which functions as a reception room and entrance hall. In this instance, however, the main stairs are not incorporated into the hall, which is only one storey high, but are set off to the side in a separate stairhall. The living rooms on the ground floor are large and generously proportioned. The study in the southwest corner and the drawing room in the southeast have southern exposures; the dining room faces east. The main stairs are in the northwest angle of the house. In the northeast corner the service stairs rise from the basement to the upper storey to provide separate access from the servants' quarters to the main house. On the second floor the bedrooms are ranged along a central corridor which bisects the house on a north-south axis.

The exterior is articulated in terms of two separately roofed rectangular blocks placed side by side. As noted in relation to the Curator's House, this was a disposition frequently used by Butterfield in his smaller country vicarages of the early fifties. The informality of the back elevation (Fig. 113) with its rubble walling, irregular, simple fenestration, and broken roof lines also recalls Butterfield's smaller cottages of the early 1850s. Otherwise there is relatively little of the purposeful irregularity of High Victorian functional expressionism. Instead the massing is regular and balanced, the contours contained, and outlines clear and simple.

The effect of Brownsbarn depends largely on the colors and textures of the materials employed. Kilkenny abounds in quarries of different types of granite and limestone, and Deane and Woodward exploited the rich natural resources of the district. The walls are banded red and gray granite, the window dressings are dark gray limestone, the voussoirs red and white banded stone, and the window shafts are of different colored marble with limestone capitals and bases. The alternating courses of rough-faced red and gray granite counterbalance the verticality of the tall, steeply gabled blocks and give the exterior a lithic "muscular" quality in effect quite different from the taut planarity of High Victorian "streaky bacon" brickwork. In keeping with the coarse texture and solid mass of the walls, the external features and ornament are necessarily bold and simple. The openings are arched and cusped with plain limestone dressings and banded voussoirs on the whole kept flush with the wall plane. The few projecting moldings are substantial and left in block while the thick stone slabs of the balconies are pierced with simple plate tracery. The windows themselves are all recessed behind the stonework, thereby increasing the sense of mass and thickness of the walls.

Because the effect of finely worked detail would be lost against the strident polychromy, there is little carved ornament on the exterior and this is restricted to the capitals on the window shafts and porch colonnettes. The carving here is stylized and in shallow relief—probably because of the hardness of the dark gray Kilkenny limestone.

As the name "Brownsbarn" suggests, Deane and Woodward looked to the simplest early vernacular structures as models for their design. The resulting sense of mass, rough surfaces, and generally big-boned quality of individual features give the building a distinctly Irish character. At the same time, however, the tendency toward unified volume, simplification of mass, and concentration on surface pattern, texture, and color are rather more Ruskinian than Irish.

Ruskin's principles concerning materials and ornament were also applied inside the house, where there are carved marble fireplaces and heavy wooden door frames with billet and cable moldings. Otherwise, the stencil-cut ornament which was noticed at Llys Dulas appears now in the wooden wainscoting and most remarkably on the balusters of the main staircase (Fig. 114). These show a lively and playful variety of motifs—leaves, rabbits, ducks, birds, lizards, and other creatures—while the ball end of the handrail is formed into a grotesque head. This ornament is difficult to characterize. Douglas Richardson has seen it as a precocious example of "Japonisme."[28] It is perhaps more correctly viewed in the context of medieval forms as a sort of naturalistic tracery.

The general quality of the workmanship, even in the most functional parts of the building, is consistently high. As always, design is conditioned by materials. Thus, where rough or motley-colored stone is used features are bold and simple. Where stone is densely textured and uniform in color it is polished, cut, and carved. Woodwork is simply chamfered, jointed, and stained to bring out the natural grain. Finally, different kinds of metal are hammered and wrought according to their tensile qualities.

[118]

The imaginative quality and vigor of the detail in Brownsbarn is rare in contemporary buildings of this type in Britain. Much of this work is only vaguely related to specifically Gothic forms. Nevertheless it conveys a thoroughly medieval spirit which is at the same time profoundly Irish. The feeling for rich interiors, for varied surface pattern and texture, for freely designed and structurally integrated ornament, is deeply rooted in Celtic design and distinguishes the Rococo work of the Irish stuccatori in preceding generations.[29] As at TCD, the architectonic sense of design and sensitivity to form and materials attest to the survival of a sound tradition of craftsmanship in Irish building.

St. Austin's Abbey, County Carlow

St. Austin's Abbey, named after the fourteenth-century friary which once stood on the site, is on the periphery of Tullow in County Carlow, approximately twenty-five miles northeast of Thomastown. The house was built for Charles N. Doyne in 1858-1859, but was burnt in the Troubles in 1922 and never rebuilt so that today only a ruin remains—a part of which is used for grain storage. The commission involved a far more extensive building program than Brownsbarn— including several outbuildings, stables, and a gate house.[30] The architects' ground plan of the house and an old photograph of the north garden facade give an impression of the building before it burned down (Figs. 115, 116).[31]

The plan is similar to Brownsbarn, being almost square with a projecting gabled porch at the entrance leading directly into a central hall. Off the hall are the reception rooms and staircase—again not in the hall itself but connected to it by a pointed-brick archway. Instead of placing the kitchen and storerooms in the basement, they are incorporated into the long service wing to the west. The kitchen, set apart on the northwest end of the wing, is formed into an independent square block with a pyramidal roof and high chimney. The idea behind this goes back to the Glastonbury Kitchen/Chemistry Laboratory at the Oxford Museum. The main house is two storeys high with the upper floor, like Brownsbarn, contained within the roof and the windows pushed up into hooded dormers. Generally the exterior is plainer than Brownsbarn. Most of the windows are simple rectangular openings with chamfered corners and otherwise undecorated stone trim and relieving arches all contained within the thickness of the wall. Cut-stone ornament is concentrated on the great staircase window on the south front and the balconies. Once again, this is simple plate tracery. There is also a limited amount of carving on the capitals of the window shafts.

St. Austin's Abbey shows a movement in Deane and Woodward's domestic designs away from structural polychromy, intricately carved foliage in capitals and string courses, and pointed Gothic windows with tracery and carved moldings toward uniform color, simple solid features, contained forms, and the deliberate primitivism of a "more archaic type."[32] These tendencies can be related to a trend in the work of other "advanced" Gothicists such as Burges, Street, Pearson, and Bodley who, in the late 1850s, were all turning to earlier, less "developed," Gothic modes, particularly "Early French" vernacular architecture.[33] Woodward may also have been inspired by the plain, solid features of French early Gothic buildings of this kind. And the nearly pyramidal roofs, simple masses, dominant horizontality, continuous surfaces, and uniform color (except in the very French detached window columns) at St. Austin's are all consistent with the mode.

Yet there are marked differences between Woodward's building and those of Street and the rest. The latter, in moving away from the jagged outlines and taut, thin, shimmering surfaces of Butterfieldian High Victorian Gothic, were clarifying the contours, unifying the surfaces, consolidating and amplifying mass in an effort to achieve a new sense of "muscularity." Woodward, on the other hand, was striving for something quite different at St. Austin's. At the same time as adopting a simpler and plainer manner he clarified the plan and composition of the building. St. Austin's shows none of the compression, interpenetrating masses, and vertical emphasis of the English buildings. Instead it moves individualistically toward elementary classicizing geometries and compartmentation, where the parts are treated as independent units, separate volumes formed into simple self-contained masses.

Glandore, County Dublin

Situated in Monkstown, a south Dublin suburb bordering on Dun Laoghaire (formerly the port and harbor of Kingstown), Glandore is now surrounded by a modern housing development, where the extensive gardens (originally part of Monkstown Castle grounds) once were. It was built for the Hon. William J. Vesey, brother of Lord de Vesci, one of the chief landlords of the district, and was named "Glandore" after the area in west Cork where the de Vescis also had land.[34]

A plan for the house inscribed "Proposed house at Monkstown for the Hon. W. J. Vesey" is dated January 25, 1858 (Fig. 117).[35] It was probably begun shortly thereafter and aside from some minor changes, including the elimination of the conservatory, it was executed according to the firm's original plan.

Glandore (Figs. 118, 119) is the largest of Deane and Woodward's Irish houses of this type, incorporating extensive service accommodations in the house itself. It exhibits the same formal qualities as St. Austin's Abbey. Built of uniformly colored Dublin granite, it has sharp regular contours, few projections, plain rectangular moldings, enveloping roofs, hipped gables, and a limited amount of Italian Gothic detail in some of the windows.

But the axiality of the main house plan and separate articulation of the service wing show an even greater clarification of parts than at St. Austin's. Here the elementary contained masses spreading horizontally outward from the main pile give it a quality of repose and balance that is totally antithetical to the intersecting, competitive forms of High Victorian Gothic composition.

At the same time it also reflects a new kind of socio-functional associationism whereby the different purposes, status, and interrelationships of the various parts of the house are clearly articulated on the exterior. Thus the north facade, though the entrance front, is, with regard to treatment, the back of the house. Asymmetrical massing, irregular fenestration, exposed chimneys, and the forward projection of the service wing at the side give this elevation a decidedly informal, private, aspect. By contrast, the regular contours and boxlike containment of the south facade clearly show this to be the formal front elevation of the house. The rationale for this treatment is immediately apparent from the plan. The main reception rooms and bedrooms are all located in the south and east portions of the house, while the north range is given over to circulation areas, servants, and utility rooms.

This simple expressive rationalism extends to every detail of the composition. On the north facade the butler's rooms on the ground floor and the small closet rooms above the porch have simple square-headed windows while the bedrooms and morning room have grander arched windows. On the south facade each room is also given distinctively individual external treatment. The drawing room has a projecting bay window and the dining room a triple arcade, while above, the bedroom windows have banded voussoirs, molded architraves, and pierced stone balconies. The landing of the main stairs, as at St. Austin's, has a great window and balcony with elaborate plate tracery. The servants' quarters are clearly set apart from the main body of the house in a dormered attic storey.

The effect of Glandore depends largely on the calculated contrasts of plain and highly ornate parts. On the north facade, where the massing is irregular, features are generally simple, workmanlike, and undecorated. On the south side where the outlines are regular and the wall plane unbroken, surface ornamentation is richer and the fenestration more elaborate. Here in particular we are reminded of the Ruskinian urban facades of the firm's large civic and commercial structures, where the contained contours likewise function as a frame for the architectural ornament. Clearly Deane and Woodward have once again followed Ruskin's counsel to balance simple building with bold concentrations of ornamental detail.

Clontra, County Dublin

Clontra is the firm's masterpiece in this group of small Ruskinian houses (Figs. 120-122). It is also the best preserved, having remained in the family of the original owners until 1930, when it was bought by its present owners who have kept the house and grounds virtually unchanged.

The house was built as a country retreat for James Anthony Lawson, a well-known Dublin lawyer, who later became Solicitor General (1861), Attorney General (1865), and Justice of the Queen's Bench (1882) in Ireland.[36] Lawson was not an unlikely client for Deane and Woodward. He was connected with TCD and was a member of the Kildare Street Club whose new premises were being built by the firm at the time. Thus, he must have been well acquainted with their work in Dublin and perhaps even in Cork, which was his wife's home.

The site chosen was in Shankill on the south County Dublin coast between the popular resort areas of Ballybrack and Bray. Following the opening of new railway lines to these districts in the mid-fifties, the Dublin bay area became the scene of rapid suburban expansion.[37] In 1858 the *Building News* noted, "There exists here [in Dublin] a tolerably strong mania . . . for building ex-urban houses, and, as everybody knows, it would be difficult to find better excuses for the mania than the exquisite scenery round Dublin bay affords."[38] Clontra is situated in one of the choicest spots on the coastline. Set in its own forested grounds with a gate lodge and conservatory—the house is directly on the sea and has views of the Killiney hills to the north and the Wicklow mountains to the south.

Building began in 1858 and was nearing completion by late September when the *Building News* gave a detailed description of it.[39] Like Brownsbarn and St. Austin's Abbey, the main house is square in plan and two storeys high with the second floor pushed up under the roof. But here a somewhat unusual arrangement was adopted. The principal reception rooms are on the top floor with their ceilings reaching up into the roof while the bedrooms are on the ground floor. A steep flight of granite steps leads directly from the veranda-covered entrance up to the second floor and into a square central hall, around which are the dining room, drawing room, and study. An internal staircase at the rear leads down to the bedroom floor and kitchen which is a self-contained unit with its own pyramidal roof, set between the back of the house and the service wing to the north.

The cross-axial arrangement of the roofs shows the internal disposition of the reception rooms. Each of these is also given distinctive external treatment, in the differently shaped oriels, bays, windows, and balconies.

The variety of forms and somewhat exotic mixture of stylistic motifs they represent reveal a wide-ranging eclecticism. The plan, original and quirky in its Gothic context, is in fact, as Mark Girouard has pointed out, a clever adaptation of an arrangement common in early-nineteenth-century two-storey Georgian terrace houses in and around Dublin, where a steep flight of external steps leads up to the second floor containing the principal apartments under a hipped roof.[40] In Clontra the stairs have been internalized and lead straight up into the center of the house. The low, dominating roofs, half-timbered oriels, stone-mullioned windows, dormers with bargeboards, tall chimneys, and the latticework of the veranda (which also appear in the small gate house) are all more picturesque cottage features drawn from a whole range of English vernacular modes. The kitchen is another variant of the Glastonbury Kitchen type—by now a familiar hallmark of the firm's work. As always, there are also North Italian Gothic motifs in the upper-storey windows and balconies and especially in the ironwork of the conservatory which is molded into "Venetian" twisted colonnettes and leafy capitals. On the whole, external ornament is kept to a minimum, consisting largely of the polychromatic effects of the inlaid red brick relieving arches and pierced stonework of the balconies.

The interior spaces (Figs. 123, 124) are arranged to create the greatest possible variety of scale, proportion, and visual richness. Entered via the steep, dark stairs, the small skylit hall is a dazzling well of light and color. Its polished yellow, green, brown, and white tile pavement and glass roof supported by massive notched and stained wooden beams resting on stone corbels is like a miniature version of Llys Dulas. The small landing and stairs directly ahead lead down to second skylit landing—another pool of light and color—that marks the intermediary stage between the upper and lower houses. Thus, the various parts of the house are clearly distinguished and their different purposes and interrelationships made explicit.

Every detail of the internal fittings is assimilated to the simple medievalism of the architecture. On the ground floor the materials and workmanship are appropriately plainer than in the "showplace" of the upper house. Here, the fireplaces are all of different colored polished marble. Notched and scalloped moldings around the door frames continue along the skirting boards. The back staircase and the original furniture designed by the architects are decorated with pounced tracery. Particularly effective are the cylindrical timber handrails in the front stairhall which pass through stone loops affixed to the walls. Thus, every detail is executed in Deane and Woodward's individual "bold and rough" medievalizing manner.

The most remarkable decorative features of Clontra—the paintings on the end walls and roofs of the stairhall, dining room, and drawing room—were not mentioned in the *Building News* review. These were designed and executed by John Hungerford Pollen in 1862.[41] Whether or not the painted decoration was a part of the original program, it seems quite certain that it was devised before Woodward's death.[42] Between the rafters of the drawing and dining room roofs Pollen painted birds, flowers, and plants in brightly colored decorative designs in the style of his other work of this kind in Merton College Chapel and Blickling Hall.[43] In the drawing room (Fig. 125) the birds are depicted flying across wavy blue, gray, and buff bands of color which are stylized representations of clouds. In the lower portion of the roof are densely clustered plants and flowers. Pollen used a similar design for the dining room involving dense foliage in the lower half of the roof and a lighter, airier design in the top portion with birds darting through fruit-laden branches and vines. On the ceiling of the stairhall (Fig. 123) the birds and sinuous plant motifs are set against a background of broad transverse bands of blue, gray, and white.

Scenes of a more allegorical nature are depicted on the walls. Above the entrance are a knight and lady in medieval dress and setting, drinking from a stirrup cup. The meaning of this scene is elaborated in a frieze carried around the walls where a series of figures represent country pursuits and hospitality—a chatelaine with keys, a servant with a dish, a boy shooting a rabbit, and other game animals.

Domestic and country themes are picked up again in the end walls of the dining and drawing rooms. The subjects in the dining room are "Spring Morning" and "Autumn Evening"—an elaboration of the theme of nature's eternal rhythms. The drawing room end walls depict the "Seven Ages of Woman." Here the themes of nature and regeneration are linked with those of domestic harmony in the personification of woman as the mainstay of home and family. All this rests on the firm foundation of faith, a sentiment graphically expressed in the quotation from Martin Luther carved over the entrance arch at the foot of the stairs: "Wer auf Gott Vertraut, Der hat auf einen Fels gebaut."

All of the paintings are framed by decorative borders of intertwined Celtic design. The paintings themselves are executed with Pollen's characteristically loose handling and saturated colors. Like the Oxford Union murals, they are most effective for their rich coloring and abstract pattern. And the combined themes of nature, domesticity, the rural idyll, and the romantic medievalism of it all are all the more fitting in their present setting than on the walls of the Oxford Union Society debating hall.

In fact, these themes are at the very root of the architecture and provide an essential clue to the wide-ranging eclecticism of Clontra. Drawing on a whole range of medieval and vernacular traditions, the effect sought, as the *Building News* aptly noted, is "highly picturesque and certainly fresh."[44]

At the same time Clontra also continues the development we have been tracing in Deane and Woodward's domestic work toward a classicizing containment of volume and mass and a corresponding richness of detail. Square in plan and blocklike in mass, Clontra, more than any of the houses we have looked at so far, was designed as a framework for the display of picturesquely conceived architectural detail on the facades and carved and painted ornament in the interior. The Kildare Street Club, our next and final building, represents the furthest advance in this movement from object to craft, and from historicism to a new sort of objective social associationism.

VII

THE KILDARE STREET CLUB AND THE END OF THE PARTNERSHIP

The Kildare Street Club, Woodward's last major building, was the culminating work of the partnership (Figs. 126, 127). Designed in 1858, the exterior was completed in 1860 and the interior in 1861, the year of Woodward's death.[1]

The club itself, founded by Nathaniel Conyngham Burton following "an act of hasty-tempered black-balling at Daly's Club" in about 1788,[2] had its first premises, bought for the members by David La Touche, at 6 Kildare Street (and hence the name). Shortly after the split, Daly's began to decline and the Kildare Street Club quickly took the lead as the "first metropolitan club of Irish noblemen and gentlemen" by gathering within its walls the leading members of Irish society.[3] In about 1856 the members decided, because of their growing numbers and the need to keep pace with the increasing size and luxury of the London clubs, to build an entirely new clubhouse.[4]

In September 1858 the *Building News* announced:

> The site, after a little Hibernian wrong-endedness, has been secured and consists of four houses in Kildare street and one in Nassau street (now Leinster street), and Sir Thomas Deane, Son, and Woodward have prepared preliminary plans, and are only waiting for the pleasure of the grouse to return a power of committee sufficient to say move on . . . about £20,000 marks the financial limit, as far as the building is concerned.[5]

Finally on March 1, 1859, the *Dublin Builder* reported that "the works for the new club-house . . . have been commenced; Messrs. Cockburns' tender in a limited competition being accepted."[6]

As the *Dublin Builder* observed, "the form of the ground suggested in a great measure the arrangement of the ground plan."[7] At the front this was, like TCD, essentially a large parallelogram. Only two sides are visible, since the range of smaller structures at the rear, containing the club's gaming rooms and sports facilities, are hidden from view by flanking buildings.

This last of Woodward's major buildings is an assimilation of the firm's earlier eclectic associationism into a remarkably original new design. Features familiar from the firm's other buildings are here presented with a monumental assurance in a whole that dominates its urban surroundings. The relation of the new building to its setting was noticed in a contemporary review:

> Certainly there are times when elbow-room is allowed in towns: and a magnificent opportunity is about to be afforded to three gentlemen (who have shown on many occasions that they know how to improve one) of trying on a large scale what can be done to humanize street architecture.[8]

Rather than "humanizing" street architecture, however, the Kildare Street Club monumentalizes it. The club expresses its size and massiveness in a similar way to TCD: broad base, low hipped roof, emphatic horizontality, and clear vertical bounding lines. The relation to TCD is intentional, especially as the two buildings were originally to face each other across the college park. In fact, as the reviewer in the *Dublin Builder* noted, the firm's original design also had "semi-circular heads to the windows like those in the New Museum building at Trinity College," which were rejected by the club's building committee.[9]

Yet, unlike TCD, the Kildare Street Club was not set in a broad expanse of grassy parkland, but on the corner of a narrow Dublin Street. Thus a number of adjustments had to be made to accommodate the building to its dense urban context. First, brick was used instead of stone for the fabric of the building in an attempt to blend in with the predominantly brick Georgian street architecture of Dublin. Further, as noted above, sash windows with rectangular frames were substituted for the round-arched ones in the firm's original design. This was largely for practical reasons. Since it was only possible to light some of the rooms from one side, it was necessary to make the openings as large and unobstructed as possible, and the "straight-sided arch" allowed for the substitution of slender columns for what would otherwise have been large piers.[10]

The novelty of Deane and Woodward's clubhouse design caused considerable contemporary comment. The *Building News* pointed out that:

Our architects have . . . gone nearly always to the later buildings of Italy for their models. The Reform Club House is based on the Farnese Palace; its neighbor, the Traveller's on that of the Pandolfini at Florence; whilst on the other side, Sansovino's Library of St. Mark has been pressed into the services of the Carlton. . . . Messrs. Deane and Woodward, in the Kildare Street Club . . . have been the first to introduce in such buildings the Italian Gothic style.[11]

The *Ecclesiologist* also exclaimed that "Dublin . . . has taken a step in advance of London in the erection of a new club house in modified Gothic."[12]

Actually, however, the form of the building does not really stray far from that of the earlier London clubhouses, a fact which was noticed by the *Building News* in 1860, which observed that "the main block or outline is as Italian as any palace in Pall-Mall."[13] Yet though the Kildare Street Club exhibits the same squared solidity as the earlier clubs, it does not follow their regularity and the symmetry of their massing. The distribution of windows and other details is constantly changing across the facades. Even the third-storey windows, which are the most regular features of the exterior, are not evenly spaced.

This asymmetry is once again a rational expression of the interior arrangement of spaces. (Unfortunately, these no longer exist in their original form. The central stairhall was taken out in the early 1960s when half of the building was sold and converted into offices for the French Embassy. In 1976 the remainder of the building was sold to the National Library and the original furnishings and fittings removed.)[14] The massive scale of the portico in proportion to the rest of the building reflects the same difference in scale between the stairhall, which rose the entire height of the building to a skylight in the roof, and the reception rooms around it. Otherwise the morning room on the ground floor and a drawing room above are given external definition by such domestic features as bay windows and balconies. The third-floor windows also express, in their domestic scale, the private nature of the rooms behind. Different degrees of privacy from passersby are shown in the relation of the window panes to the external wall surface. On the ground floor they are deeply recessed behind the window piers; on the second floor they are flush with the piers; and on the third floor they are almost flush with the jambs. This arrangement, as Douglas Richardson has pointed out, also serves as a rational expression of the decreasing load by an effective thinning of the walls.[15] In still another way the architects have managed to insure the privacy of the members by surrounding the building with a walled moat. Behind this, and beneath the level of the street are the kitchens, servants' bedrooms, and spacious wine and beer cellars.

The plan shows a masterful use of the limited available space. The arrangement of the entrance lobby and waiting room leading into the central court is perhaps derived from Barry's Reform Club. The idea of the court itself (though Barry did not incorporate the stairs in the hall) also has its origins in the Reform Club plan, as do the placement of the coffee and morning rooms and the members' private entrance.

Though the style of the club was identified as "Italian Gothic," in fact only isolated ornamental details such as the carved capitals, stringcourse moldings, quoin colonettes, and more loosely the balcony and balustrade above the portico can be related to Italian Gothic prototypes.[16] The portico itself is clearly modeled on the south porch of St. Mark's, which Ruskin illustrated in his *Examples of the Architecture of Venice*.[17] This feature, together with the generally big-boned quality of the building, probably prompted a reviewer in the *Dublin Builder* to dub the design "Byzantine," a term used rather loosely in contemporary architectural jargon to designate a wide variety of round-arched styles with massive "bold and ornamental" features.[18]

Concerning the ornament, the writer in the *Building News* noted that "the details . . . are all suggested by the Gothic which prevailed in [Italy]. We say advisedly *suggested* because we would not detract from the originality with which the building has been in many portions treated."[19] Indeed, the design and execution of the ornament is by far the firm's greatest achievement in this area.

There is a certain amount of controversy concerning the authorship of the stone carving on the exterior of the Kildare Street Club. C. P. Curran noted that the O'Sheas are "associated by a firm tradition" with the work, while Charles W. Harrison, a Yorkshireman who came to Dublin in 1857, also "did his first Dublin work on this building . . . working side by side . . . with the O'Sheas."[20] More recently Raymond McGrath attributed all of the carving to the O'Sheas. Since then, however, on the basis of some newly discovered sketches by Harrison, Peter Harbison gave all the carvings to Harrison.[21] It would, in fact, seem that much of the carving on the exterior of the Kildare Street Club was executed by Harrison. This claim is supported by a reference in the *Dublin Builder* in 1861 to the fact that "an enormous sum . . . is now being expended on the decoration of the new . . . Kildare Street Club, all of which was paid to English and foreign workmen."[22]

Earlier the *Dublin Builder* had noted that a "professional firm" was responsible for "supervising the work."[23] This was probably the English firm of C. W. Purdy and John Henry Outhwaite, "architectural sculptors," who came to Dublin in the mid-1850s and were also responsible for executing the carving on two drinking fountains in the city designed by Deane and Woodward in 1860.[24] Charles Harrison was the most talented carver in Purdy and Outhwaite's employ at this time and it is possible that he was brought over by that firm, who had a reputation for their very liberal practice of allowing "competent workmen a consistent latitude in producing forms," expressly to work on the club.[25] While in all of these contemporary accounts no mention is made of the O'Sheas, it is nevertheless possible that they were also involved in a later stage of the work on the interior.[26]

The *Dublin Builder* reported that "no drawings have been made in detail for any of the carved work in the building, a careful supervision and rough sketches, to ensure a certain character of foliage, being all that was deemed necessary."[27] A number of such sketches by Harrison have survived that clearly show this claim to be true.[28] These include a variety of fine drawings of flowers and leaves, evidently studied from nature. In other drawings these have been arranged into decorative designs which are clearly sketches for the external capitals and friezes. Thus, a sketch of a bird's nest resting in the leafy branches of a tree was used as the basis for one of the portico capitals (Figs. 128, 129). Harrison's distinctive style is easily recognizable, and from the drawings it would appear that most of the deeply undercut, vivid, and exuberant carving on the external capitals and string courses is his work (Figs. 130, 131).

Otherwise, carved animals and figures disport themselves around the bases of the external columns, rather like the curious anthropomorphic creatures with which medieval illuminators decorated the margins of their manuscripts (Figs. 132-134). There are a number of drawings by Harrison for these carvings of birds, dogs, rabbits, squirrels, snakes, and monkeys. Some are carefully studied, delicate, and graceful naturalistic representations; others are like the grotesque creatures of the medieval bestiary. They are all remarkable for their intricacy and variety of subject and fully evoke the spirit and wit of Ruskin's idea of the medieval craftsman. Some represent scenes from Aesop's fables. The best, however, are a pointed, though humorous, comment on the members of the Club— "an institution famous for aristocracy, claret and whist"—and their pastimes.[29] Monkeys playing billiards and scenes of the hunt are a satirical commentary on the amusements of the landed gentry. A more ominous scene of a bear-baiting is depicted on one of the second-storey bases. The enraged bear is unable to defend himself against his semi-human tormentor. The reference to the Anglo-Irish situation seems clear.

The interior detailing follows the large scale of the exterior. As the *Ecclesiologist* noted, "instead of shirking detail as he might have done, [the architect] has carried out every minutia with scrupulous attention to his general idea."[30] This was "that construction should be visible, and ornament added to construction."[31] Thus carved detail appears on marble chimney pieces and massive stone cornices and corbels. The timber roof beams resting on the corbels were left uncovered, to be decoratively painted at a later stage of the work in the event that additional funds would be forthcoming. Beneath this the plant and flower motifs of the stone carving are repeated in plaster friezes.

Constructive realism is most striking in some of the rooms at the back of the house. The skylit billiard room and racquet court both have open timber roofs (Fig. 135). The private staircase to the bedrooms is a wooden dog-leg construction with revealed joints and stencil-cut ornament like those in Brownsbarn and Clontra. The floors in the passages, dressing rooms, and bathrooms all have different patterned tile pavements.

However, the most striking feature of the interior—the main stairhall—has disappeared and is now only known from photographs (Figs. 136, 137). This was another example—the most original and excitingly complex—of a grand and richly decorated main hall which was a central feature of so many of Deane and Woodward's interiors. As in TCD, the Oxford Museum, Llys Dulas, and Clontra the hall is naturally lit from a skylight in the roof and surrounded by a double arcade. The dominating feature of the hall is the massive stone staircase which rises gradually behind the arcade along the wall, thus leaving the central area open, and then thrusts out in a powerful diagonal flying flight across the hall. As in TCD, the changes in scale as one moves through the hall and up the stairs, the colored marble shafts, the elaborate geometry of the floor and skirting tiles, the pierced, thick stone slabs of the balustrade, and the organic forms of the great carved free-stone capitals, moldings, and beltcourses all give the hall the effect of surprise, drama, and infinite variety. It is a bold adventure where every part and detail is calculated for effect and expresses the excitement of the enterprise and delight in the complexity and diversity of the work.

This hall, as indeed the entire design of the Kildare Street Club where "the spirit . . . [is] namely, that of imparting a Gothic feeling into a building in which the pointed arch either does not appear at all, or in a very modified form," carries further the development traced in Deane and Woodward's domestic work toward a freer sort of eclecticism.[32] It also carries forward the progressive tendencies of these houses toward contained monumental forms, elaborate window design, and rich decoration—expanding and urbanizing their program into a town house on a truly monumental scale.

The Kildare Street Club was the last complete building designed by the firm before Woodward's death in May 1861. In December 1860, when work on the club was nearing completion, he embarked on a journey to the south of France, from which he was never to return.

In the last decade of his life, Woodward suffered from recurring and increasingly severe bouts of the consumption which he had contracted as a young man. As early as 1854 Rossetti recalled on first meeting him that he had "the look of having gone through some narrow escape of illness which might come again and be ever narrower and narrower."[33] Tuckwell also noted that at this time Woodward had "the shadow of an early death already stealing over him."[34] But the serious decline began in 1857 and was brought on by the strain of work on the Oxford Museum and the Government Offices competition. Of the latter, Woodward wrote prophetically to Henry Acland, "I think they will be the death of me."[35]

As if sensing that time was short, the next years were a period of frenetic activity during which he strove to complete the Oxford Museum, the Crown Life Company building, and the firm's numerous institutional and domestic projects. This necessitated continuous travel back and forth between sites in Ireland, Wales, Oxford, and London. It all took its toll. By November 1858, Woolner reported to Mrs. Tennyson that "Woodward is in a most delicate state of health, in fact his life looks as weak as a little candle in the open air."[36] That year Woodward was forced to spend his first winter abroad in more temperate climates. But even there, as Rossetti recorded, he was "unalterably devoted to his own pursuits— the art which he loved . . ."[37]—and was constantly on the move, traveling throughout France and Italy, visiting Paris and Venice among other places.[38] By April of the following year his condition had worsened and he was again forced "to give up all work and go on the continent for a change of air."[39] In 1859, Woodward spent several more months in southern France and Algiers. But to no avail. In March 1859, Miss Acland wrote to her father that Woodward was "very thin and looks very poorly."[40]

[132]

Finally, after a brief "fortnight's excursion on the Continent" for "a little rest and relaxation" in August, Woodward embarked on his final journey to France in December 1860.[41] From Paris on December 14 he wrote to his friend and patron, Lady Trevelyan:

> I am here for some days, perhaps a week, it is cold, but much more bracing than in England. I am thinking of remaining at Marseilles and Hyères and returning early in March to England . . . and much sooner if wanted.[42]

But over the months Woodward's health continued to decline. He stayed on in Hyères in the vain hope that he might yet recover. Though his health showed no signs of improvement he finally began his homeward journey in early May 1861. Unable to proceed farther than Lyon he died on May 15, 1861, in the Hotel de L'Universe on the rue Bourbon. His body was discovered two days later and his death registered at the Mairie in Lyon on May 17, 1861.

News of Woodward's death reached England in June. In July the *Art Journal* reported:

> An influential committee has been already formed for the purpose of securing the erection of such a public memorial as may worthily commemorate Mr. Woodward. . . . At present it would be premature to suggest any form for the proposed memorial, but we may at once declare our readiness to do all in our power to co-operate with the "Woodward Memorial Committee."[43]

More information on the project and committee appeared in the *Dublin Builder* on August 1:

> Propositions are being circulated [it reported] by a committee consisting amongst others, of the Dean of Christchurch and Dr. Acland, Messrs. Holman Hunt, G. Richmond, and G. E. Street, which has been formed for obtaining subscriptions for a memorial to the late Benjamin Woodward, architect, of Oxford and Dublin. . . . The plan for the memorial is somewhat a novel one, comprising, first, a biographical and critical sketch, of his life and his works; secondly, a series of photographic illustrations of his principal public and private works, to accompany the above-named sketch, and to include both general views of eleva-

tions, and also numerous details, such as roofs, windows, doors, and interiors; thirdly, a bust, in marble, to be presented to the Oxford New Museum.[44]

The idea for the memorial—itself unusually comprehensive—was probably originally proposed by Henry Acland who threw himself into the project with his customary energy and enthusiasm. Work began immediately. The first meeting of the committee was held on July 2, 1861. And soon the ranks of the committee members swelled to include Dr. William Stokes, William Shaen, and F. T. Palgrave, among others.[45] These last and Acland took upon themselves the preparation of the biographical and critical sketch. "Mind not a word of praise in the biography—only principles inculcated by 'quotations,' " Acland wrote of the sketch to his wife.[46]

Ruskin and other associates of Woodward's were consulted for their suggestions and for further information on the architect. Ruskin's response was singularly cool: "I wonder," he wrote to Acland, "who will write a memoir of me." And continued,

> I'm very sorry for Woodward. Rossetti's brother could do the work you want better than anybody else, if it was in any bricklayers rate of wages likely to be paid for. If it is not—truly—it had better not be done. There is nothing whatever to criticise in the Oxford Museum or this other thing [the Oxford Union]. Nothing bad and nothing good. Your wife's regret is the reasonablest . . . I will write to Rossetti about this business if you like.[47]

Rossetti was more forthcoming and contributed his account of all he knew of Woodward in the series of letters addressed to Gilchrist, which have been extensively quoted from in the foregoing pages.

Dr. Stokes was charged with gathering subscriptions and material in Ireland for the memoir. He raised £80, much of which came from the Woodward family, and compiled a biographical sketch of Woodward from information gathered in interviews with Charles Woodward, the architect's father, or some other relation. This material, together with notes of conversations between Woodward and Margaret Stokes, a writer on Irish art and history and the doctor's daughter, were assembled and sent on for approval to Acland, William Shaen, and F. T. Palgrave, who was to write the memoir.[48]

After this initial burst of activity, however, the project began gradually to falter and lose impetus. Little was done by the English members of the committee and in his correspondence with Acland, Stokes repeatedly asked "to learn what progress has been made" on the project in England.[49] Finally in November 1861 he wrote complaining, "I too have heard nothing from Mr. Shaen for a very long time and this puts me in a very unpleasant position—for the family of Woodward's have been writing to me to learn what is likely to be done with the money that has been subscribed by them."[50]

But the major obstacle to the committee's progress on which the project ultimately foundered was the violent opposition to the scheme by the Deanes. In September 1861, Stokes wrote to Acland, "I have as yet got nothing from Deane— no letters, no photographs, no money."[51] Later he wrote again, "I fear that we shall get no help from the Deanes—they are opposed to the appearance of any memoir—as if the history of a remarkable man should not be written because he had the misfortune to be a partner in their house—they are perfect specimens of Corkmen!"[52]

The Deanes' reluctance to support the project is understandable. The works of the partnership in the 1850s had established the firm among the leaders of the profession at home and in England—a position jealously guarded by the Deanes and which they were anxious to retain. No doubt sensitive to the fact that the firm's high standing rested on the reputation and achievement of their more talented partner, they naturally felt threatened by the memorial committee's un-disguised bias toward Woodward to whom they attributed all the firm's major works. Thus the Deanes withheld information and denied the committee access to other material in their possession in a concerted effort to obstruct its progress.

In the face of such opposition work on the Woodward Memoir ground to a halt. It is possible that in their effort to suppress the memoir the Deanes actually destroyed papers and other documents concerning Woodward which have never come to light. In so doing they obliterated the details of Woodward's life and work and consigned him to the obscurity where he has remained to this day.

The material gathered by Dr. Stokes fared no better. Over the years this too disappeared. The memoir was never written. The only part of the project actually executed was the stone portrait bust of Woodward by Alexander Munro which was placed in the Oxford Museum, where it still is (Fig. 138). Munro's portrait showing Woodward's features worn by work and wasted by disease, with the deep-set eyes sadly surveying his greatest unfinished work, is a poignant tribute to the architect and a sad memorial to his partially realized dreams.

Woodward's obituaries paid him further tribute. The *Dublin Builder* named him "the author of some of [the firm's] most important works."[53] A memorial paper was read at the Royal Institute of British Architects on June 24, 1861 (an unusual honor in itself for a non-member), by James Bell, who also noted that the firm's designs were "chiefly due to Mr. Woodward's inspiration."[54] The *Art Journal* hailed him as "preeminently an artist-architect," and added, "Had he been spared to a prolonged life, what he has actually accomplished gives more than reasonable hope that he would have been recognized as the first of English, if not of European architects."[55]

T. N. Deane, who was just thirty-three when Woodward died, had a long career ahead of him and continued to practice until his death in 1899. Sir Thomas Deane, who was almost seventy at the time Woodward died, retired completely from active practice. In 1861 he moved from Dundanion Castle in Cork to Dublin where he lived at 26 Longford Terrace in Monkstown until his death in 1871. In the last decade of his life he became increasingly involved in the corporate activities of the professional associations to which he belonged. In 1861 he was elected to the Royal Hibernian Academy. Two years later he was made vice-president of the newly organized Royal Institute of the Architects of Ireland, and later became president of both.[56]

When T. N. Deane began practicing on his own he already enjoyed a position of high standing in the profession—a position which, it was generally acknowledged, he owed to the talents of his late partner. Nevertheless professional recognition brought work with it and his practice thrived. Deane's achievement after Woodward's death lies outside the scope of this book. Most of his work in the 1860s and 1870s was done in Dublin and Oxford, where the firm still had strong ties, though some domestic work was executed elsewhere in Ireland.[57] These buildings show a considerable dependence on Woodward's designs of the 1850s. Unsure of his own creative abilities, Deane often relied heavily on the firm's earlier achievements.

The O'Sheas, who last worked for Woodward on the Kildare Street Club, gradually disappear from record after his death. In 1861 they are found working in Oxford on S. L. Seckham's Corn Exchange.[58] At about the same time they were employed in Oxford by G. G. Scott to carve the Credence Shelf in Exeter College Chapel.[59] In December 1861 one of the O'Sheas was in London working on Woolner's studio in Welbeck Street, about which the latter wrote to F. T. Palgrave,

O'Shea is doing his work like a man, and the corbels are bursting forth

[136]

into violets, roses, thistles, ivies, geraniums, and other things lovelier than their names . . . so fast is his progress that unless your brother comes early O'Shea will have done and fled, for such rapidity of work-manship I never saw, he does three corbels a day! I thought he would take a day each.[60]

The O'Sheas are next found working under Woolner's supervision on the sculpture for Waterhouse's Manchester Assize Courts.[61] But in 1862 they were back in Oxford working for T. N. Deane on the carving in Cowley House—their last work for the firm.[62] The O'Sheas are last heard of in 1863 when they executed some of the sculpture for John Hungerford Pollen's Catholic Church in Rhyll, North Wales.[63] But neither they, nor Charles Harrison, nor T. N. Deane ever again aspired to the level that Benjamin Woodward, while he was living, had brought them.

CONCLUSION

The career of the Deanes spanned the nineteenth century and constituted one of the longest, most successful, and productive practices in Ireland. Yet it was only during that brief period of the partnership with Woodward, the period with which this book is mainly concerned, that their work was marked by true originality. Woodward's creative ability, artistic range, and grasp of theory quickly led to the first embodiments, in actual buildings, of Ruskin's writings and teachings.

We are returned to the questions raised in the Introduction: What was Ruskin's role in the formation of the Ruskinian Gothic style that has always been identified with Deane and Woodward's work, especially the Trinity College and Oxford Museums? Or rather, what was *Woodward's* role in the episode? That, we can now see, is the proper way to frame this question.

Analysis of TCD showed it on one level to be the architectural embodiment of Ruskin's richly embellished, monumental, symmetrical, essentially classicizing, formal ideal of the *Seven Lamps* (1849) and the *Stones of Venice* (1851-1853). Yet that classicism was already there in the firm's pre-Puginian works. Many of Ruskin's ideas in these books deal with the importance of sound and truthful construction, expressive architectural ornament, an honest use of materials that exploits their natural qualities of color and texture, close attention to detail and workmanship, and the proper employment of the workmen. But these very principles had already been at least partially realized in Queen's College, Cork (1846-1849) and the Killarney Lunatic Asylum (1847-1850). Meanwhile, Ruskin's stylistic recommendations, followed at TCD and the Oxford Museum, can be traced to non-Ruskinian sources.

Nevertheless, Deane and Woodward's acknowledged debt to Ruskin is evident in these works. Ruskin's writings not only served to articulate ideas already nascent in Deane and Woodward's architecture, but they also gave direction and form to these ideas. Thus on the one hand Ruskin's precepts regarding the role of the craftsman and the social responsibility of public art can be seen as providing

[138]

CONCLUSION

the ideological framework for Deane and Woodward's architecture, while his more precise prescriptions concerning the "noble characters" of buildings, the use of particular materials, types of ornament and surface patterns, account for some of the formal qualities of their work.[1] On the other hand, taken all together Ruskin's precepts do not really constitute a style. They are a program for reforming the processes with which builders, carvers, and architects work, and a set of analyses of good and bad architectural forms. To build an actual building, however Ruskinian, required more than this moralism and formalism. It required all the constituents of style. Hence, much of what has been identified as "Ruskinian" Gothic, and much of Woodward's architecture—including even his most Ruskinian buildings—have nothing at all to do with Ruskin.

The reasons for this have been more than hinted at. Ruskin himself was unconcerned with space, structure, or function. While he talks about proportion, massing, and composition in the *Seven Lamps*, he does so only in the broadest and most general terms.[2] And nowhere in the *Seven Lamps* or the *Stones of Venice* does he deal in any real sense with the problems of structure, planning, or the architect's basic concern of providing space. Thus these crucial aspects of even the Trinity College and Oxford museums, and the decisions and artistic choices involved in their design, are due to Woodward.

Ruskin, on the other hand, was concerned with facades, and it is here that his real influence lies. His preoccupation with the subject matter and the execution of architectural sculpture led him to concentrate on what he called "surface Gothic" and to emphasize both the "readability" of these surfaces and their pictorial qualities of light, shade, and color.[3] These aspects of Deane and Woodward's architecture are indeed deeply influenced by Ruskin.

This Ruskinian facade treatment is best exemplified by the firm's large public and civil buildings: TCD, the west front of the Oxford Museum, the Government Offices design, and the Crown Life office, where the contained contours of the facades, like the bordered pages of Ruskin's illustrations in the *Stones of Venice*, provide a frame for an eclectic assembly of architectural details, richly associational story-telling sculpture, naturalistic relief carving, and constructive color. The compartmentation and balanced composition of these monumental, regular facades represent a completely different aesthetic from the taut planes, truncation, compression, slicing, irregularity, and harsh outlines of Butterfieldian High Victorian Gothic, and constitute the identifying characteristics of Ruskinian Gothic.

Thus Ruskinian Gothic is correctly seen as antithetical to the compositional

[139]

and organizational principles of the Ecclesiologists. In fact, the Ruskinian mode established in Deane and Woodward's secular civic buildings was primarily suited to large public buildings requiring monumental facade treatment, and that is where it also had its greatest influence.

Deane and Woodward's domestic works of the later 1850s are neither Ruskinian in this sense nor High Victorian Gothic—nor, for that matter, do they fit Douglas Richardson's classification "Hibernian Monumental."[4] Though the planning and composition of these structures do owe something to the Ecclesiologists, the richness of the decoration, the emphasis on craft and materials, the tendency toward simple contained masses, and the preoccupation with window design reflect a Ruskinian aesthetic. At the same time, however, the firm's use of vernacular construction and ornamentation in these buildings moves individualistically away from these mid-century styles.

This returns us to Germann's point, mentioned in the Introduction, that Ruskin's "one really independent and fertile argument" in his early architectural writings was the importance of craft and the workmen's creative contribution to the building.[5] This is, of course, not Ruskin's only "really independent and fertile argument." But it was crucial for the development of much late-nineteenth- and early-twentieth-century architecture. It is hoped that the foregoing pages have established that this development is probably due as much to Deane and Woodward's activities in architectural design in its fullest sense as to Ruskin's writings. Indeed, the idea has a new importance today, now that the the post-modern aesthetic—which is in so many respects neo-Victorian—returns once more to the ideals of idiosyncrasy, ornamental exuberance, facadism, color, eclecticism, and the power of associations.

APPENDIX: MINOR WORKS AND PROJECTS

Oxford, 1857-1861

Woodward was responsible for a number of small projects executed in Oxford while work on the Museum progressed. The commissions, for additions or alterations to existing buildings, are direct offshoots of the Oxford Museum. Though these works were often credited to the firm as a whole in contemporary reviews and notices in the building press, they were almost all designed by Woodward. Various members of Woodward's Oxford artistic circle often collaborated in their decoration.

Library and Study in Dr. Acland's House, 40-41 Broad Street

In February 1857, Acland engaged Woodward to design an extension to the back of his house for a study and library. Construction of the extension was entrusted to Woodward's assistant in Oxford, W.C.C. Bramwell, who later rebuilt No. 42 Broad Street for Dr. Acland. Woodward also did some alterations to rooms inside the house. But since it was demolished in 1937 to make way for the New Bodleian Library it is difficult to tell from existing photographs what parts he was responsible for.[1]

However, the library and study extensions, built in brick with a banded "streaky bacon" effect, are easily distinguished and formed self-contained units at the back of the house (Fig. 139). The library ("A" on the photograph) is a simple rectangular block with a hipped roof resting on large stone brackets. The study ("B" on the photograph) is another variant of the Glastonbury Kitchen type.

These simple structures display the characteristics of Woodward's brick style: volumetric spatial planning resulting in a variety of clearly articulated forms which are dramatized by the bold, large-scale detailing, deep voids of the openings, and "brick-massiveness" of the walls. Much use is also made of rustic cottage features, gables, dormers, brackets, and tall chimneys.

Like the Oxford Museum and Union, the work involved a certain amount of amateur collaboration. In particular both Acland and Ruskin took advantage of the opportunity to try their hands at bricklaying.[2]

Woodward also designed two chimneypieces for the rooms which were carved by O'Shea with foliage and animals.[3] Both chimneypieces are inscribed with domestic proverbs. The one in the study carries the simple homily "There is no place like home," while the loftier sentiment "Type of the wise who soar but never roam, True to the kindred points of Heaven and Home" appears in the library.

[141]

RUSKINIAN GOTHIC

Middleton Hall

The Rev. Bartholomew Price, Professor of Natural Philosophy at Oxford, commissioned Woodward in 1857 to build a red brick extension to the south side of his house, at 11 St. Giles' (now a part of St. John's College and known as Middleton Hall after a medieval house that once stood on the same site). Another addition, recently removed, was made to the back by Price in 1875.[4]

Woodward's structure (Fig. 140) is a plain three-storey brick block with a high saddleback roof. He used unevenly colored red brick which, as in the firm's other brick buildings, produces a rich surface texture and variegated color on the large areas of flat wall. Asymmetrically grouped windows of different shapes, some with Bath stone trim, are arranged in an irregular grid across the facades. Most interesting are the "Venetian" cusped or trefoil-headed windows on the south facade. To accommodate the square-headed sashes their arched tops were filled in with Bath stone slabs, since blackened by soot.[5]

Every feature of the facades, including the saw-tooth edged brick archivolts, is kept tightly within the thickness of the wall. Only the dripstones, sills, and tall chimney project forward from its plane. The starkness, severe outline, asymmetrical fenestration, verticality, and angularity of this building are rather more Butterfieldian than Ruskinian. There are also none of the rustic cottage features that livened the outlines of the firm's other brick buildings in Oxford. Yet the urban containment, and emphatic fenestration are still characteristically Ruskinian.

Very little of Woodward's alterations to the interior still exist. Only the familiar carved oak door frames and a fireplace attributed to O'Shea remain.[6]

St. Frideswide Window, Latin Chapel, Christ Church Cathedral

In 1860 Woodward was commissioned by the Dean of Christ Church to design the stonework for the St. Frideswide window at the east end of the Latin Chapel in Christ Church Cathedral. The window, erected on the bequest of Dr. John Bull who died in 1858, was executed by James Powell and Sons of Whitefriars. Cartoons for the stained glass were prepared by Edward Burne-Jones and the stonework was carved by James O'Shea.[7] The subject of the window was chosen to celebrate the life and deeds of St. Frideswide, the patroness in the eighth century of an extensive priory on the site of the Cathedral where she was supposed to have lived and died in 740.

The St. Frideswide window was one of Burne-Jones' earliest commissions for stained glass, and he prepared a very elaborate design—somewhat overambitiously crowded with descriptive incident. The four lights of the window are packed with sixteen narrative scenes from the saint's life. In the six-foils of the tracery are the trees of life and knowledge, and in the roundel at the top of the window is the ship of souls conveyed

[142]

by angels. The brilliant color of the glass is the result of experiments Powells were making at this time to recreate the effects of medieval glass.[8]

The fault for the overcrowding of the small panels was Woodward's. He apparently gave the wrong set of measurements to the artist, which resulted in the compulsory reduction of each panel afterwards, and adversely affected the proportions of the design. In the end Burne-Jones was dissatisfied with his work and offered to supply another design free of charge.[9]

The architectonic qualities of the stonework designed by Woodward are strikingly different from the flowing, lacy late Gothic-inspired tracery of the other nineteenth-century windows in the chapel. Even here, Woodward followed Ruskin's preference for the broad sculptured forms of "surface Gothic."

Library Bookcases, Blickling Hall, Norfolk

Though not in Oxford, Woodward's work at Blickling is also a direct offshoot of the Oxford Museum. In 1861 he was engaged by the eighth Marquess of Lothian, a generous contributor to the Museum carving fund, to design carved oak bookcases to be fitted along the walls of the 130 x 24 foot library at Blickling. This was currently being redecorated by John Hungerford Pollen with mural painting, a carved stone chimneypiece, stained glass, and frieze decoration.[10]

Woodward's design for the bookcases, probably executed early in 1861 and completed in that year, is similar to the Union bookcases—though more elaborate and involving entire fitted casements. In keeping with Pollen's richly decorated walls, they are carved with a dense pattern of naturalistic foliage that does not however detract from the simple and solid character of the structural principals.

DUBLIN, 1854-1860

In the mid-1850s Deane and Woodward built a group of smaller, little-known buildings in and around Dublin. A combined police court and barracks, and three parochial schools are modest, provincial, and essentially utilitarian structures. They were executed on limited budgets and built with inexpensive rubble masonry or brick. Almost devoid of carved ornament and elaborate stone detailing, the effect is reduced to the contrasting qualities of the different materials used. In treatment and pragmatism of approach these buildings relate to the firm's early institutional works in Ireland, particularly the Killarney Lunatic Asylum, where the emphasis is likewise on the material purposes of the buildings.

The formal characteristics of these smaller works also seem closer to the Ecclesiologists than to Ruskin. This is partly due to the fact that Ruskin was not directly involved with these projects and had little interest in such structures. The Ecclesiologists, on the other hand, were very much concerned with such buildings. Deane and Woodward's designs in fact owe a great deal to the Ecclesiologists' parish schools of the early 1850s and the Society's precepts concerning the proper arrangement of such buildings. But while Deane and Woodward adopted the constructional and organizational principles of the Ecclesiologists, they were unconcerned with the Society's doctrinal prescriptions regarding the "fitness" of particular forms to the various parts of the building. Instead, their approach was essentially pragmatic reflecting Ruskin's attitude that architecture, in the absence of sculpture, can have no meaning beyond its physical attributes—the materials of which it is built and the way in which it is constructed.

Three of the four commissions discussed here, the Dundrum police court and barracks, the parish schools in Dundrum, and St. Stephen's Schools in Ballsbridge, are all closely connected and originated from the same source. In the nineteenth century the south Dublin suburbs of Dundrum and Ballsbridge, along with most of the southeastern districts and outlying areas of the city, belonged to the Earls of Pembroke.[11] In the 1850s the principal proprietor of the Pembroke Estates was Lord Sidney Herbert, the second son of the 11th Earl of Pembroke. Herbert, a statesman and philanthropist, was regarded as a "model Anglo-Saxon landlord" who laid out large sums of money on improvements— including the police court and schools—on his Dublin estates.[12]

Dundrum Police Court and Barracks

In May 1854 the magistrates of Dundrum applied to Herbert for new constabulary buildings to replace the "very wretched accommodation afforded to the Magistrates by the existing Court House."[13] The sum of £1600 was allocated for the purpose, and Deane and Woodward were commissioned later in that year to design a courthouse, attached barracks and furnishings for both. Construction on the new buildings began in 1855. They were substantially complete in June 1856 and finally finished by the end of March 1857 when they were given over to the police.[14] Today only the courthouse remains, the barracks having recently been torn down and replaced by another structure.

The original court and barracks buildings (Fig. 141) comprised two independent blocks of about equal size and height with steeply pitched roofs and free gable ends placed at right angles to each other, with the courthouse on north-south axis fronting onto Eglinton Terrace and the barracks adjoining it on the west. Both were built of rough-cut local granite with limestone window dressings and red brick relieving arches.

As in the firm's early Irish work, in particular the Killarney Asylum, the architects also responded to local building traditions by employing indigenous materials and adopting the simplified medieval forms of the local vernacular. The resulting sense of mass, thick walls, rough surfaces, and big-boned quality of individual features, give the buildings a distinctly Irish character.

APPENDIX: MINOR WORKS

The buildings are also functionally expressive in the way of the Killarney Asylum. The residential purpose of the barracks is shown by irregular massing, dormers, and prominent chimneys, and the unified space of the courtroom by the external regularity and containment of the courthouse block.

In building *type* the combined court and barrack buildings are not unlike the traditional country schoolhouse program with large schoolroom and attached teacher's residence. Indeed, the Ecclesiologists' precepts for structures of this type suggest a possible source of inspiration for the design.[15] These were first laid down in the *Ecclesiologist* in 1847.[16] The basic principle to be followed was simply that the schoolrooms and master's house were to be treated as independent units with separate roofs and to be disposed in a cross-axial arrangement.[17] This formula was easily adapted to the functional requirements of the provincial police court and barracks. So too were several features from William Butterfield's designs for model schoolhouses published in *Instrumenta Ecclesiastica* in 1853, such as the high open-timber roofs with exposed rafters, plain stone fireplaces, and carpenter-like wooden benches and desks with revealed joints and simply chamfered corners.[18]

Of the actual buildings erected under the auspices of the Ecclesiological Society, the police court is closest in treatment to G. E. Street's early country schools. At Inkpen in Berkshire of 1850, Street adopted a plain vernacular mode involving rubble walling, a dominating roof, dormers, and windows with red brick trim instead of the elaborate cut-stone tracery of Butterfield's designs.[19] In both Street's and Deane and Woodward's buildings the simple features and plain undecorated surfaces show a conscious striving for a certain primitivism evocative of an older and simpler vernacular.

Dundrum Schools

Shortly after construction on the police court was under way the manager of the Pembroke Estates requested the firm to draw up plans for a parochial school in Dundrum (Fig. 142). Slow progress was made on the plans.[20] Finally in February 1859 additional funds were raised making it possible for the firm to prepare plans for both a schoolhouse and teacher's residence. The tender of Gilbert Cockburn and Sons, the Dublin contractors, was accepted for £750. On March 1, 1859, the site was officially laid out and the building was finally finished at the end of December 1859.[21]

None of the firm's original plans exist. However, a site plan in the Pembroke Estates Office shows the school situated directly north of Deane and Woodward's courthouse on Eglinton Terrace. L-shaped in plan, the schoolrooms are parallel to the road, while the master's residence, placed at right angles to these, adjoins them to the north.

Again, the Ecclesiologists' organizational recommendations were followed. The school and residence are separate, self-contained blocks with independent roofs and freestanding

[145]

gable ends. Internally the school is divided into two classrooms which are separated, as in Butterfield's designs, by a movable screen. The cloakrooms, toilets, and other offices are set apart from the classrooms at the back of the building. Also following the Society's specifications, the front entrance is covered by a separately gabled projecting porch. The master's house, in keeping with William White's recommendations for schools in "Causes and Points of Failure in Modern Design" also published in the *Ecclesiologist*, in 1851, is set back from the road and thus in a subordinate position in relation to the school.[22]

Generally, no doubt due to restricted funds, the Dundrum schools are plainer than the police buildings. Details and outlines have been greatly simplified. The walls are plain and unbuttressed, the windows are all simple rectangular openings with hardly any cut-stone trim. As a result the effect depends largely on the contrasting tones of the black and gray granite used.

St. Stephen's Schools

St. Stephen's School (Figs. 143, 144), begun in April 1859 and completed in 1860, was from the beginning, a larger, more complex and expensive structure than the Dundrum schools.[23] Like these, it is essentially a single-storey building with a few upper-storey rooms contained within the low dominating roof. Fronting onto the Northumberland road, it is H-shaped in plan with classrooms in each of the principal ranges and the school master's house (Fig. 145), with projecting porch and round stair tower, situated at the rear of the north wing.

While retaining the clear separation of parts and cross-axial plan of the Ecclesiologists' model, the architects also aimed for a more unified composition and for greater clarity of outline and surface. The red brick walls are unbuttressed and their sheer blank surfaces terminate in clean, sharp corners. The taut planes, purity of line and contour, and generally sharp-edged quality of the building are largely due to the dense texture, smoothness, and evenness of the brick itself.

The end effect is very different from the rough primitivism of the Dundrum buildings and comes closer to Butterfield's plainer brick schools of the mid-fifties as at Cowick and Pollington, both designed in 1854.[24] Yet the broad expanses of blank wall, regular fenestration, and balanced massing are distinctly un-Butterfieldian and consistent with tendencies recognized in Deane and Woodward's work elsewhere. At the same time, the simple, regular forms, the low encompassing roofs, tall chimneys, and round tourelle also suggest that Deane and Woodward, like many other architects in the late 1850s, may have looked to Early French vernacular architecture for their design.

Close attention to detail is evident even in the most pragmatic aspects of the design. Indeed, it would seem that Deane and Woodward were at their best in this respect when dealing with limited funds and space. There are hidden trap doors in the corridor ceilings to allow for furniture and other objects too large for the narrow staircases to be lifted into the upper rooms. Elsewhere fly-leaf tables built into the walls can be extended or folded away according to need. The most ingenious construction is a movable wall panel between the two adjoining classrooms. The panel, shaped like a large wooden barn door, can be raised like a sash window into the gable of the roof to create one large L-shaped room, making it possible for both classrooms to be monitored at the same time by a single teacher.

St. Anne's Parochial Schools

The firm's next school building was for the parish of St. Anne's, the most important and wealthiest in the Diocese. The site, on Molesworth Street, was directly behind Old St. Anne's Church in the fashionable center of Dublin. The building (demolished in 1979), was begun in 1857 and completed in 1858.[25]

The design reflected its urban setting (Fig. 146). A large rectangular block with a tall hipped roof, the street elevation had two principal storeys and a third attic storey in the roof marked by gabled dormers of different sizes and shapes. It was set back from the street on a high base behind a masonry wall approximately four feet high. The materials were rough-faced Calp or black limestone and granite laid in alternate horizontal bands across the facade, with Caen stone and red brick dressings. The doorway, raised above street level, was deeply recessed behind a massive imbricated Caen stone arch carved with nailhead, billet, and other moldings.

A clear distinction was made between the formal, public street front and the informal, private back of the building, where random granite rubble was substituted for the ashlar masonry of the front and simple rectangular windows were asymmetrically grouped to create an irregular grid across the facade. The same distinction was made inside. At the front were the large committee rooms and classrooms; at the back the smaller offices, toilets, and cloakrooms, and on the dormered top floor were domestic apartments to accommodate eighteen boarders.

Clearly, the Ecclesiologists' village school prototype was abandoned here in favor of a more urban type.[26] But not entirely. While gathering the different parts of the school together into a monumental contained urban block with continuous arcading across the principal facade, the architects nevertheless consciously strove to maintain some of the solid, simple and functionally expressive features of their country schools: the pitched roofs, heavy brackets, tall chimneys, and dormers. The rough-cut and quarry-faced stone give the walls a coarse, lithic quality which is accentuated by the broad bands of structural color. This contrasts strikingly with the fine dense texture and smooth brick surfaces of T. N. Deane's adjacent Molesworth Hall built in 1867.[27] In his elegantly detailed parish hall Deane also made some use of structural polychromy in the form of alternating bands of yellow and red brick and a continuous arcade of blue-gray relieving arches above the upper windows which, unlike the earlier building, tend to emphasize the surface rather than the depth of the walls.

SMALLER HOUSE COMMISSIONS AND PROJECTS NEAR DUBLIN, C. 1860

In about 1860, the firm commenced a series of domestic projects in the outskirts of Dublin. While notices of the commissions appeared in the *Dublin Builder* and there are references to the houses and their clients in the recently discovered ledger of Benjamin Patterson, the firm's Dublin bookkeeper from 1855 to 1861, few of these projects were actually brought to completion or even beyond the design stage.[28] However, a small number of the firm's designs have survived and appear to relate to some of these domestic commissions.

House for Arthur Guinness, Shanganagh Grove, Ballybrack

In the National Library in Dublin are a set of plans and a watercolor drawing of the front elevation of a small house for "Arthur Guinness Esq." (Figs. 147, 148).[29] The house was probably commissioned by Arthur Guinness, the brewer, for a clergyman whose living was in his bestowal.[30] It was, in fact, built in Ballybrack on the Wyattville Road, and was known as Shanganagh Grove. Demolished in c. 1964, no trace of the structure now remains except for a single piece of carving.[31]

The plan shows a small two-storey house well suited to the modest needs of a country cleric. It has neither the extensive household accommodations and service wing nor the spacious reception hall of Deane and Woodward's other Irish houses. Instead, the ground floor has a dining room and drawing room with bay windows and the curate's office at the back. The kitchen, scullery, and larder are also in the main body of the house on the ground floor. A single staircase at the center of the house leads up to a landing on the second floor on which there are four bedrooms and a dressing room.

The design is most like the firm's first unexecuted plan for the Curator's house in Oxford. It has the same modest proportions, massing, simple stone-finished gable ends, and prominent chimneys.

A single carved pier and capital were preserved by the last owner of the house (who made them into a sundial). The freestone capital is deeply undercut so that the carved flowers, plants, birds, snakes, and other small animals stand out in high relief from the bell. The design and style of this work suggest that the carving was executed by Charles Harrison.

In general less individual than some of Deane and Woodward's earlier domestic designs, the plan, massing and ordonnance—in fact, everything but the detail—adheres closely to the strict Tractarian line of the Ecclesiologists' country vicarages. This is not surprising, since here, for the first time, Deane and Woodward were also building for a clergyman rather than a prosperous middle-class man of affairs.

Carrigbraec, Howth

In 1861, Woodward designed a gatelodge for Dr. William Stokes, his Dublin physician (who had sometime earlier, "snatched Woodward . . . from the very brink of the grave"), at his mountain cottage at Howth, a popular suburban resort area on a peninsula jutting out into Dublin Bay. Woodward was particularly fond of the lodge, and often as Stokes reported, "when asked for a design for a gatelodge would say 'you may copy the lodge at Carraigbraec, I can do nothing better than that.' "[32]

The building, though still standing, has been much altered in recent years. All that remains of the original is the half-timbered porch with its trefoil-headed lancet windows.

It would seem from a drawing in the National Library in Dublin (Fig. 149) that Woodward also drew up plans for extensive alterations to the main house at Carraigbraec.[33] This involved the addition of a tall rectangular block to the back of the house (the square block at the front being the original house) with a bay window on one corner, colored marble shafts and carved capitals and imposts, an arched doorway, chamfered and molded stone window dressings and wooden dormers in the high pitched roof. Tall chimneys and delicate wrought iron finials on the roof add to the generally picturesque effect of the design. It is difficult to tell how much, if any, of Woodward's design was executed as the house has undergone many subsequent alterations.

TOWN HOUSES, 1855-1861

Deane and Woodward's two urban domestic commissions discussed here were for minor alterations to a late Georgian terrace house in Dublin and a private house in London. Built in confined urban spaces, they reflect an urban sensibility: frontality, emphasis on exterior surface embellishment, and use of manufactured building materials, which is quite different from the freestanding houses in country settings with their emphasis on picturesque planning, simple cottage features, and local stone.

28 Fitzwilliam Place, Dublin

In 1855, Deane and Woodward were commissioned to remodel 28 Fitzwilliam Place in central Dublin (Fig. 150), the end house in a late Georgian terrace on the Earl of Pembroke's Fitzwilliam Estate.[34] This involved refacing the exterior, providing new internal fittings, adding a conservatory or study at the back, stables, and boundary walls.

As in the Crown Life offices, the original massing of the row house was retained. The sheer surface of the brick wall is also unbroken save for the projecting stone and saw-tooth edged brick course just below the second floor windows. Similar patterned brickwork is used for the cornice and chimney ridges. The windows all have shallow segmental arches and red brick relieving arches above, but otherwise plain chamfered jambs. Those on the first three floors have cast iron tracery balconies.

The central feature of the street facade is the massive imbricated stone entrance arch carved with billet and cable moldings and the occasional cluster of foliage in the interstices. The trefoil above the doorway is a clever "Gothic" modification of the distinctive Dublin Georgian fanlight.

Originally the two-storey rear extension was hexagonal in shape before an elaborate oriel window was added to one end by another architect. The upper windows are arched like the front entrance and have stone dressings. Those on the remaining apsidal end have pointed stone hood moldings with carved label stops. Once again this simple structure displays the characteristics of Woodward's brick style, volumetric planning leading to simple geometric forms.

Little of Deane and Woodward's interior has survived since the building was converted into offices, but similar medievalizing ornamental motifs as those on the exterior are still to be found. Thus, the wooden doorframes are notched, there is foliate tracery above some of the doors and naturalistic carving in some of the moldings.

28 Fitzwilliam Place is truly a "Dublin rarity," combining the restrained and regular proportions of the Georgian town house with boldly expressive Gothic detail.[35] The individual character of the detail strikes an unusual but not discordant note in Dublin's distinctive Georgian street architecture.

15 Upper Phillimore Gardens, London

The firm's only private house in London was designed by Woodward for William Shaen, a solicitor and social reformer who was a friend of the Italian Revolutionaries Garibaldi and Mazzini, and was involved with Ruskin at the Working Mens College.[36]

The house was begun in 1859 and finished in 1861. But very little of the original red brick structure remains today. In 1936-1937 it was completely reconstructed, inside and out, by G. Grey Wornum. The only surviving visual documentation of Woodward's building is an illustration (Fig. 151) in A. Trystan Edwards' *Good and Bad Manners in Architecture* (1924). Edwards described the house as "a quite unique work which has the distinction of being the only authentic example of a design conceived and inspired by Mr. Ruskin himself."[37]

The composition of 15 Upper Phillimore Gardens, with steps leading up to a side entrance, is very much in the mold of late Georgian and early Victorian double-fronted suburban villas. In the late 1840s and 1850s these were becoming increasingly eclectic and a "Gothic" formula involving two gables facing the road, bay windows, and brick facing was well-established in London suburban architecture.

Woodward's design, however, is unusually eclectic, with features derived from a variety of Gothic sources and modes of street architecture. The stepped gables and steeply pitched roofs are Dutch or German, the balconies and some of the windows are Venetian and Veronese Gothic, while the cylindrical stair tourelle with its conical spire is Early English or Irish. Woodward also used a rich variety of different materials: red brick for the fabric, stone window dressings and balconies, marble window shafts, and slate roof tiles. In every way the design strives for the maximum picturesque effect possible within the confines of the restricted urban site.

FINAL PROJECTS, 1860-1861

A few minor works designed by the firm in 1860-1861, were begun before Woodward's death and brought to completion by T. N. Deane in the early 1860s.

Public Drinking Fountains, Dublin

The first of these were two public drinking fountains in Dublin (Fig. 152). Both were commissioned and built in 1860 by the Earl of Carlisle, Lord Lieutenant of Ireland from 1859 to 1864, who had them erected as part of a program of municipal improvements and presented them as a gift to the people of Dublin.[38]

The first, on Beresford Place on the north bank of the Liffey, constructed on a granite base, was a square limestone pillar six feet high with a carved Caen stone basin and a tall pointed spire surmounted by a wrought iron vane.[39] The second, on Park-Gate Street, near the city entrance to Phoenix Park, was a mural fountain recessed into the wall under a stilted, segmental banded brick arch. Both fountains were fitted with cups to drink from and charcoal filters "which rendered the water exceedingly pure."[40]

The fountain designs fulfill both their practical and decorative functions. They are simple architectonic forms: the pillar and the arch. Ornamental carving, as on the firm's buildings, is concentrated in areas of structural significance.[41]

Kilkenny Castle, County Kilkenny

The firm's extensive alterations to Kilkenny Castle, the ancestral home of the Butlers, one of Ireland's oldest Anglo-Irish families and the chief seat of the earls, dukes, and marquesses of Ormonde since the fourteenth century, were completed after Woodward's death. The original castle, built entirely of Kilkenny black marble, was begun in 1192.[42] Over the centuries it was extended and rebuilt according to the tastes and needs of successive generations of Butlers. The last occasion, prior to Deane and Woodward's work, was in 1825 when William Robertson, a local architect, transformed it from a seventeenth-century French chateau into a Neo-Gothic machicolated castle, and rebuilt the eastern wing as a picture gallery to house the Ormondes' great art collection.[43] In 1858, the second Marchioness of Ormonde commissioned Deane and Woodward to carry out a survey of the Castle preliminary to further alterations. These were begun in 1859 and completed under T. N. Deane's supervision in 1863.[44]

Some of the firm's survey plans survive along with their proposals for alterations to the north front, the picture gallery, and staircase in the east wing.[45] On the north front these alterations consisted of reroofing the corner towers and replacing Robertson's plain cross-windows with cusped arches and marble shafts with carved bases and capitals.

The firm's proposal for the east wing, containing the picture gallery, was only partially executed (Figs. 153, 154). This involved inserting plate tracery in the windows and adding high-pitched roofs with wrought iron finials to the towers, turrets, and gallery. The gallery roof, an open-timber construction, was to be pierced by star-shaped glass skylights. Aside from the rather French roofs the design was rich in local associations: the unusual cusped window heads are derived from the thirteenth-century Cistercian Abbey at Graiguenamanagh and the east window of St. Canice's Cathedral in Kilkenny, where alone they appear in Irish medieval work. The simple geometric forms of the other plate tracery can also be related to Irish types.

In the final execution much of this scheme for the exterior was abandoned (Fig. 155). None of the roofs were executed; the traceried side windows were replaced by projecting oriels in alternate bays; and the end lights were simplified.

Inside, the enclosed staircase (Fig. 156) at the north end of the east wing is built in Caen stone, the half-turn stairs rising around a square skylit well with a winter garden at the bottom. A pointed arcade and stone molding climb alongside the stairs up the inside of the well. The syncopated rhythms of the alternating long and short columns, the different levels from which the arches spring, and the engineered collisions of structural parts at the angles of the landings add up to a composition of considerable dynamic force. Carved clusters of foliage and animals by Charles Harrison are tucked in between the springing of the arches in the stair passages.[46]

More of Harrison's work is to be found inside the picture gallery on the chimneypiece and massive stone corbels supporting the roof (Fig. 157). The gallery itself extends the length of the east wing with a skylight along the full length of the roof ridge, giving the room appropriate natural overhead lighting. Every part of the roof, including the vertical supports, was carved by Harrison and brilliantly painted by John Hungerford Pollen.[47] The wall plate, arched braces, hammer beams, curved struts, and purlins are all decorated with abstract Celtic designs. Great gilded dragons' heads terminate the hammer beams. Richly colored Celtic motifs are carried over onto the principals of the roof itself. The rafters are painted with fanciful landscapes of lush vegetation, waterfalls, richly laden fruit trees, and every variety of birds and small animals; motifs which spill out into the carved foliage of Harrison's corbels (Fig. 158). This is without doubt Pollen's best work of this kind. Gone is the unsure, loose handling of the Clontra murals. Instead, the saturated colors, abstract Celtic designs, and graceful flowing forms of the plants and trees behind work together to create a dense, tightly controlled composition that has an almost electric vibrancy.

The centerpiece of the hall is the double-fronted fireplace designed by Pollen and executed by Harrison. This is decorated with seven panels depicting incidents from Butler family history.[48] The chimney breast, capitals, and soffits of the arches are further ornamented with relief carving, the criss-cross pattern of which echoes the rhythms of Pollen's paintings above. The Marchioness, who took a great interest in the work is said to have arrived daily with flowers and leaves to serve as models for the carving.[49] The rich texture and color of the gallery must have appeared even more luxurious when the paintings were hung from floor to ceiling on the original dark red walls. Altogether, the Kilkenny picture gallery is one of Deane and Woodward's more dazzling pieces of interior design and one of their most successful collaborations with Pollen.

Alterations to Trinity College Library, Dublin

Trinity College Library, originally built in 1712-1722 by Thomas Burgh, and modeled on Sir Christopher Wren's Trinity College Library, Cambridge, begun in 1676, was approximately 200 feet long and 40 feet wide, with the bookcases at right angles to the walls, and a low flat paneled ceiling (Fig. 159). Burgh, however, added a gallery above the bookcases which ran round the entire room. This remained empty and unused for years until the Copyright Act of 1801 made it compulsory for a copy of every book published in Britain to be deposited in the library. By the mid-1850s the shelf space provided along the walls of the gallery and the cases below proved insufficient and various ways of enlarging the library's storage capacity were considered. At about the same time it was also found that the timbers of the roof and floor were in very poor condition.[50] An examination of the structure was held in November 1856, and designs for remodeling the room were solicited from Deane and Woodward and the college engineer, John McCurdy.[51] McCurdy and Deane had already proved to be ill-matched collaborators on TCD and naturally old rivalries flared up again. Both parties gave opposing advice with the result that negotiations were deadlocked for years.[52]

Deane and Woodward's first proposal involved stopping up the windows of the Gallery to increase the shelf space along the walls, replacing the ceiling with an open timber roof, and lighting the room from above—rather like the gallery in Kilkenny Castle. This was abandoned and other plans were made in which the original ceiling would be kept and bookcases inserted in the gallery at right angles to the wall.[53] The firm's final proposal, involving both construction of a new roof and book cases was accepted by the Board in January 1858.[54] But work only began in 1860. Construction of the new roof took approximately two years and was supervised by the Deanes, who also represented the firm at all of the Board meetings.[55]

Deane and Woodward's design (Fig. 160) was a remarkably successful and effective solution. All of the work was executed in American and Canadian white oak, selected by Sir Thomas and stained to match the older wood in the room.[56] The transverse bookcases inserted in the gallery doubled the accommodation for books at the same time as providing additional support for the new roof. Each of the upper alcoves thus created was covered by a barrel vault which permitted the maximum of daylight to enter from the side windows. The ceiling was raised by inserting a long barrel vault over the central nave of the room. The transverse ribs of this vault were brought down to the piers at the end of the gallery bookcases, thereby relieving the outer walls (which were already found to be out of plumb), and throwing the whole weight of the roof on the floor which was underpinned with stone columns.

Similar long barrel-vaulted ceilings had been used in earlier library designs, notably by C. R. Cockerell in the University Library, Cambridge in 1837-1840 and by Labrouste in the Bibliothèque Ste. Geneviève in Paris in 1843-1850, both of which Deane and Woodward must have known.[57] The idea for combining the transverse gallery bookcases and barrel-vaulted nave may have come from W. H. Playfair's Old University Library in Edinburgh, built in 1831-1834, which uses the same system. But these are all essentially "phantom prototypes," and Trinity Library is as far removed in spirit and character from Playfair's library as it is from the broad, horizontal, flowing spaces of Burgh's original light and airy Augustan classicism. More likely sources of inspiration were the great tunnel-vaulted naves of Irish Romanesque churches. Deane and Woodward's design captures both the form and feeling of these ancient medieval monuments; their sense of compression and weight which dramatizes volume as it emphasizes mass and structure.

The Kilkenny Picture Gallery and Trinity College Library exemplify the particularly Irish qualities of Deane and Woodward's interiors: rich detailing and freely designed ornament, which is always subordinated to the stronger rhythms of the structure. The resulting sense of architectonic reality, of structural mass and spatial compression within contained forms, creates a drama of these interior volumes.

[154]

APPENDIX: MINOR WORKS

WOODWARD'S WORK FOR THE TREVELYANS AT SEATON, DEVON, 1860

Woodward's final project, a series of designs for the Trevelyans' "Marina" at Seaton, a village on the South Devon coast, was undertaken independently of the firm and left unfinished at his death.[58]

Woodward met the Trevelyans in Oxford while working on the Museum. Sir Walter, well known as a "liberal supporter of all efforts for the augmentation of knowledge" (among others of the erection of the museum building at Oxford), was also a liberal patron of the fine arts.[59] In this activity he was largely guided by his wife, Pauline, patroness of the Pre-Raphaelites, and an amateur artist in her own right.[60] The scientific and artistic interests of husband and wife converged in the Oxford Museum, and through their associations with the prime movers of the scheme they were both drawn into the project. Sir Walter assisted with the selection of plants for the courtyard capitals and Pauline contributed designs for the carving.

Lady Trevelyan, whose patronage of the Pre-Raphaelites also extended to their associates—including William Bell Scott, Woolner, and later, most notably, Swinburne—took a special interest in Woodward.[61] He, like the others, was invited to Wallington. On one of these occasions the idea of transforming the Trevelyans' property at Seaton into a "Venetian Gothic Eden" was hatched.[62]

Sir Walter had inherited the manor and lands of Seaton in 1846 when he succeeded to the baronetcy and family estates in Somerset, Devon, Cornwall, and Northumberland. Originally acquired through marriage by the first baronet in 1655 Seaton had since then been tied to the Trevelyan estates at Nettlecombe in Somerset. In 1788, however, it passed out of Trevelyan hands to Thomas Charter, steward to Sir Walter's father, Sir John Trevelyan of Nettlecombe. But in 1845 it was discovered that the transfer had been fraudulently obtained by Charter, and Seaton was returned by a judgment in Chancery to the Trevelyans.[63]

In the same year Sir Walter and Lady Trevelyan paid their first visit to the site. They were enchanted with the place; Sir Walter because of the multitude of archaeological remains and unique geological features of the locality and Pauline because of the still-surviving tradition of lacemaking in the district. Both were deeply impressed by the poverty of the inhabitants and the unsanitary and neglected look of the place and determined then to modernize and "develop" Seaton into a seaside spa for the "right sort" of visitors, much like the neighboring resort towns of Sidmouth and Lyme Regis.[64]

Plans for the redevelopment of Seaton began immediately. A new bathhouse, a modern sewage system, an esplanade along the seafront, and other improvements—all to be executed at Trevelyan's expense—were projected. As it turned out, only the bathhouse was actually built at this time, since for the next ten to fifteen years Trevelyan was forced to turn his attention and capital to the management of the family's principal estates in Somerset and Northumberland. However, in the late 1850s and 1860s he was once again able to return to Seaton and begin his program of improvements. These included plans for the installation of waterworks, gas lighting, a branch railway between Seaton and Beer, new roads, the demolition of unsanitary buildings, the construction of a model farm and the improvement of others in the district.[65]

Sir Walter's first completed project was a schoolhouse. This was opened in 1860. The building, a single-storey rectangular block with high pitched roof, separately gabled entrance porch, rubble flint walling, limestone quoins, and a small amount of red brick trim, has been attributed to Woodward.[66] Though the simple, saddleback-roofed block and the rubble walling can be related to the firm's police court in Dundrum and while the gabled porch tower and limestone quoins recall Llys Dulas, the resemblance to Woodward's work is superficial and the uninspired composition, awkward proportions, and crude and dessicated detailing make this attribution unlikely. Furthermore, the schoolhouse is never mentioned by Woodward in his correspondence with the Trevelyans. Instead, these letters, all dating from 1860, are primarily concerned with Woodward's designs for the esplanade houses.

The esplanade was a part of Trevelyan's original plans for Seaton in 1845.[67] It was to be situated along the seafront between the railroad station and the bathhouse (Fig. 161). The houses themselves were to be small single-family dwellings, durably built so as to withstand the continuous assault of sea spray and the prevailing southwesterly winds and storms, as well as providing an attractive backdrop to the waterfront promenade.

It would seem that Trevelyan's program for the houses was based on a combination of philanthropic principles and commercial speculation similar to that of the suburban housing projects of the Land Societies. Like the "Artisans' Labourers' and General Dwellings Company" in London in the 1870s, the purpose here was to provide lower-middle-class housing which working men could then purchase and own.[68] Thus, the original building program was to be paid for by Trevelyan probably with a view to selling the leaseholds to prospective tenants. In this scheme the designs for the row houses along the esplanade were also to function as models for later speculative building.

The idea of designing the esplanade houses was first proposed to Woodward in the summer of 1860. In August of that year he wrote to Lady Trevelyan, "I shall try and design the nicest and most rational and the most taking with the sea side resorting people that I can."[69] Trevelyan was most concerned that the buildings should be economical and impressed this point on Woodward, who responded:

Though I cannot say at present what the houses should cost, I think I can safely say they need not cost anything more for being designed in good taste

[156]

than if they were as bad as speculative builders' architecture usually is, i.e., provided they are not more durably built in the one case than the other.[70]

It would seem that the original proposal, again like the Artisans' Labourers' and General Dwellings Company programs, was to have pairs of semi-detached houses or continuous rows of houses designed so as to give a semi-detached impression.

In October 1860, Woodward visited the Trevelyans in Seaton and brought with him a number of sketches for the houses. Some of these appear to have survived and are now in the National Library in Dublin.[71] The four drawings in question are all elevations of semi-detached and terrace houses, executed in pen and color wash, some with penciled-in detail, which seem to have been prepared as "presentation" rather than working drawings.

The first of these shows a pair of semi-detached houses (Fig. 162). Here Woodward adopted a traditional suburban semi-detached house site plan involving twin gables facing the road, bay windows, separately gabled side porches, and a taller unifying rear block with a high pitched roof.[72] The double gabled front recalls Woodward's house for William Shaen, then building in London, about which he wrote to Lady Trevelyan, sketching the profile of the roofs and explaining the rationale behind this composition.

> Though I think high roofs stand better against storms than low ones and keep their slates on better—I don't go with Ruskin in thinking all architecture (in England) hopeless without them. The house I spoke of [15 Upper Phillimore Gardens] has high roofs, but presents its gables towards the street.

Such an arrangement, he argued, could be practicably adopted in the esplanade houses "if that position [gables facing the street] coincided with presenting them to the prevailing winds. . . ."[73]

From the drawing it would appear that the houses were intended to be built of red brick or possibly the red sandstone of the locality with alternating brick and stone relieving arches and window dressings. The surfaces are smooth and the corners sharp and regular. The banded relieving arches are flush with the wall surface while the stone dressings are boldly three-dimensional and make much of the play of light and shade across their molded surfaces. The dominant symmetry of the laterally balanced masses is counter-balanced by the irregular rhythms of the windows across the front. This centers on the dramatic structural gesture of the central chimney shaft locked into the V of the roof gables. Woodward's design is tightly controlled and dynamically balanced. The stand-ardization—use of a traditional semi-detached house plan, regular window shapes and sizes, and the absence of intricate, individualistic detailing—is due to the fact that here

[157]

for the first time Woodward was designing a large-scale speculative building project rather than a single house for an individual client.

Woodward himself was not particularly fond of the semi-detached house type, as he wrote to Lady Trevelyan, "I confess I do not like rows of double houses." He made an alternative proposal for the esplanade houses: "I should like to make them in groups of sometimes two sometimes three, some one, or else in a continuous terrace. But if they must for any reason, be on the binary principle I should like to join their porches together by some connecting link."[74] Another drawing in the National Library collection is just such a design for either semi-detached or a row of coupled houses with joined porches (Fig. 163). Like the first, this design also has a twin-gabled front, but the doorways are now side by side in the center between the symmetrical gabled front blocks. The porch roofs cut back from this front plane to the transverse rear block, where the two quatrefoil openings probably, as at Clontra, light the front stairhalls.

In the absence of plans it is difficult to judge the internal arrangements of the houses, but from the placement of the entrances and stairs it seems possible that this also followed Clontra with the main stairs leading directly from the front entrance up to the second floor containing the principal apartments and a second internal staircase giving access to the lower level. Over the quatrefoils another roof slopes back to triangular dormers above which a recessed wall rises vertically between two acute dormers with trefoil openings.

Woodward's complex composition of receding wall planes, shifting cornice lines, and roof angles tends to emphasize the shimmering and brightly colored surfaces of his design. The walls are coursed with red brick or sandstone, limestone, and inlaid bands of lozenge-shaped dark brown stone or brick. Their surfaces are sheer and taut, their stretched planes unbroken by projections except for the molded stone dressings. The angularity, sharp edges, and richly patterned fabric have a Butterfieldian clarity of outline and surface. But the effect is quite different and depends largely on the areas of "broad sunlight" and "starless shade" shifting across the different wall planes which enforce the direction of their masses and create a sense of spatial depth and volume which is nevertheless subordinated to the dominant frontality of the whole.[75]

Two further drawings in the National Library are designs for continuous terraces of two-storey houses with dormered attic storeys in the roof (Figs. 164, 165). Each house is expressed as a unit, marked off from the next by tall chimney shafts and ridges. The houses in the first of the two drawings are three bays across with evenly spaced segmental windows and projecting gabled porches.

Woodward did not stray far from the traditional small terrace house massing, siting, and proportions. The detailing, however, is unusually lavish for such modest housing. Much of this, including the ornamental brickwork of the discharging arches, the wrought iron balcony, gas lamps, door hinges, and brackets, was penciled in over the original pen and wash drawing and suggest that the latter may have been done by someone else in the firm's office and the pencil additions made later by Woodward. As in the other designs, Woodward intended to use a variety of materials: red brick or sandstone for the walls, darker sandstone belt courses, and limestone with red sandstone trim for the porches. The emphasis is likewise on the rich surface embellishment of the principal facades.

The second drawing of terrace houses shows two complete units. Here the windows of the second floor are gathered together to form a sort of arcaded loggia; an "Italianate" modification of the familiar bow-fronted Georgian seaside terrace. As in the latter, this *piano nobile* probably contained the drawing room.

Inside, Woodward proposed to Trevelyan that the floors could be "made of chips of (Plymouth) marble in cement, so much used in Italy and which I am very anxious to try here—for making fireproof floors." Trevelyan who was a campaigner for more extensive use of concrete, no doubt approved of Woodward's argument that "tiles are so troublesome to get, hard to get properly laid, cost so much and are (for colour and beauty) worth so little, i.e., as they are made as yet in England (and speculative builders I should think abhor them)."[76]

Though he retained the form of traditional English terraced artisans' dwellings in these designs, Woodward made liberal use of structural polychromy and Continental Gothic motifs. All of the designs are essentially facade architecture, frontally oriented and with contained outlines to provide a suitably cohesive yet varied backdrop for the esplanade.

Woodward's letters to Lady Trevelyan of these years contain references to a number of other projects for the Trevelyans, including a carved stone cross for the Trevelyan Chapel in St. Mary's Church, Nettlecombe, and a church in Seaton, neither of which was executed.[77]

Another letter from Woodward to Lady Trevelyan in the Newcastle University Library collection, written from Paris on his last trip to the Continent, deals with his final project for them. This was a design for the Trevelyan's own house in Seaton. Regarding it he wrote, "I have been unable to get Sir Walter's house out of the hands of Mr. Bramwell [Woodward's Clerk of the Works in Oxford] and into mine. But I shall not wait for that to show you the architecture, but proceed to invent it forthwith."[78] It is not known whether Woodward's design was ever made or seen by the Trevelyans. Their house (Fig. 166), however, called "Calverley Lodge," was actually built after Woodward's death in 1865-1866 by Charles Edwards, a young Exeter architect—though the responsibility for the design has recently been given to Woodward.[79] In the absence of plans, drawings, and further documentation this is difficult to verify. But on the face of it this attribution seems unlikely. Indeed, the house, which still stands on a high cliff overlooking the sea to the west of Seaton village, and is now known as "Check House," does have certain affinities with Woodward's work. The variety of roof shapes, the gabled porch and windows, the glass and iron structure of the conservatory, and finally the close attention to detail in the interior—the carved wooden door frames and cut-stone fireplaces—are features which also characterized some of Deane and Woodward's houses. But whereas these are generally tightly composed with simple rational plans, clear bounding lines, functionally expressive massing and vigorous structurally integrated detailing, Edwards' composition is loose, rambling, and awkwardly planned with the rooms arranged along either side of narrow central corridors. Calverley Lodge lacks the clarity and concentration of Woodward's designs and instead relies on a gratuitous irregularity of overscaled and crudely detailed, vaguely Gothicizing, features to create a facile picturesqueness. The strident polychromy of the different local materials used—flint, sandstone, freestone and brick— also characterized Woodward's designs for the esplanade terraces, but here the exotic checkerboard effect is overdone in a way that Woodward would never have sanctioned, much less have designed himself.

Taken together Woodward's projects for the Trevelyans, had they been executed, would have comprised a comprehensive building scheme comparable to Butterfield's Baldersby St. James village estate for the Downes in Yorkshire. Like the latter, Seaton was to be a "model village" with school, church, terraces, cottages, and villas of different types conceived and designed by the architect in conjunction with his patron. However, Woodward did not live long enough to realize any of these projects and all that remains of his work is a meager and tantalizingly incomplete record of his intentions and ideas expressed in his correspondence with the Trevelyans.

NOTES

INTRODUCTION

1. Sir Thomas Drew, "The Late Sir Thomas Deane, RHA," *Journal of the Royal Institute of British Architects* (9 December 1899), 48 (hereinafter cited as *JRIBA*).

2. The most complete account of the firm's work is given in my "The Architecture of Deane and Woodward, 1845-1861" (Yale University, Ph.D. dissertation, 1978).

3. Douglas Richardson, *Gothic Revival Architecture in Ireland* (New York, 1978).

4. For a more detailed discussion of the Woodward Memoir and its suppression see Chapter VII.

5. The Woodward Sketchbooks (cat. nos. 7381, 7384, 7385, 7386, 7387, National Gallery, Dublin) were given to the National Gallery by Thomas Manly Deane in 1921. Appended to them is a note from T. N. Deane, "These little books contain much of Woodward's views on architecture . . ." (n.d.). I am indebted to Jeanne Sheehy, who discovered the sketchbooks in 1973, for directing me to them.

6. E. T. Cook and Alexander Wedderburn, eds., *The Works of John Ruskin*, Library Edition, 39 volumes (London, 1902-1912), X, 459 (letter to *Pall Mall Gazette*, March 15, 1872).

7. Charles L. Eastlake, *A History of the Gothic Revival* (London, 1872), pp. 264-280.

8. Kenneth Clark, *The Gothic Revival* (1928; reprinted Harmondsworth, Middlesex, 1962), pp. xiv-xv.

9. Ibid., p. 196.

10. Ibid., Chapter 10, pp. 176-196.

11. Henry-Russell Hitchcock, "Ruskin or Butterfield? Victorian Gothic at the Mid-Century," *Early Victorian Architecture in Britain* (New Haven, 1954), pp. 572-613.

12. Ibid., p. 588. Hitchcock discusses the relation of *Seven Lamps* to All Saints in detail on pp. 584-597.

13. Ibid., p. 610.

14. Paul Thompson, *William Butterfield* (London, 1971), p. 4.

15. Ibid., p. 165.

16. Georg Germann, *Gothic Revival in Europe and Britain: Sources, Influences and Ideas* (London, 1972), p. 34.

17. Stefan Muthesius, *The High Victorian Movement in Architecture* 1850-1870 (London, 1972), p. 38.

18. Ibid.

19. George L. Hersey, *High Victorian Gothic—A Study in Associationism* (Baltimore, 1972), pp. 186-188.

20. Ibid., p. 184: Hersey maintains that Ruskin "was, in fact, in disagreement with the ecclesiologists on every principle of their style, though rather inconsistently he could praise examples of it."

21. Ibid., p. 191. Probably taking the lead from Hersey, Roger Dixon and Stefan Muthesius in *Victorian Architecture* (New York, 1978), have also noted the anti-High Victorian Gothic classicism of Ruskin's early architectural writings: "In 'The Lamp of Power' Ruskin goes back to the eighteenth-century concept of the Sublime. The most important element in architecture is size, combined with simplicity of outline. . . . Thus Ruskin helped to turn the tide from Picturesque variety towards massive uniformity" (p. 202). Dixon and Muthesius do not, however, relate these formal qualities to Deane and Woodward's work.

22. Hersey, *High Victorian Gothic*, p. 209.

23. For the early history of the firm in Cork see Eve M. Blau, "The Earliest Work of Deane and Woodward," *Architectura*, 2/1979, 170-192.

24. The most thorough published histories of the Deanes are: J(ames) C(oleman), "Sir Thomas Deane, P.R.H.A.," *Journal of the Cork Historical and Archaeological Society*, 2nd ser., XXI (1915), 180-186 (hereinafter cited as *JCHAS*); *Irish Builder*, LXIII (February 13, 1901), 633-635.

25. James Coleman, *JCHAS* (1915), 180-186. For further biographical notes on Sir Thomas Deane, see "The Dublin Builder's Photographic Album," *Dublin Builder*, V (15 March 1863), 49; and his obituary, "Sir Thomas Deane, Architect," *Builder*, XXIX (14 October 1871), 804.

26. For a detailed discussion of Deane's early buildings see Eve M. Blau, *Architectura*, 2/1979, 170-192.

27. These previously unknown facts concerning Woodward's parentage, birthdate and place, were obtained from Baptismal Records, St. Catherine's Church (Church of Ireland), Parish of Kilbride, Tullamore, County Offaly, and Death Certificate of Benjamin Woodward, 17 May 1861, in the Archives Municipales de Lyon, France.

28. Major Benjamin Woodward is mentioned in a letter from Dr. William Stokes to Henry Acland, 19 August 1861, *MS. Acland. d. 65. fol. 131*, Bodleian Library, Oxford (hereinafter cited as *MS. Acland*). This Benjamin Woodward is also mentioned in *The Memoirs of Edward Ludlow*, 2 vols. (Oxford, 1894). John O'Hart, *The Irish and Anglo-Irish Gentry* (Dublin, 1969), p. 423, lists "Benjamin Woodward, Meath—Soldier of the Commonwealth of Ireland" as one of those who claimed land in Ireland in c. 1648. The Woodwards are mentioned among the principal families in Ireland at the close of the seventeenth century in John O'Hart, *Irish Pedigrees* (Dublin, 1878), p. 697. Benjamin Woodward is also listed as an Adventurer for Lands in Ireland under various Acts and Ordinances of Subscription, ibid., p. 704. Seamus Pender (ed.), *A Census of Ireland Circa 1659* (Dublin, 1939), lists "Benjamin Woodward, Esq., High Street, Kells, Meath." Most of the big estates in County Meath were appropriated by Cromwell and given to English settlers. *Griffiths' Primary Valuation of Meath*, 1854 (National Library, Dublin), lists a Robert Woodward as the proprietor of 654 acres and a house at Drumbaragh. This Woodward sold the property and house in 1869. A plaster frieze dating from the late eighteenth century in the entrance hall of Drumbaragh depicting the Woodward arms and a variety of martial trophies suggests that the Woodwards were a military family.

29. "Memoir of the late Mr. Woodward, Architect," *Dublin Builder*, III (1 July 1861), 563. Obituary of "Sir Thomas Deane, Architect," *Builder*, XXIX (14 October 1871), 804, calls Woodward "an old pupil of Sir. Thomas." This probably refers to the fact that Woodward entered Deane's office sometime before he was actually made a partner in the firm.

30. There was a great deal of bridge-building undertaken in Cork City and County in the 1830s and Woodward may well have been apprenticed to any one of the many civil engineers involved in this work and construction at Cork harbor, which was also under way at the time.

31. The possibility of Woodward being related to the Woodwards of Cork has also been suggested by C. P. Curran in "Benjamin Woodward, Ruskin and the O'Sheas," *Studies*, XXIX (June 1940), [255]-268. There seems to be further evidence for the connection. The Woodward crest in the plaster frieze at Drumbaragh (see n. 28, above) has a bishop's crozier, which suggests that the two families were related.

32. *Dublin Builder*, III (1 July 1861), 563.

33. Between 1833 and 1846 the Ordinance Survey was carried out and a large number of Irish medieval monuments recorded. At the same time the shortlived but widely read *Dublin Penny Journal* (1832-1836) and the *Irish Penny Journal* (1840-1841) began circulation. Both journals contained a great deal of information on Irish antiquities and Irish crafts. Samuel Lewis' *Topographical Dictionary of Ireland* was first published in 1837 and was succeeded in the mid-forties by George Petrie's *The Round Towers and Ecclesiastical Architecture of Ireland*, 1845; George Wilkinson's *Practical Geology and Ancient Architecture of Ireland*, 1845; and Mr. and Mrs. C. S. Hall's *Ireland, Its Scenery and Character*, 1846, all of which dealt extensively with Irish antiquities and medieval monuments.

34. Pugin suggested, in a note to *An Apology for the Revival of Christian Architecture in England* (1843), that "if the clergy and gentry of Ireland possessed one spark of real national feeling, they would revive and restore those solemn piles of buildings which formerly covered that island of saints, and which are associated with the holiest and most honourable recollections of its history. Many of these were indeed rude and simple; but, they harmonized most perfectly with the wild and rocky localities in which they were erected."

35. "Benjamin Woodward measured drawings of Holy Cross Abbey, County Tipperary, June 1844," nine mounted drawings, MS.3.B.59, Royal Irish Academy, Dublin.

36. For discussion of Woodward's possible association with the Morrisons, see Eve M. Blau, *Architectura*, 2/1979, 189-190.

37. Sir Thomas Deane appears to have written to Sir Thomas Acland in Oxford of his concern. Letter from Sir Thomas Deane to Sir Thomas Acland, 18 December 1854, *MS. Acland.* d.71. fol. 71; "[M]y early debut, the Queens College Cork (how well I recollect your anxiety for me)." Deane is also reported to have borrowed drawings of the Oxford colleges from Henry Hill, another Cork architect, to help him with the designs. See Henry H. Hill, "Cork Arcitecture," *JCHAS*, XLVIII (1943), 97.

38. Quote from *Building News*, V (1 January 1858), 2.

39. *Builder*, XXIX (14 October 1871), 804.

40. Letter from D. G. Rossetti to Gilchrist, June 1861, *MS. TOP. OXON. D.144*, Bodleian Library, Oxford (hereinafter cited as *MS. TOP. OXON. D.144*).

41. Quoted in C. P. Curran, "Benjamin Woodward, Ruskin and the O'Sheas," *Studies* (1940), p. 263.

42. Letter from Richard Brash to Wyatt Papworth, 3 March 1866, in Sir John Soane's Museum, London. (I am indebted to Sir John Summerson for showing me this letter and allowing me to quote from it.)

43. Letter from Rossetti to Gilchrist, June 1861, *MS. TOP. OXON. D.144.*

44. Ibid.

CHAPTER I

1. The fortunes of Sir Thomas Deane's firm throughout the decade of the 1840s were closely linked to these national fluctuations. Politically a staunch conservative, Deane was violently opposed to the Repeal Movement and even proposed an anti-Repeal petition in the early 1840s when national feeling in favor of independence was at its highest. Thus swimming against the popular political tide, his practice suffered accordingly. In 1843 he found himself totally without business. The architectural profession was in any case hard hit by the famine, and for Deane's firm it brought both heavy personal and professional losses. His two brothers and early partners, Kearns and Alexander Sharp Deane, died in early 1847. For Kearns Deane, see Thomas Crofton Croker Correspondence, unpublished letters, City Library Cork, V.64 (hereinafter cited as *Crofton Croker Correspondence*); *Builder*, V (13 February 1847), 79. For Alexander Sharpe Deane, see J. Gwilt, *An Encyclopedia of Architecture*, new ed. rev. by Wyatt Papworth (London, 1867), p. 248.

2. For reports of famine relief projects, see Board of Public Works Ireland, Reports to Commissioners of Public Works, in *Parliamentary Papers* (annually from 1845).

3. The best history of the founding of the Queen's Colleges (now University Colleges) and educational reform in Ireland in the nineteenth century is Theodore William Moody and James Camlin Beckett, *Queen's Belfast, 1845-1949: The History of a University*, 2 vols. (London, 1959), pp. xxxv-lxvii, 1-39.

4. Board of Public Works, Ireland, *Sixteenth Report from the Board of Public Works, Ireland with Appendices*, rev. ed. (London, 1848), p. 16.

5. *Builder*, VI (30 December 1848), p. 631.

6. "Irish Colleges and Lunatic Asylums," *Ecclesiologist*, IX (April 1849), 289-291.

7. For a thorough and penetrating discussion of the other Queen's Colleges, see Douglas Richardson, *Gothic Revival Architecture in Ireland*, pp. 311-345.

8. Twenty-one in all have survived in a somewhat tattered condition, including twelve of the original contract drawings, five tracings, and four drawings for the medical buildings, which were drawn up under separate contract in 1850. College Archives, University College, Cork.

9. Moody and Beckett, *Queen's Belfast*, p. 8. The opening ceremony and speeches are described in some detail by Sean Petit, "The Queen's College, Cork—The First Session 1849-50," *University College, Cork Record*, No. 49 (1974), 5-14. Further contemporary accounts appeared in the *Freeman's Journal* and the *Cork Examiner* on November 9, 1849.

10. See n. 8, above. All of the wooden beam roofs are diagrammed in section, and details of the joints are given, as well as profiles of the string courses.

11. In the 1840s a number of articles on wooden structures appeared in the *Ecclesiologist* and elsewhere: Ecclesiologist, III (1843-1844), 72ff.; *A Few Words to Church Builders* (1841), pp. 16-18; *Transactions of the Ecclesiological Society* (1845), 105 ff.; *The British Critic*, No. 58, April 1841. In 1849, R. and R. A. Brandon published their widely influential *Open Timber Roofs in the Middle Ages* (London, 1849), a detailed illustrated study of the development of medieval timber roofs which included all of the different types used by Deane and Woodward at Queen's College. Brandon also recommended their use in collegiate work.

12. Henry H. Hill in "Cork Architecture," *JCHAS*, XLVIII (1943), 97, recalled that Sir Thomas Deane "borrowed a large number of my grandfather's sketches of the Colleges at Oxford" at the time. Otherwise, the *Builder* IV (20 June 1846), 295, called the design "Elizabethan" while the *Illustrated London News* (17 November 1849), 327, called it "Collegiate or Domestic Architecture of the 15th century." In fact, the use of Tudor domestic models for college buildings became a stylistic convention for such work in the first half of the nineteenth century, as it had been throughout so much of medieval Oxford and Cambridge. When Deane and Woodward came to design Queen's College, it was already a firmly established collegiate style.

13. A.W.N. Pugin, *An Apology for the Revival of Christian Architecture in England* (London, 1843), p. 31.

14. Ibid.

15. A.W.N. Pugin, "Ancient Residences for the Poor," *Contrasts: or, A Parallel Between the Noble Edifices of the Fourteenth and Fifteenth Centuries, and Similar Buildings of the Present Day*, 2nd ed. (London, 1841).

16. *Builder* VI (1 April 1848), 162. *Illustrated London News* XIII (1847), 5. Butterfield's work at St. Augustine's consisted of rebuilding and restoring the old buildings.

17. For Deane's earlier buildings, see Eve M. Blau, *Architectura*, 2/1979, 170-192.

18. Woodward was elected a member at the Annual General Meeting on 7 January 1852. *Journal of the Royal Society of Antiquaries of Ireland*, Vol. 2 (1852-1853), 184.

19. The drawings of Holy Cross Abbey (nine in all) are in the Royal Irish Academy Library, Dublin: (RIA Ms. 3.B.59).

20. *Builder*, VI (6 May 1848), 222-223.

21. See n. 8, above. The tracings show that a number of minor alterations and additions, mostly of decorative details, were made to the original design after construction of the buildings was well under way. It would appear that Woodward was primarily responsible for these alterations and for designing the architectural ornament sketched onto the tracings and accompanied by notations in his hand.

22. The earliest record of the O'Sheas is in connection with Deane and Woodward's Museum at Trinity College in Dublin of 1853-1857, see Chapter II, below.

23. Unpublished diary of Henrietta Falkiner (neé Deane), daughter of Thomas Newenham Deane, written in 1950. (Private Collection)

24. A drawing of the fireplace is in MS. 4824, National Library, Dublin. Woodward's study of the Waking Bier is in the Royal Irish Academy (see n. 19, above).

25. *Builder*, VI (25 March 1848), 150-151, 595.

26. The name of the wrought-iron workshop, "Robert Merrick, Cork," where the gates, railings, etc., were made, was stamped on the gates, but it has been painted over many times and is now indecipherable. Deane and Woodward continued to employ local craftsmen for all of the wrought-iron work used in their buildings.

27. *University College Cork Development Plan Report* 1972 (Cork, 1972), p. 23; *Irish Builder*, L (1909, Jubilee Issue), 29-30.

28. As was the case with the Queen's Colleges, the necessary legislation had been enacted long before the famine. See Metropolitan Commissioners in Lunacy, 8 August 1844, Report to Lord Chancellor, with Statistical Appendix, *Parliamentary Papers*, 1844; A Bill to Amend the Laws for the Provision and Regulation of Lunatic Asylums for the Counties and Boroughs, and for the Maintenance and Care of Pauper Lunatics in England (8 and 9 Vict. cap. 100), 15 July 1845, 8 August 1845, *Parliamentary Papers* IV, 1845.

29. Reports from Commissioners, *Parliamentary Papers* 1847-1848, XXXII, p. 410.

30. "Rules for selection of sites," *Parliamentary Papers*, 1845 (Appendix E), p. 323.

31. Ibid., pp. 324-325.

32. The eight asylums and their architects were listed in Board of Works, Ireland, *Sixteenth Report from the Board of Public Works, Ireland with Appendices*, rev. ed. (London, 1848), p. 14. For discussion of the seven other asylum buildings see Richardson, *Gothic Revival Architecture in Ireland*, pp. 347-350.

33. Board of Works, Ireland, *Sixteenth Report* (Appendix B), pp. 236-237.

34. For earlier asylum planning see "Plans of Lunatic Asylums," *Builder*, IV (25 July 1846), 349-350, 354-355; "Asylums and Asylum Planning," *Irish Builder*, XLII (27 February 1901), 644.

35. The most advanced plan of the group was William Atkins' Eglinton Lunatic Asylum in Cork. Built to accommodate five hundred patients, it is the largest of all the asylums—and no doubt the size had a lot to do with the complexity of the plan. The main front is over a thousand feet long. Along this spine projecting bays of pavilions grouped at regular intervals contain the dormitories and day rooms. A plan and elevation of the Cork Asylum were published in Board of Works, Ireland, *Sixteenth Report* (Appendix B), pp. B16-B18; *Builder*, IX (27 November 1852), 754-755.

36. MS. 4824, National Library, Dublin. The sheet is unsigned and undated.

37. Board of Works, Ireland, *Seventeenth Report* p. 26.

38. In 1856 some minor works were carried out, and in 1864 the first major series of alterations was undertaken on the asylum. In 1888 further additions were made by J. F. Fuller. At that time the east and west wings were extended and outbuildings were added at the back. In 1930 there was some demolition, extensive additions were made to the rear of the main building and the lodge was built adjacent to the main entrance block at the front. See: *Builder*, XIV (9 February 1856), 74.; "Killarney Lunatic Asylum," *Building News*, X (26 August 1864), 644; "Tenders," *Irish Builder*, XXIX (15 February 1888), 55.

39. John Connolly, M.D., *The Construction and Government of Lunatic Asylums and Hospitals for the Insane (with Plans)* (London, 1847).

40. Ibid., p. 13.
41. A.W.N. Pugin, *True Principles of Pointed or Christian Architecture* (1841), p. 1.
42. Ibid., p. 42.
43. Ibid., p. 1.

CHAPTER II

1. *Builder*, X (18 September 1852), 589: "The new Lunatic Asylum here, which has been built for the county, under the direction of Sir Thomas Deane, is now finished. This, too, is Early Pointed in style, and is beautifully placed. With nothing adventitious, or introduced merely for the sake of ornament, the building is very picturesque and effective. It has cost about £30,000 we understood, and will lodge 250 patients."

2. For the School see "Cork School of Design," *Builder* V (3 April 1847), 161; Francis H. Tuckey, *The County and City of Cork Remembrancer* (Cork, 1837), p. 348; and Schools of Design, Reports and Returns relating to Head and Provincial Schools; Reports on Branch Schools for the year ending July 1850; The Government School of Design, *Parliamentary Papers*, 1850, XLIII, 730; Reports and Papers relating to Head and Branch Schools, *Parliamentary Papers*, 1850-1851, XLIII, 1423; "Cork School of Design," *Dublin Builder*, III (1 February 1862), 30; First Report of the Department of Practical Art, *Parliamentary Papers*, 1852-1853, LIV (1615), 43. It is probable that the O'Sheas, Deane's protegés from Ballyhooly, attended the school in its early years. In any case, Deane continued to take an active interest in the progress of its pupils and gained a reputation as a benefactor and supporter of struggling artists and craftsmen about which he complained to Crofton Croker, "It is a bore forever to be considered as having money and energy to forward sculptors," *Crofton Croker Correspondence*, V1.11.

3. Deane's influence is evident in some of the items exhibited, especially "some carvings by Irish peasants [that] show what might be done there in this way with proper encouragement [and provide] the most satisfactory proof . . . that there are workmen in the country capable of carrying out, under proper direction, any undertakings that may be entrusted to them," *Builder*, X (31 July 1852), 483. For the National Exhibition, see John Francis Maguire, *The Industrial Movement in Ireland as Illustrated by the National Exhibition of 1852* (Cork, 1853), p. 439; Henry Parkinson and Peter Lund Simmonds, *The Record and Descriptive Catalogue Dublin International Exhibition 1865* (London, 1866), p. 5; "National Exhibition of the Arts of Ireland," *Builder*, X (22 May 1852), 328. The space originally chosen when the exhibition was only contemplated to display the products of the province of Munster, was a large room (75 square feet) in the Corn Exchange which had in the past been used for concerts and other public purposes. The original building with a small dome in the center, facing onto Albert Quay, had been built in 1835 by Deane's firm. As applications for exhibition space became more numerous, it was found necessary to enlarge the building. Therefore, a gallery or transept 300' x 30' was built across the back or southern facade of the Hall and was roofed with glass. At the beginning of April 1852 it was found that even more space was needed and the Southern Hall was added onto the original building on a north-south axis. The extension, designed and built by John Benson, City and County Engineer for Cork, was 177' x 53' bringing the entire exhibition area to 42,525 square feet.

There is some confusion concerning the authorship of the Corn Market or Exchange building. The *APS Dictionary* II, C.147, lists the corn market as by W. and H. Hill in 1835. However, Henry H. Hill in "Architecture of the Past in Cork," *JCHAS*, XLIV (1939), 91, notes that the firm of Sir Thomas Deane built the Cornmarket even though the competition was won by Hill. *Builder*, X (21 August 1852), 534, noted: "that Mr. Benson, in conjunction with Sir Thomas Deane, was the architect for the building of the Cork Exhibition."

4. Deane and Woodward entered a design in the competition for the exhibition building (won by John Benson) which was awarded second prize. For the Dublin Exhibition and Benson's building see Parkinson and Simmonds, *The Record and Descriptive Catalogue, Dublin International Exhibition*, p. 1; *APS Dictionary*, II, D.76; *Builder*, X (21 August 1852), 534; ibid., (18 September 1852), 589, 593; *Builder*, XI (1 January 1853), 1, 8-9; ibid., (12 May 1853), 321-323, 329.

5. *Thoms Dublin Directory*, 1853, lists 3 Upper Merrion Street as the offices of the Great Industrial Exhibition, while in 1854 the same address is given as the offices of "Messrs. Deane and Woodward, architects," and the residence of Thomas Newenham Deane. Letter from Sir Thomas Deane to Sidney Herbert (proprietor of the Pembroke Estates in Dublin, see further, Appendix: Dublin 1854-1860), 5 November 1853, *Correspondence Pembroke Estates*, Pembroke Estate Office, Fitzwilliam Place, Dublin: "When Trinity College employed me as an architect, I resolved to open an office in Dublin and that my second son, my partner, should reside there." (There follow details of the lease, explaining that his son had "a slender purse.")

6. "Royal Institute of Architects in Ireland," *Builder*, XII (25 November 1854), 606; "A Short Sketch of the Early History of the Institute, 1839-71," *Journal of the Royal Institute of Architects in Ireland*, 1909 (hereinafter cited as *JRIBA*).

7. For Thomas Newenham Deane see, *DNB*, s.v., Deane, Sir Thomas Newenham; "The Late Sir Thomas Deane, R.H.A.," *JRIBA* (9 December 1899), 48-49; "Sir Thomas N. Deane," *Builder*, LXXVII (18 November 1899), 471; "Death of Sir Thomas Deane," *Irish Builder*, XLI (15 November 1899), 180; "The Late Sir Thomas Deane," *Irish Builder*, XLI (1 December 1899), 196-197.

8. Quote from *Crofton Croker Correspondence*, VI.16. T. N. Deane's favorite subjects were seascapes and sailing boats, recalling his early naval ambitions and love of the sea. Otherwise there are the usual Victorian travel sketches. Though most of these (which are in a private collection in London), date from the 1870s and 1880s, two of Deane's early drawings executed when he was in Switzerland in the summer of 1852 have survived and show that he made his first visit to the Continent shortly after the opening of the National Exhibition in Cork.

9. The exact date when T. N. Deane and Woodward were made partners is uncertain, but from 1851 onward the firm was known as "Messrs. Deane and Woodward." In June 1851 Woodward and T. N. Deane traveled together to London to see the Great Exhibition where a design by Woodward for a roof ridge carved in slate by machinery had been entered by the slate manufacturing firm of Blackburn and Bewicke, Island of Valentia, Kerry. For Woodward's design see *Official Catalogue Great Exhibition of 1851*, II, class 27, section 3, number 21: "Roof ridge carved in slate by machinery, designed by Benjamin Woodward, Esq., architect." (I am indebted to John O'Callaghan for this reference.)

10. For the competition see *Builder*, IX (13 December 1851), 791; *Builder*, X (31 July

1852), 483. The firm's drawings, which have not survived, were exhibited at the RHA, see *Exhibition Catalogue of Royal Hibernian Academy*, 27th Exhibition, July 30, 1853, no. 390: "Three elevations of the proposed town hall of Cork, Sir Thomas Deane, Son, and Woodward." (I am indebted to John O'Callaghan for bringing the lithograph of the firm's design, which is in his possession, to my attention.)

11. *Builder*, X (31 July 1852), 483.

12. It is possible but unlikely—in view of Deane and Woodward's later work—that they may have been influenced by Ruskin's *Seven Lamps of Architecture* (London, 1849) in the use of such features. Of course the *Seven Lamps* had been preceded by numerous well-illustrated books on Continental medieval architecture.

13. Letter from Sir Thomas Deane to Dr. Lloyd, 21 August 1852, MUN/P/2/325, TCD Library Dublin. Letters from Charles Lanyon to Dr. Lloyd, 15, 22 September, 8 November 1852, MUN/P/2/322, TCD Library, Dublin (expressing gratification at being included and discussing the plans he is sending); Letter from Decimus Burton to Dr. Lloyd (declining invitation), 27 August 1852, MUN/P/2/326, TCD Library, Dublin. (All material from the Trinity College Muniments is consulted, quoted, and otherwise reproduced here by permission of the Board of Trinity College, Dublin.)

14. "University of Dublin Competition," *Builder*, XI (9 July 1853), 228.

15. "Addition to Trinity College, Dublin," *Builder*, XI (2 July 1853), 420.

16. For the competition of 1833, see MUN/P/261, and *TCD Register and Board Minutes*, 1830-1840, TCD Library, Dublin; Henry Fulton, *Remarks on Irish Collegiate Architecture* (Dublin, 1837); Henry Fulton, "Remarks," *Civil Engineer and Architect's Journal*, I, 93. A more recent account of the building of the college and especially the New Square is given by Edward McParland, "Trinity College Dublin," *Country Life* (May 20, 1876), 1312-1313. Darley's plans are in MS. 5203, TCD Library, Dublin.

17. Report from Decimus Burton, April 30, 1849, *TCD Register*, TCD Library, Dublin.

18. Plans and section for a museum building, by John McCurdy, architect and civil engineer (5 sheets), MUN/MC/99, TCD Library, Dublin.

19. Entry for 11 February 1853, *TCD Register, 1851-1856*, TCD Library, Dublin: "The Board authorized the Bursar to inform Sir Thomas Deane that they . . . would propose the following form in the hopes that it might be satisfactory to both parties. 'Design (on the basis of Mr. McCurdy's ground plans as modified by the Board) by Sir Thomas Deane etc.' This form to be signed by Mr. McCurdy as superintending architect." Entry for 25 February 1853: "The following resolutions were adopted, relating to the plans for the new lecture room building. Resolved— that Mr. Lloyd's modification of Mr. McCurdy's plan No. 1 be adopted, subject to the consideration of a committee of the Board in reference to minor details. Sir Thomas Deane's plans (Nos. 2 and 3) having been deemed by the Board next in suitability to that of Mr. McCurdy, in preparing designs for the elevations and detailed specifications on the understanding that the usual architect's fees (5%) be divided equally between the two parties." Letter from Sir Thomas Deane, Son and Woodward to Dr. Todd, MUN/P/348, TCD Library, Dublin: "In reply to your letter announcing the decision of the committee appointed by the Board to consider the question at issue, between

us and Mr. McCurdy. We deeply regret that, feeling as we do, most anxious to comply with every wish of the Board and to stand high in their estimation, we cannot acquiesce in the decisions of the committee 'that Mr. McCurdy is fully entitled to sign the ground plans.' We beg respectfully to offer the following solution of the question viz. On the ground plan and plan of upper storey to take out the words 'designed by' and write underneath the title of the plan as follows. 'Ground Plan: Altered (with the approval and authority of the Board) from the modification of Mr. McCurdy's Ground Plan supplied by the Board as a basis—By Sir Thomas Deane etc. Architects. J. McCurdy, Superintending Architect.' We submit the plan, so altered from the modification, is essentially a different plan. That the superstructure designed by us, could not by any possibility be adapted to any ground plan of Mr. McCurdy's, or the modification. That he had no share whatever in such alterations, and that even if the modified plan, had not been altered at all by us, it would not have been according to the usual practice for him to have signed it." Privately, however, Sir Thomas Deane wrote to Crofton Croker concerning TCD that "They [TCD] sent for me to do the *aesthetics* of a new Building to be erected in the Park. . . ." 11 October 1853, *Crofton Croker Correspondence*, VI.139.

20. The argument began with a letter from McCurdy to the *Builder* XI (16 August 1853), 351, objecting that "the Board awarded the designs sent in by me the first place, those by Sir Thomas Deane the second; who in conjunction with me, has been appointed to carry out the building on my plans, with some trifling modifications suggested by a member of the Board. The elevations submitted by Sir Thomas Deane since the competition, have been approved of . . . but they have been drawn to suit the plans sent in by me, which were adopted." Deane and Woodward responded in the next edition of the *Builder*, XII (26 August 1854), 453, stating that the proposition of the Board to design "jointly with Mr. McCurdy, the elevations and the whole of the superstructure . . . was respectfully but at once declined on our part, and an intimation made, that if the designing of the superstructure were confided to us, and the superintendence of the execution of our designs were given to Mr. McCurdy, such an arrangement would be acceptable to us; and on this understanding, as is distinctly expressed in the resolution of the Board, we were 'employed to design the building,' taking as a basis the modified ground-plan mentioned above. The elevations, sections, and decorations, external and internal (to which Mr. McCurdy admits he has no claim) include everything in a building that is properly called architecture. It is clear that, on the same ground plan (i.e., arrangement) may be erected the worst possible architecture as well as the best. We know very well that the ground-plan has an influence on the general form of the super-structure, and therefore, the first thing we did on receiving the instructions of the Board was to obtain their consent to an alteration of the ground-plan, from a form somewhat resembling a Greek cross to a simple parallelogram, the general design of the building as now in course of erection having been originally preconceived by us in that form." Before this, however, another letter from McCurdy appeared in the *Builder*, XII (19 August 1854), 443: "This building, which is now being erected, *on my plans and under my superintendence*, the elevations and external decorations being from the office of Messrs. Deane and Woodward. I must regret the temerity which has caused your informant to give so unfair and incorrect a statement to the public. I wish in no way whatever to appropriate to myself the portions of this

building which have been designed by Messrs. Deane and Woodward, or rather . . . by the workmen; but while giving those gentlemen all merit for their portion of the edifice, I am quite as determined that the plans and internal arrangements which have been made by me, and to one line of which they have not the most remote title, shall not be put to the credit of the Messrs. Deane and Woodward." At the foot of McCurdy's letter the *Builder* inserted an editorial note: "It is due to ourselves to say that in the correspondence we had on the subject with the Messrs. Deane and Woodward, Mr. McCurdy's name was never mentioned, and that all the working drawings of the exterior, to which our illustrations refer, are signed by the first-named architects alone. This it will be seen, is quite consistent with Mr. McCurdy's claim; but a little more candour, if that claim be correct, would have prevented misconstruction." Deane and Woodward answered this accusation in *Builder*, XII (26 August 1854), 453: "In our former communication to you we could not place Mr. McCurdy's name in a position that would be perfectly acceptable to him, therefore we confined ourselves to a description of the building." Finally the last editorial note appeared in the *Builder*, XII (2 September 1854), 467: "We did not intend to print anything more on this subject, but observing in the Irish newspapers that an inference is wrongly drawn from our remarks, to impute an untruth to the Messrs. Deane and Woodward, it is necessary we should say, in confirmation of Messrs. Deane and Woodward's statement, that in the descriptive particulars with which they furnished us, no names were given. The working drawings of the elevations were signed by them (correctly so, according to Mr. McCurdy's statement), and we, therefore, as a matter of course, introduced their names into the account. The position of the several parties is now made clear by their statements, and we sincerely hope that no angry feeling will be permitted longer to exist, and that all will concur to render the building worthy of the beautiful capital of beautiful Ireland." Neither McCurdy's nor Deane and Woodward's original plans still exist. However, tracings from a working plan of the second floor, signed "Sir Thomas Deane Knt., Son and Woodward, showing the modified arrangement are in MUN/P/2/365, TCD Library, Dublin. The plans of both floors inscribed "John McCurdy, Architect" were published in the *Civil Engineer and Architects Journal*, XVIII (1855), 48.

21. Entry for April 16, 1853, *TCD Register 1851-56*, TCD Library, Dublin.

22. Entry for October 22, 1853, *TCD Register 1851-56*, TCD Library, Dublin. Information concerning the contracts is in MUN/P/2/330, TCD Library, Dublin.

23. "New Churches," *Ecclesiologist*, XV (October 1854), 356.

24. The second floor of the interior has been changed, since the building no longer functions as a geological and mineralogical museum and is now a part of the Engineering School. The upper storey has been divided into two half-storeys and the museums and drawing room have been subdivided into smaller classrooms and offices.

25. The warehouse analogy is also associationally apt, and the physical similarities—the blockiness and round-arched facade—may be a conscious reference to their related functions.

26. "Ireland," *Building News*, IV (26 June 1857), 662. The reviewer noted that "the College structure seems to have provoked more criticism, and elicited a greater variety of opinions than any building erected of late years in the Irish metropolis."

27. *Builder*, XI (2 July 1853), 420.

28. *Builder*, XII (12 August 1854), 425.

29. "New Churches," *Ecclesiologist*, XV (October 1854), 356.

30. *Works of Ruskin*, XVI, xliv. The letter from Ruskin to Woodward has not been traced.

31. *Crofton Croker Correspondence*, VI.139.

32. "Il Palazzo dei Pergoli Intagliati, Venice," *Builder*, IX (15 March 1851), 170-171; "Casa Visetti, Venice," *Builder*, IX (24 May 1851), 330-331; "The Palazzo Dario," *Builder*, IX (29 March 1851), 202; "Palazzo de'Cornari, Venice," *Builder*, IX (23 August 1851), 530-531; "Capitals: Ducal Palace, Venice," *Builder*, IX (27 December 1851), 815.

33. These similarities to Venetian palaces have also been noted by Douglas Richardson, *Gothic Revival Architecture in Ireland*, pp. 392-394.

34. For the influence of J. W. Wild's St. Martin's Northern Schools, 1849, on Victorian commercial architecture see Henry-Russell Hitchcock, "Victorian Monuments of Commerce," *Architectural Review*, CV (February 1949), 65.

35. These relations were also suggested by Douglas Richardson, *Gothic Revival Architecture in Ireland*, p. 394.

36. *Ecclesiologist*, XV (October 1854), 356.

37. *Builder*, XI (19 March 1853), 185. This was also noted by Douglas Richardson, *Gothic Revival Architecture in Ireland*, p. 391.

38. "Ancient Doorway Killeshin Church," *Builder*, XII (7 January 1854), 2-3. For Irish and Celtic Revival work exhibited in the Great Exhibition of the Works of Industry of All Nations in London, 1851, see *Official Descriptive and Illustrated Catalogue*, 3 vols. (London, 1851). For Irish crafts exhibited in the Cork exhibition of 1852 and the Dublin exhibition of 1853, see John Francis Maguire, *The Industrial Movement in Ireland As Illustrated by the National Exhibition of 1852* (Cork, 1853); Parkinson and Simmonds, *The Record and Descriptive Catalogue Dublin International Exhibition* (Dublin, 1853); and J. Sproule (ed.), *Irish Industrial Exhibition of 1853* (Dublin, 1854). For the Irish Vestibule at Sydenham which was part of the Byzantine and Romanesque Court in the Crystal Palace, see M. Digby Wyatt and J. B. Waring, *The Byzantine and Romanesque Court in the Crystal Palace* (London, 1854). Generally at this time, "Byzantine" was often used to refer to Irish Romanesque architecture, and was seen as a link between classical and Gothic periods, which may account for some of the confusion concerning the style of TCD. Finally, concerning the Celtic Revival in Ireland in the 1850s, see Stephan Tschudi Madsen, *Sources of Art Nouveau* (trans. Ragnar Christophersen, New York and Toronto, 1956), pp. 201-221.

39. Plans of the Traveller's Club were published in W. H. Leeds, *The Traveller's Club House* (London, 1839). Plans of the Reform Club were published in *Civil Engineer and Architect's Journal*, III (December 1840), 409.

40. The Murphy manuscript is mentioned in *Crofton Croker Correspondence*, I.143. The manuscript is now in the collection of the Society of Antiquaries in London.

41. Ruskin's "Byzantine" chapter in the *Stones of Venice II* deals largely with St. Mark's, Venice, and was one of the first detailed studies of Byzantine art, which had previously been

considered "a stumbling block and a mystery to all persons, architects, or amateurs, who beheld it." Quoted from *Works of Ruskin*, X, 1-1ii.

42. *Works of Ruskin*, XI, 229n.

43. Deane and Woodward's own comments on the style of the building were also somewhat confused as can be seen from the article in the *Builder* based on information sent from the firm: *Builder*, XII (12 August 1854), 425: "The building is the Venetian form of the Renaissance or Cinque-Cento style. The mouldings and carved work are, however, intended by the architects to be of somewhat earlier character, that is to say, as far as is attainable, Trecento or 'Giottesque.' " (Ruskin's praise of Giotto's tower in *Works of Ruskin*, VII, 187, no doubt strongly influenced Deane and Woodward here.)

44. *Works of Ruskin*, VIII, 258.

45. Ibid., p. 21.

46. Ibid., p. 187.

47. Ibid., p. 106.

48. For alterations of McCurdy's plans see note 20, above.

49. *Works of Ruskin* , VIII, 108.

50. The domes over the central hall are also masked on the exterior by the hipped roof and cannot be seen above the roof line.

51. *Works of Ruskin*, VIII, 134.

52. Ibid., p. 106.

53. Ibid., p. 61.

54. *Builder*, XII (12 August 1854), 425-426. A similar system was devised by Francis Lloyd whose book *Practical Remarks on the Warming and Ventilation and Humidity of Rooms* (London, 1854) was reviewed in the *Builder*, XII (3 June 1854), 288-289.

55. *Works of Ruskin*, VIII, 106.

56. *Building News*, IV (26 June 1857), 662: "The details, however, are bold and effective, and the carvings, which are executed by, and in many instances from designs of, native workmen, are admirable." "Ireland—Its Progress in Architecture," *Builder*, XIV (15 March 1856), 143: the writer noted that the sculpture was "most elaborate, and as yet unique . . . so diverse, so diffuse, so graceful, that the very diversity establishes its beauty."

57. *Works of Ruskin*, VIII, 47-48.

58. Ibid., p. 163.

59. *Works of Ruskin*, X, 146-155.

60. *Works of Ruskin*, VIII, 204.

61. Ibid., p. 163: "Any succession of equal things is agreeable; but to compose is to arrange unequal things, and the first thing to be done in beginning a composition is to determine which is to be the principal thing. . . . Having one large thing and several smaller things, or one principal thing and several inferior things, and bind them well together."

62. Ibid., pp. 66-67.

63. Letter from Sir Thomas Deane to the Rev. Dr. Sadlier, May 4, 1855, MUN/P/2/340,

TCD Library, Dublin. The Cork and Dublin exhibitions did a great deal to encourage the use of Irish marble. Articles on Irish marble appeared in *Builder*, X (31 July 1852), 483; *Builder*, XI (21 May 1853), 323. The publications of George Wilkinson were also important for their information on Irish marbles: G. Wilkinson, *The Practical Geology and Ancient Architecture of Ireland* (London, 1845); and further "On the Marbles of Ireland," *Builder*, III (7 June 1845), 273-274.

64. *Works of Ruskin*, VIII, 66-67.

65. Ibid., p. 45.

66. Letter from Sir Thomas Deane to the Rev. Dr. Sadlier, May 4, 1855, MUN/P/2/340, TCD Library, Dublin.

67. *Works of Ruskin*, VIII, 176.

68. Ibid., p. 80.

69. *Works of Ruskin*, IX, pl. I: "Wall Veil Decoration, Ca'Trevisan and Ca'Dario," pl. II: "Decoration by Discs," pl. XIV: "Spandril Decoration, Ducal Palace."

70. *Works of Ruskin*, VIII, 81.

71. Ibid., p. 184. Ruskin illustrated this type of ornament in the *Stones of Venice I*, "Edge Decoration," in *Works of Ruskin*, IX, pl. IX.

72. *Works of Ruskin*, VIII, pl. VII.

73. Ibid., p. 184. This type of ornament was also illustrated in the *Stones of Venice II*, "Inlaid bands of Murano," Pl. III; "Archivolt in the Duomo of Murano," Pl. V, in *Works of Ruskin*, X.

74. *Works of Ruskin*, VIII, 183. Ruskin distinguishes between "Surface Gothic" and "Linear Gothic" in *Stones of Venice II: Works of Ruskin*, X, 261-266.

75. *Works of Ruskin*, VIII, 183.

76. *Works of Ruskin*, X, 230.

77. *Works of Ruskin*, VIII, pl. V. In 1851 Ruskin published as a supplement to the first volume of the *Stones of Venice*, a separate collection of plates: *Examples of the Architecture of Venice, Selected and Drawn on Measurement from the Edifices*, which included lithographs of capitals from the Ducal Palace, in *Works of Ruskin*, XI, 309-353; "Capitals: Ducal Palace, Venice," *Builder*, IX (27 December 1851), 815.

78. *Builder*, XIV (15 March 1856), 143.

79. *Works of Ruskin*, XI, 200: "In examining the nature of Gothic we concluded that one of the chief elements of power in that and in *all good* architecture, was the acceptance of uncultivated and rude energy in the workmen." See also *Works of Ruskin*, X, 180-269.

80. *Builder*, XII (12 August 1854), 425.

81. The sketchbook of Woodward's mentioned here is one of five in the National Gallery, Dublin (cat. no. 7381).

82. "Workmen's Capitals, Trinity College, Dublin," *Builder*, XIV (29 March 1856), 171.

83. *Works of Ruskin*, X, 215: "For, so soon as the workman is left free to represent what subjects he chooses, he must look to the nature that is round him for material, and will endeavour to represent it as he sees it . . . with much play of fancy, but with small respect for law."

84. Curran, *Studies* (1940), 260. There are further references to the O'Sheas' use of plants from the Botanical Gardens in the Papers of Sir Shane Leslie, TCD Library, Dublin.

85. *Building News*, IV (19 November 1858), 1146.

86. *Works of Ruskin*, VIII, 218.

87. Henry W. Acland and John Ruskin, *The Oxford Museum* (London, 1859), pp. 42-43.

88. *Works of Ruskin*, VIII, 215.

89. *Works of Ruskin*, X, 180-269.

90. This attitude is expressed by Lord Granville in a review of the Dublin Exhibition of 1853 in *Builder*, XI (21 May 1853), 322: "With reference to the imaginative powers exhibited by the Irish . . . in the works of their sculptors and their painters . . . this faculty, directed by a sound art-education, will give us crowds of inventive designers from that country; and that Irish cleverness and English practical working united will be more than a match for all the nations of the earth."

91. *Works of Ruskin*, VIII, 48: "There is no way in which work is more painfully and unwisely lost than in its over delicacy on parts distant from the eye."

92. Ibid., p. 230.

93. *Building News*, IV (19 November 1858), 1146.

94. *Works of Ruskin*, XVIII, 149-150.

95. *Works of Ruskin*, VIII, 21.

96. Ibid., p. 230.

97. Ibid., p. 187.

98. *Works of Ruskin*, VIII, 176.

99. *Dublin Builder*, VIII (15 May 1866), 121.

100. *JRIBA* (9 December 1899), 48.

101. *Dublin Builder*, VIII (15 May 1866), 121.

102. *JRIBA* (9 December 1899), 48.

103. *Dublin Builder*, VIII (15 May 1866), 121.

104. Ibid.

CHAPTER III

1. The principal collection of documents relating to the Oxford Museum are contained in the *Papers of the Oxford University Museum* (UM/M), in the Oxford University Archives. Within this collection material of particular relevance to Deane and Woodward's activity and the building of the Museum is in the "Minutes of the Delegates Meetings 1853-1905," 8 vols. (UM/M/1); "Original Plans" (UM/P/3); "Papers Concerning the Carving Fund" (UM/F/7); "Miscellaneous Files" (UM/F/11). This documentation is, however, incomplete. Gaps in the history of the Museum and the progress of the work are partially filled by the personal accounts and correspondence of various individuals involved. The correspondence of Ruskin, Acland, and others relating to the Museum is contained in the *Acland MSS* in the Bodleian Library, Oxford. Additional material and correspondence was assembled by E. T. Cook and A. Wedderburn in *The Works of Ruskin:*

Library Edition, 39 vols. (London, 1902-1912), and William Rossetti, *Ruskin, Rossetti, and Pre-Raphaelitism* 1854-1861 (London, 1899). Between December 31, 1858, and April 8, 1859, the *Building News* did a series of eight articles on the building in which the controversy over the Museum and the progress of the work were discussed in detail. The most important manifesto on the Oxford Museum is Acland and Ruskin's *The Oxford Museum* (London, 1859). William Tuckwell's *Reminiscences of Oxford* (London, 1901) is another important personal chronicle of events and Oxford personalities. An early history of the Museum was compiled by H. M. and Dorothea Vernon, *A History of the Oxford Museum* (Oxford, 1909). A more recent article is Peter Ferriday's "The Oxford Museum," *Architectural Review*, 1962. Since then, however, little new has been written on the Museum. Because so much of the primary source material contained in contemporary accounts is colored by personal bias, the history of the building has remained controversial. Thus, this study of the Oxford Museum is as much an attempt to unravel the history of the Museum and the roles played by the different personalities involved as it is a strictly art-historical assessment of the building.

2. Quote from *Building News*, VI (21 January 1859), 59.

3. John Summerson, *Victorian Architecture in England; Four Studies in Evaluation*, (New York, 1970), pp. 83, 91.

4. "What are the Gothic Leaders Doing?," *Building News*, V (11 June 1858), 589.

5. *Works of Ruskin*, XVI, xli.

6. "Minutes of the Oxford Museum Committee Meeting," June 6, 1850, *Papers of the Oxford University Museum*, Oxford University Archives. Hereafter cited as *Papers of OUM*. (All material from the Oxford University Archives is consulted, quoted, and otherwise reproduced here by permission of the Keeper of the Archives, University of Oxford.)

7. "Meeting of Convocation," May 1, 1849, *MS. Acland*. d. 95 fol. 71.

8. A hand-written note dated June 19, 1849, added to the "Minutes of Oxford Museum Committee Meeting," June 15, 1849, *Papers of OUM*. "Minutes of Oxford Museum Committee Meeting," June 19, 1849, *Papers of OUM*.

9. *Works of Ruskin*, XIV, xli.

10. "Minutes of Oxford Museum Committee Meeting," February 28, 1853, and "Report of Delegates," February 17, 1853, *Papers of OUM*.

11. *MS. Acland*. d. 95, fol. 73.

12. "Memorial on the (proposed) Oxford University Lecture Rooms, Library, Museums, etc., addressed to Members of Convocation by the Rev. Richard Greswell," May 20, 1853, N.W. 2/1/8, *Papers of OUM*.

13. "Prometheus," May 21, 1853 (Pamphlet arguing against building of Museum—that money is needed for other purposes); "Prometheus Vinctus," n.d. (Pamphlet answering "Prometheus"—that the museum is absolutely necessary); "To Members of Convocation from a Member," n.d. (Pamphlet arguing that fees of pupils should pay for building); "Report of Delegates," May 3, 1854 (regarding purchasing of Parks grounds), *Papers of OUM*.

14. "Report of Delegates," December 7, 1854, N.W./2/1/16, *Papers of OUM*.

15. Ibid.

16. "Report from Referees received by the Committee," November 28, 1854, *Papers of OUM*.

17. *Builder*, XII (2 December 1854), 622. The competition was closely followed in the *Builder*, XII (1854), 388, 562, 606, 622, 631, 641.

18. "Report of Delegates," November 28, 1854, *Papers of OUM*.

19. "Report by George Butler, Secretary Museum Delegacy," December 11, 1854, *Papers of OUM*. E. M. Barry later received a £100 award.

20. George Edmund Street, *An Urgent Plea for the Revival of True Principles of Architecture in the Public Buildings of the University of Oxford* (Oxford and London, 1853). Street presented his proposal as a lecture before it was printed.

21. Ibid., pp. 2, 17.

22. "The Old English Style of Architecture as Applicable to Modern Requirements or, Suggestions for the New Museum at Oxford," *Papers of OUM*.

23. "ΕΡΤΑΤΗΣ," December 11, 1854, N.W.2/1/21, *Papers of OUM*.

24. "Report of Delegates," April 25, 1855, *Papers of OUM*; also *Building News*, V (31 December 1858), 1291.

25. *Building News*, V (22 October 1858), 1054.

26. *MS. Acland*. d. 95, fol. 58.

27. For designs for furnishings see "Original Plans" (UM/P/3), Oxford University Archives; and for carvings see "Carving Fund" (UM/F/7), Oxford University Archives.

28. The manifold problems, intervention of professors, and lack of funds are discussed in Vernon, *A History of the Oxford Museum*, pp. 58-71; and *MS. TOP. OXON*. D. 144.

29. *Building News*, V (31 December 1858), 1291.

30. The proposed alterations and Woodward's response are in: Woodward letter to Vice Chancellor, December 18, 1854, *Papers of OUM*. "Report to Delegates," February 23, 1855, *Papers of OUM*. For site plan see "Original Plans," No. XIV (UM/P/3/8), Oxford University Archives. Woodward Sketchbook: 7387, National Gallery, Dublin. For the drawings and plans showing alterations see "Original Plans" (UM/P/3/1-9), Oxford University Archives.

31. "Report of Delegates," February 23, 1855, *Papers of OUM*.

32. *Building News*, VI (21 January 1859), 59.

33. The Pitt Rivers extension was built by T. N. Deane, 1882-1885. In 1867-1869, T. N. Deane also built the Clarendon Laboratory adjacent to the Oxford Museum on the northwest corner. For contemporary references to the Clarendon Laboratory see *Jacksons Oxford Journal*, 16 October 1869, 14 October 1871; *Oxford Chronicle*, 15 October 1870. For both the Pitt Rivers and Clarendon Laboratory see Sherwood and Pevsner, "Oxfordshire," *The Buildings of England* (Penguin, 1974), pp. 278-282.

34. These alterations can be seen on the plans and drawings in "Original Plans" (UM/P/3/5 + 6), Oxford University Archives.

35. *Building News*, VI (14 January 1859), 29.

36. *Building News*, VI (21 January 1859), 59.

37. S. F. Petit, "The Queen's College, Cork: Archival Sources, 1849-1850," *University*

College, Cork Record, No. 51 (1976), 25-26. In the "Statement of the Requirements of the Oxford University Museum," April 8, 1854, *Papers of OUM*, it was also specified that the curator's residence, chemistry lab, and "such work-rooms or dissecting rooms as may cause offensive exhalations" should be detached from the main pile.

38. The roof of the Chemistry Laboratory is described in *Building News*, VI (18 March 1859), 269.

39. Quoted in *Works of Ruskin*, XVI, xlii.

40. *Building News*, VI (14 January 1859), 29.

41. Acland and Ruskin, *The Oxford Museum*, p. 39. This is also noted by Hersey, *High Victorian Gothic*, p. 193. John Henry Parker published the first volume of T. Hudson Turner's *Some Account of the Domestic Architecture of the Middle Ages*, on the Norman and Early English periods, in Oxford in 1851. He continued the second volume on the Edwardian and Early Decorated periods himself after Turner's death. The second volume was published by Parker (who also published Street's *Urgent Plea*) in 1853.

42. Hersey, *High Victorian Gothic*, p. 192 [197].

43. *Building News*, VI (14 January 1859), 29.

44. *Works of Ruskin*, XI, 230.

45. Ibid., p. 230.

46. Paper for the Oxford Architectural Society, *Ecclesiologist*, XIII (1852), 247-262.

47. G. E. Street, "On the Revival of the Ancient Style in Domestic Architecture," *Ecclesiologist*, XIV (1853), 70-77.

48. Parker, *Some Accounts of the Domestic Architecture of the Middle Ages* (Oxford, 1853).

49. *Works of Ruskin*, XI, 229. Here Ruskin praised Butterfield's All Saints: "It is the first piece of architecture I have seen, built in modern days, which is free from all signs of timidity or incapacity. In general proportion of parts, in refinement and piquancy of mouldings, above all, in force, vitality, and grace of floral ornament, worked in a broad and masculine manner, it challenges fearless comparison with the noblest work of any time. Having done this, we may do anything. . . ."

50. *Building News*, V (31 December 1858), 1291.

51. *Building News*, VI (14 January 1859), 29.

52. Hitchcock, *Early Victorian Architecture*, pp. 576-577, 605, lists books and articles dealing with Continental Gothic, including those by the Ecclesiologists.

53. *Building News*, VI (14 January 1859), 29.

54. *Building News*, V (11 June 1858), 589.

55. *Building News*, V (31 December 1858), 1291.

56. Ibid.

57. For the use of iron in architecture of the 1850s see Stefan Muthesius, "The 'Iron Problem' in the 1850s," *Architectural History*, 13 (1970), 58-63. Quote from *Building News*, VI (8 April 1859), 338.

58. Published in *Ecclesiologist*, XV (1854), 124; *Ecclesiologist*, XVII (1856), 221-222, 333-338.

59. "Report of Delegates," February 23, 1855, *Papers of OUM*.

60. Quoted in Vernon, *A History of the Oxford Museum*, p. 69.

61. *Builder*, XIII (7 July 1855), 318. Woodward's diagram was printed in a pamphlet soliciting subscriptions for shafts and capitals for the main court: "Oxford University Museum," June 1, 1855, *Papers of OUM*.

62. *Building News*, IV (9 January 1857), 34.

63. Vernon, *A History of the Oxford Museum*, p. 70; *Building News*, VI (18 February 1859), 161.

64. "Report of the Museum Delegacy," May 1, 1863, *Papers of OUM*.

65. The relation between the church design and the Museum roof has been discussed by Hersey, *High Victorian Gothic*, p. 182; Richardson, *Gothic Revival Architecture in Ireland*, p. 410; and Muthesius, *Architectural History*, 13 (1970), 59-60.

66. *Works of Ruskin*, VIII, 66-67.

67. Acland and Ruskin, *The Oxford Museum*, pp. 30-31.

68. Eastlake in *The Gothic Revival*, p. 284, objected to the construction of the iron capitals on the grounds that "they appear unnecesary not because they are simply decorative . . . but because they are confessedly *applied* decorations to a feature whose very form is regulated by practical considerations."

69. The phrase "principle of diversity in unity" is from "F.G.S.," "The Oxford University Museum," *Macmillan's Magazine*, V (November 1861—April 1862), 527.

70. Quote from Acland and Ruskin, *The Oxford Museum*, p. 88. Cook and Wedderburn record that Ruskin did designs for six brackets for the roof, though only one of these has survived, *Works of Ruskin*, XIV, xlvi.

71. *MS. Acland*. d. 22, fol. 114-118.

72. *MS. Acland*. d. 71, fol. 71.

73. *Works of Ruskin*, XI, 228.

74. *MS. Acland*. d. 72, fol. 39.

75. *MS. Acland*. d. 72, fol. 44-45.

76. Ibid.

77. *MS. Acland*. d. 72, fol. 41.

78. *MS. Acland*. d. 72, fol. 43.

79. *Works of Ruskin*, XVI, xliii. Cook and Wedderburn maintain that Ruskin and Woodward were brought together by Rossetti, with whom Woodward was already acquainted. This is unlikely since Rossetti has recorded that he met the architect through Ruskin, *cf. MS. TOP. OXON*. D. 144: "I first met him [Woodward] at dinner at Ruskin's, I should think about the end of 1854. I never knew anything of the progress of architecture nowadays, and was quite ignorant of who he was. . . ."

80. See *Works of Ruskin*, XVI, xli-xlvii, li-liii, lxiii-lxxv. Acland and Ruskin, *The Oxford Museum*; Tuckwell, *Reminiscences*, p. 49.

81. *Works of Ruskin*, XVI, xlvi. Furnivall had provoked this response from Ruskin in the following manner, "I met frequently at Mr. Ruskin's, and liked much, a very handsome and

elegant Mr. Woodward, whom Mr. Ruskin treated as the architect of the Oxford Museum, and the designer of its ornamentation. One day I came across a man who knew the firm, and he assured me that Sir Charles [sic] Deane, and not Mr. Woodward, was the real designer of the whole building and decoration always accepting the capitals, etc. that the working mason-carvers did. I told Mr. Ruskin this—and got scolded accordingly."

82. Tuckwell, *Reminiscences*, p. 49.

83. *Works of Ruskin*, XVIII, 150.

84. Tuckwell, *Reminiscences*, p. 48.

85. For references to Woodward and Ruskin staying with the Aclands, see *MS. Acland*. d. 11, fol. 27, 123. For Ruskin's supervision of the work in Woodward's absence, see *Works of Ruskin* XVI, p. xlvi.

86. For Professor Phillips' plan dated November 5, 1858, see "Carving Fund" (UM/F/7/7), Oxford University Archives.

87. See "Carving Fund" (UM/F/7/1), Oxford University Archives; and Vernon, *A History of the Oxford Museum*, p. 85.

88. *Builder*, XVII (18 June 1859), 401: "The carving of the capitals and corbels has been mostly designed and executed by the O'Sheas . . . and their nephew, James Whelland [sic]." (The name of the O'Sheas' nephew was Edward Whellan; James was the first name of one of the O'Sheas, hence the confusion.)

89. Letter from Woodward to William Bell Scott, March 25 [1859], W. C. Trevelyan Papers (WCT 70), University Library Newcastle (By permission of the Trevelyan Family). Hereinafter cited as WCT 70, Newcastle.

90. "Capitals: Ducal Palace, Venice," *Builder*, IX (27 December 1851), 815; "Capital from the Lower arcade of the Doge's Palace, Venice," Pl. V, *Works of Ruskin*, VIII; "Examples of the Architecture of Venice," *Works of Ruskin*, XI, 304-353.

91. "Examples of the Architecture of Venice," *Works of Ruskin*, XI, opp. 318; and "Leafage of the Venetian Capitals," Pl. XX, *Works of Ruskin*, X, 430.

92. Earp and Nicholls' work is discussed in Muthesius, *High Victorian Movement*, pp. 151-159; C. Handley-Read, *Victorian Architecture*, pp. 187-220; C. Handley-Read, "Sculpture in High Victorian Architecture," *The High Victorian Achievement*, 2nd Conference Report, Victorian Society (1964), 22-31.

93. See C. P. Curran, *Newman House and University Church* (Dublin, 1953), pp. 29-56.

94. *Works of Ruskin*, XVI, liii.

95. Diagram elevation of exhibition court in pamphlet: "Oxford University Museum," June 1, 1855, *Papers of OUM*.

96. The drawing (neither signed nor dated) now hangs in the office of the Secretary of the Oxford Museum. The painting, a few square inches of which were executed, is also referred to in *Art Journal* (1858), 62.

97. *Builder*, XVII (18 June 1859), 401.

98. For Pollen see Anne Pollen, *John Hungerford Pollen 1820-1902* (London, 1912). Pollen and Woodward probably met in Dublin in c. 1855 when Woodward was working on TCD and

Pollen on University Church. The former was no doubt strongly influenced by Woodward's employment of his workmen and his ideas on ornament. Though there is no record of Pollen having executed any of the painted work at TCD or the Oxford Museum, he did do a great deal of similar work for the firm in England and Ireland in the later 1850s. For Merton Chapel see Paul Thompson, *William Butterfield*, pp. 234, 422.

99. Some of the showcases and furnishings in the Museum were also designed by Bramwell, see "Original Plans and Drawings" (UM/P/3/24, 29), Oxford University Archives. Woodward may have been influenced here by Street's ideas on furniture design published in *Ecclesiologist*, XIV (1853), 70-77, where he recommended solid, simple, economic design for medievalizing furniture.

100. E. T. Cook, *Life of Ruskin*, 2 vols. (London, 1911), p. 447; Hort, *Memoir of Acland*, p. 223.

101. *MS. Acland*. d. 72, fol. 66.

102. "Statement of the Requirements of the Oxford University Museum and Plan of the Site," April 8, 1854, *Papers of OUM*.

103. *MS. Acland*. d. 72, fol. 66.

104. Quoted in Cook, *The Life of Ruskin*, p. 484.

105. *Works of Ruskin*, XVI, xlv.

106. *MS. Acland*. d. 73, fol. 1.

107. *MS. Acland*. d. 72, fol. 75.

108. *MS. Acland*. d. 72, fol. 79.

109. *MS. Acland*. d. 95, fol. 38.

110. Woodward's studies for the portal and base of the tower are in his private notebook.

111. For Ruskin's letter to Acland regarding the portal, see Acland and Ruskin, *The Oxford Museum*, pp. 44-53. Woolner letter in *MS. Acland*. d. 95, fol. 62. Woolner's original drawing is now in the Ashmolean Museum, Oxford.

112. Amy Woolner, *R. A. Thomas Woolner: His Life in Letters* (London, 1917), p. 194.

113. Quoted in Vernon, *A History of the Oxford Museum*, pp. 84-85. Pollen's drawing now hangs in the office of the Secretary of the Museum.

114. Also noted by Hersey, *High Victorian Gothic*, p. 193.

115. There is a commemorative plaque in the Museum of the debate which took place in June 1860.

116. Pamphlet, *MS. Acland*. d. 95, fol. 81-82. Sherwood and Pevsner, *Oxfordshire*, p. 280, note that Woolner carved the portal from Pollen's design. This is very unlikely. In fact both William and D. G. Rossetti record that O'Shea was responsible for the executed carving; *MS. TOP. OXON*. D. 144: "the decoration designed by Pollen and executed by Woodward's excellently trained workmen the brothers Shea. . . ." Wm. Rossetti, *Ruskin, Rossetti, and Pre-Raphaelitism*, p. 283: "Woolner . . . says that Ruskin at Oxford has compelled a carver he had sent down to discontinue carving a figure by Pollen on the arch at the Oxford Museum, on the ground of its being sensual."

117. *Works of Ruskin*, XIV, xlv.

118. *MS. Acland*. d. 72, fol. 92.

119. *MS. TOP. OXON.* D. 144.

120. For Woodward's request to Rossetti, see William Rossetti, *Ruskin, Rossetti, and Pre-Raphaelitism*, pp. 97, 98. Ruskin approved of Rossetti's decision: "I think you and your pupil have judged very wisely in this matter, and I will so arrange it with Woodward, and let you know his ideas as soon as may be." For Siddal's drawings, see *Works of Ruskin*, XVI, xliv.

121. From William Rossetti, *Ruskin, Rossetti, and Pre-Raphaelitism*, p. 132. References to Morris' and Rossetti's work are also in Georgiana Burne-Jones, *Memorial of Edward Burne-Jones*, 2 vols. (London, 1904), I, 104, and Philip Henderson, *William Morris* (London, 1966), p. 45.

122. Regarding the Hogarth Club, see William Rossetti, *Ruskin, Rossetti, and Pre-Raphaelitism*, p. 216; *Art Journal*, XX (December 1858), 374; ibid., XXII (May 1860), 159; *Building News*, VI (18 February 1859), 154; Letter from Rossetti to Acland, 1855 *MS. Acland.* d. 71, fol. 94: "Woodward was here Sunday and we called on Munro to find him gone to you. I introduced Woodward to Woolner. . . ."

123. For W. C. Trevelyan, see *DNB*, s. v. Trevelyan, Walter Calverley. For Pauline Trevelyan, see Raleigh Trevelyan, *A Pre-Raphaelite Circle* (London, 1977). The friendship between the Trevelyans and Woodward led to future projects. In 1860-1861, Woodward and Lady Trevelyan devised plans for turning the Trevelyan property at Seaton in Devon into a "Venetian Gothic Eden," see Appendix, above.

124. *Builder*, XVII (18 June 1859), 401.

125. Letter from Woodward to Lady Trevelyan, 26 September 1859, WCT 70, Newcastle.

126. *MS. Acland.* d. 72, fol. 75; *Works of Ruskin*, XVI, xlvii.

127. *Works of Ruskin*, XVI, xlvi.

128. Acland and Ruskin, *The Oxford Museum*, p. 44.

129. Ibid., pp. 44-53.

130. Ibid., pp. 48-53.

131. "A Joy Forever," *Works of Ruskin*, XVI, 37-38.

132. *Works of Ruskin*, XVI, xlviii. It would seem that Woodward brought over several Irish workmen aside from the O'Sheas.

133. Letter from O'Shea to Acland, October 14, 1859, *MS. Acland.* d. 95, fol. 42. O'Shea also donated five pounds out of his own pocket to pay for one of the capitals in the Museum.

134. Letter from Ruskin to Miss Heaton quoted in *Works of Ruskin*, XVI, xlvi.

135. *MS. Acland.* d. 95, fol. 38; *MS. Acland.* d. 72, fol. 90.

136. There are many contradictory accounts of O'Shea's dismissal. The story, which has become legendary, is told in Ferriday, "The Oxford Museum," *Architectural Review* (1962), 415-416. Ruskin noted in *Arata Pentelici* that O'Shea's dismissal was due to "the unnecessary introduction of cats," quoted in E. T. Cook, *Life of Ruskin*, p. 157.

137. *MS. Acland.* d. 72, fol. 93.

138. *Works of Ruskin*, XVI, liii.

139. Acland and Ruskin, *The Oxford Museum*, p. 44.

140. Ibid., p. 76.

141. *Works of Ruskin*, XXII, 524.

142. Ibid., p. 523.

143. *MS. TOP. OXON.* D. 144.

144. "Sir Galahad and an Angel," also known as "Alma Mater and Mr. Woodward," V. Surtees, *Paintings and Drawings of Dante Gabriel Rossetti*, 2 vols. (Oxford, 1971), n. 96.

145. The replications of the Oxford Museum are discussed by Hersey, *High Victorian Gothic*, pp. 198-203.

146. *Building News*, VI (14 January 1859), 29.

147. The phrase "informational appliance" comes from Hersey, *High Victorian Gothic*, p. 198. Hersey also notes the influence of the Oxford Museum type on Waterhouse, ibid., p. 203.

148. *Building News*, VI (8 April 1859), 338.

149. Quote from *Ecclesiologist* (1856), 221.

CHAPTER IV

1. *Building News*, V (1 January 1858), 2. For histories of the Union Society see H. A. Morrah, *The Oxford Union 1823-1923* (London, 1923); C. Hollis, *The Oxford Union* (London, 1965).

2. *Building News*, V (1 January 1858), 2; *The Victoria History of the County of Oxford*, III, 59.

3. *Building News*, V (1 January 1858), 2.

4. Hollis, *The Oxford Union*, pp. 94-96.

5. *Illustrated London News* (1863), 348.

6. The bookcases which are now fitted along the lower walls were put in when the new debating hall was built by Waterhouse in 1878 and this room became the Union library.

7. *Victoria History of the County of Oxford*, III, 59-60.

8. *Ecclesiologist*, XIX (1858), 243.

9. The fireplace design was not altogether successful as it tended to smoke, and the soot contributed to the progressive disintegration of the mural paintings.

10. *Illustrated London News* (1863), 348.

11. *Building News*, V (1 January 1858), 2.

12. Stefan Muthesius, *The High Victorian Movement*, p. 165.

13. For Butterfield, see Thompson, *William Butterfield*, passim. For Street's early village schoolhouses, see Hitchcock, "G. E. Street in the 1850s," *JSAH*, XIX (1960), 145-171.

14. *Saturday Review*, IV (26 December 1857), 62; *Building News*, V (1 January 1858), 2; *Ecclesiologist*, XIX (1858), 243.

15. *Works of Ruskin*, XI, 230.

16. *Works of Ruskin*, X, 305.

17. *Works of Ruskin*, VIII, 177-178.

18. Ibid., p. 178.

19. Ibid., p. 183.

20. *Building News*, V (1 January 1858), 2. For Ruskin on "surface deceits," see *Works of Ruskin*, VIII, 70-71.

21. The mural paintings and their history are described by Morrah, *The Oxford Union*; and Hollis, *The Oxford Union*. William Holman Hunt, *Oxford Union Society* (London, 1923), includes photographs of the paintings taken in 1906.

22. *MS. TOP. OXON.* D. 144.

23. Ibid.

24. Mackail, *The Life of William Morris*, 2 vols. (London, 1899), I, 125-127.

25. *MS. TOP. OXON.* D. 144.

26. K. L. Goodwin, "William Morris' 'New and Lighter Design,' " *Morris Society Journal*, II, no. 3 (Winter 1968), 24-31. For Morris' and Burne-Jones' admiration of Pollen's painted roof at Merton Chapel, see Ray Watkinson, *Pre-Raphaelite Art and Design* (London, 1970), p. 196.

27. Patmore, *Saturday Review*, IV (26 December 1857), 62.

28. For process used, see Philip Henderson, *William Morris: His Life, Work, and Friends* (London, 1967), p. 43. (However, when the paintings were recently cleaned in 1975-1976 evidence of a blue ground was found in places.)

29. Mackail, *The Life of William Morris*, I, 127.

30. *Ecclesiologist*, XIX (1858), 243.

31. Ruskin quoted in William Rossetti, *Ruskin, Rossetti, and Pre-Raphaelitism*, p. 193.

32. For the Palace of Westminster frescos, see T.S.R. Boase, *English Art 1800-1870* (London, 1959), pp. 203-222.

33. *Works of Ruskin*, VIII, 185.

34. Patmore, *Saturday Review*, IV (26 December 1857), 62.

35. *Works of Ruskin*, VIII, 185.

36. *Works of Ruskin*, X, 235n.

37. Ibid.

38. For Scott, see D. Cole, "Some Early Works of G. G. Scott," *Architectural Association Journal*, LXVI, 98ff. For Street, see Hitchcock, " G. E. Street in the 1850s," *JSAH*, XIX (1960), 155. In All Saint's, Boyne Hill, 1855, Street painted a large fresco on the east wall.

39. The term "art-architect" was first used by Burges in 1864, cf. *Building News* (1864), 460-462.

40. *Ecclesiologist*, XIX (1858), 232-240.

41. *Builder* (1857), 730.

42. *Building News*, V (1 January 1858), 2.

CHAPTER V

1. *Westminster City Directory*, 1857-1861: "Deane and Woodward, architects," are listed at the address from 1857 to 1860. In 1861 only "Benjamin Woodward, architect," is listed.

2. G. G. Scott, *Personal and Professional Recollections* (London, 1879), pp. 177-192. Other accounts are given in John Summerson, *Victorian Architecture in England*, pp. 79-91; Kenneth

Clark, *The Gothic Revival*, pp. 169-172; Christopher Hussey, "Foreign Office's Threatened Glory," *Country Life* (6 April 1964), 272-275.

3. *Building News*, III (8 May 1857), 441.

4. The premiated designs were illustrated in the *Illustrated London News*, 31 (1857), passim. The competition was also covered thoroughly and the designs listed and reviewed in the *Building News*, III (1857), passim. Regarding the Gothic designs the *Building News*, III (22 May 1857), 501, noted "the small band of Gothic supporters, under the inspiration of Mr. Scott and Mr. Ruskin, exhibit a degree of vigour and ability which has gained attention for them, and which, in many instances, will entitle them to applause."

5. Quote from *Works of Ruskin*, VIII, 21.

6. *Hansard* (164), 535: "men above sixty still love Palladian, men below sixty hate it."

7. "What are the Classicists Doing?," *Building News*, IV (16 July 1858), 714.

8. *Art Journal* (1 August 1857), 253-254.

9. Quoted from *Builder*, XV (16 May 1857), 270.

10. Ruskin quoted in *Building News*, III (12 June 1857), 615.

11. Hitchcock, "G. E. Street in the 1850s," *JSAH*, XIX (1960), 160.

12. For history of the Government Offices see, "The Story of the Government Office," *Builder*, XXXIV (25 August 1877), 852-856; "Her Majesty's Office of Works and Public Buildings," *Builder*, XXXIV (8 September 1877), 897-899; "The New Government Offices," *Builder*, LVII (25 March 1899), 289-291; *Building News*, XLV (24 March 1899), 397-398.

13. No specifications were made concerning style. See "Foreign and War Office, Rules of Designs, guidelines for architects entering in Competition," *Works*: 12/86/1, Public Record Office, Chancery Lane, London. But it was generally felt (not without reason, as it turned out) that the Government would be inclined to favor classical designs. Thus, only 19 of the 218 designs entered in the competition held in the summer of 1857 were Gothic. As suspected, none of the Gothic entries received any of the first awards. However, five Gothic designs were premiated. In the Foreign Office list the Gothic design of G. G. Scott came third, Deane and Woodward fourth, Buxton and Habershon sixth, and G. E. Street seventh. Pritchard and Seddon's design was awarded fourth premium in the War Office competition. A complete list of the 218 entries and commentary were given in *Building News*, III (8 May 1857), 441-443, 445, 447.

14. Hersey, *High Victorian Gothic*, p. 142. The relation between Street's design and the traditional medieval collegiate program has also been pointed out by Hitchcock, in "G. E. Street in the 1850s," *JSAH*, XIX (1960), 161.

15. Woodward Sketchbook: "Government Offices," 7384, National Gallery, Dublin.

16. *Illustrated London News*, 31 (1857), 348; *Builder*, XV (16 May 1857), 270-271.

17. *Builder*, XV (16 May 1857), 270.

18. Ibid.

19. Ibid. "The Foreign Office with residence form an oblong block, with internal courts, and a staircase in the centre. It has three storeys, and a mezzanine in one part, in addition. Windows, with pointed arches, and shafts coupled in the thickness of the wall; a range of windows, circular or multi-foil, in the basement of the War-office; and of square form, with shafts, in the

corresponding position of the Foreign-office; stairs at the angles, which are marked externally by stepped openings, and raking lines in the fronts; high truncated roofs to square portions of the plan; dormers; a recessed porch; the alternate voussoirs of arches marked by darker-colored materials; enriched strings and bands; and generally a profuse application of sculpture in relief— on piers and spandrils—are the prominent characteristics of this design."

20. For a discussion of the influence of Deane and Woodward's Government Offices design on commercial architecture, see Hitchcock, "Victorian Monuments of Commerce," *Architectural Review*, CV (February 1949), 71.

21. *Building News*, III (22 May 1857), 501.

22. Ibid.

23. Like TCD the design is a direct transcription of the monumental, symmetrical, and classicizing formal ideal of the *Seven Lamps*. See *Works of Ruskin*, VIII, 187.

24. Ibid., p. 171: "I believe it properly consists only in a due expression of their subordination, an expression varying according to their place and office."

25. *Works of Ruskin*, VIII, 10.

26. Ruskin quoted in *Building News*, III (12 June 1857), 615.

27. Ibid.

28. *Works of Ruskin*, X, 240.

29. *Works of Ruskin*, VIII, 11.

30. Ibid., pp. 183-184.

31. Ibid., p. 229.

32. Ibid., p. 225.

33. Ibid., p. 230.

34. Woodward's sketch shows the same portion of the facade as Pollen's finished competition elevation and was probably made as a guideline for Pollen, who was responsible for the design itself. There are further sketches for the foliate relief carving at basement level which suggest that this was Woodward's conception.

35. Pollen's finished competition elevation is reproduced in Anne Pollen, *John Hungerford Pollen*, pl. 10. A wood engraving of the design was published in the *Builder*, XV (3 October 1857), 563. Pollen's preliminary study for the same section of the facade sculpture is in the RIBA Drawings Collection, London (RIBA Cat. II, p. 57).

36. It is perhaps for this reason that a reviewer in the *Building News*, III (22 May 1857), 501, called the design "Pre-Raphaelite."

37. *Builder*, XV (16 May 1857), 271.

38. *Building News*, III (12 June 1857), 615.

39. *MS. Acland*. d. 95. fol. 58.

40. *Building News*, IV (16 July 1858), 725.

41. *Building News*, X (23 June 1865), 438-439.

42. Eastlake, *Gothic Revival*, no. 125, p. 92.

43. Board and Committee Minutes of the Crown Life Assurance Company, 1 August 1856.

Archives of the Royal Insurance Group, Broad Street, London. (Hereinafter cited as *Board Minutes*.) I am indebted to H.A.O. Cockerell for directing me to these company records.

44. *Board Minutes*, 14 September 1855.

45. Details of the commission from *Board Minutes*, 8 August 1856. Information regarding the contracts was published in the *Building News*, IV (16 July 1858), 725.

46. *Board Minutes*, 22 August 1856.

47. *Board Minutes*, 14 May 1858.

48. *Building News*, IV (16 July 1858), 725.

49. Ibid.

50. *Building News*, XI (23 June 1865), 438.

51. J. Elmes, *Metropolitan Improvements, or London in the nineteenth century displayed in a series of engravings of the new buildings, improvements, etc. from drawings by T. H. Shepherd* (London, 1827).

52. For the history of nineteenth-century commercial architecture see Hitchcock, "Victorian Monuments of Commerce," *Architectural Review*, CV (February 1949), 63-74; and Nicholas Taylor, *Monuments of Commerce* (London, 1968).

53. Hitchcock, *Architectural Review*, CV (February 1949), 61-70.

54. Quote by Palmerston regarding Scott's design of 1868 for the India Office in Clark, *Gothic Revival*, p. 258.

55. "The New Government Offices," *Illustrated London News*, 31 (1857), 348: "With reference to the prevailing prejudices against Gothic architecture, on the score of certain alleged inconveniences, especially the (supposed necessary) deficiency of light, it should be observed that the windows in their [Deane and Woodward] designs are quite as wide as, if not wider, in clear opening, than those usual in Italian designs; as may be instanced in the windows of the new Museum at Oxford, and the Oxford Union Society's new Debating-room already built."

56. Hitchcock has noted the importance of the Government Offices designs for engendering a pointed-arch Italian Gothic style for commercial work. Hitchcock, *Architectural Review*, CV (February 1949), 71.

57. *Works of Ruskin*, IX, 10.

58. Street, "On the Revival of the Ancient Style in Domestic Architecture," *Ecclesiologist*, XIV (1853), 70-77; *Builder*, X (1853), 140.

59. Scott, *Remarks on Secular and Domestic Architecture Present and Future* (London, 1858), pp. 207-209.

60. Ibid., pp. 195-196.

61. Ibid., p. 205.

62. *Building News*, X (23 June 1865), 439.

63. *Works of Ruskin*, VIII, 50: "It is to be remembered, however, that while the ornaments in every fine building, without exception so far as I am aware, are most delicate at the base, they are often in greater effective *quantity* on the upper parts."

64. The drawing is in the RIBA Drawings Collection (RIBA Cat. II, p. 45). It is also reproduced in Anne Pollen, *John Hungerford Pollen*, pl. 30.

65. *MS. TOP. OXON.* D. 144.

66. *Works of Ruskin*, VIII, 12.

67. *MS. Acland.* d. 95. fol. 63.

68. *Building News*, X (23 June 1865), 438-440.

69. Ibid., p. 439.

70. *Building News*, IV (16 July 1858), 725.

71. There has been some question as to the date of the building. Hitchcock gives the date as 1864-1865 in *Architectural Review*, CV (February 1949), 66; Eastlake gives the date 1861-1862 in *Gothic Revival*, p. 406; the *Builder* noted in 1865 that the building was still under construction when reviewed—"Offices of the Crown Life Assurance Company, Fleet Street, London," *Builder*, XXIII (15 July 1865), 502-503; *Board Minutes*, February 5, 1864, record that T. N. Deane was appointed architect of the new building at that date. Further from the *Board Minutes*, 13 April 1866, the last meeting of the Board of Directors was held in the New Bridge Street Offices. The first meeting in the new premises took place on 20 April 1866.

72. The building is illustrated in *Builder*, XXIII (15 July 1865), 503. A photograph showing part of the building, taken in June 1920 shortly before it was demolished, is in Greater London Council, London.

73. *Builder*, XXIII (15 July 1865), 502.

74. Ibid.

75. *Building News*, XIII (15 March 1867), 186-187.

76. See Hitchcock, *Architectural Review*, CV (1949), 66-74; Nicholas Taylor, *Victorian Monuments of Commerce*, pp. 53-63.

77. Hitchcock, *Architectural Review*, CV (1949), 72, Hitchcock calls the style "Old Irish." For Douglas Richardson's more detailed treatment of the genre see *Gothic Revival Architecture in Ireland*, pp. 381-384, 416-421, 423-425; for later developments in Belfast, pp. 437-448.

78. The mode had been used a few years earlier by Wyatt and G. G. Scott in the design for the India Office of 1860 which is itself an assimilation of Deane and Woodward's TCD and Government Office designs. Scott's drawing of the India Office, in a "Byzantine-Italian" style, was recently discovered in June 1975 in the basement of the National Monuments Record in London and is now in the RIBA Drawings Collection (uncatalogued). The drawing is illustrated in *Architectural Review* (June 1975), 323.

79. Further examples are the undated and anonymous shop front of 4 Merrion Row in Dublin with sculpture also executed by Charles Harrison; W. G. Murray's Gilbey's Office and Warehouse, 45-46 O'Connell Street of 1865, and the shop front of 36 Dawson Street of the late 1860s; T. N. Deane's Premises for J. G. Mooney, Sackville Street of 1872, and his Scottish Widows Assurance Company Offices on Westmoreland Street of 1875.

80. For Harrison, see "Obituary," *Irish Builder*, XLIV (18 June 1903), 1811. Born and trained as a stone carver in Yorkshire, Harrison came to Dublin in the mid-1850s. He was employed by Deane and Woodward from c. 1858 to 1861 and worked on the Kildare Street Club, Kilkenny Castle, and other works by the firm. Harrison succeeded the O'Sheas as the "master carver" in Dublin—working in their manner—when they remained in England after Woodward's

death in 1861. For references to Harrison's works, see "St. Finbarr's Cathedral, Cork," *Irish Builder*, XIII (1 January 1871), 2, 6, 7, 88; "Royal Insurance Office, Dame St.," ibid., XIII (1 February 1871), 31; "English and Scottish Law Life Ass. Assoc., Lower Sackville St.," ibid., XIII (15 February 1871), 40, 44-45; "Hibernian Bank, College Green," ibid., XIII (15 May 1871), 131, 134.

81. The date of this building is also uncertain. Douglas Richardson gives the date 1871 or earlier in *Gothic Revival Architecture in Ireland*, p. 416. See also Irish Builder, XIII (1 May 1871), 112-113; *Architect*, IX (4 January 1873), 8. The *Board Minutes*, 19 December 1856, also record that Deane and Woodward did some alterations to the Company's original premises in Dublin.

82. Quote from *Building News*, XIII (15 March 1867), 186-187.

83. Quote from Ruskin printed in *Building News*, III (12 June 1857), 615.

CHAPTER VI

1. James E. Rodgers (1838-1896), was a pupil of Woodward's who trained with the firm in the 1850s. In the 1860s he practiced independently in Ireland. In 1876 he moved to London and gave up architecture for painting. Rodgers' works of the 1860s in Ireland include Carmichael School of Medicine, New Brunswick St., Dublin: *Dublin Builder*, VI (1 April 1864), 61-62; ibid. (15 October 1864), 208-209; ibid. (1 November 1864), 200; alterations to Cashel Town Hall: *Dublin Builder*, VIII (15 June 1866), 152; Howth Church: *Dublin Builder*, VIII (15 July 1866), 175; St. Patrick's Church, Kilcock: *Irish Builder*, XII (15 February 1870), 82. See also Walter G. Strickland, "James Edwards Rodgers ARHA," *A Dictionary of Irish Artists*, 1913.

2. For the history of the detached house in England, see Hitchcock, "The Development of the Detached House in England and America from 1800-1900," *Architecture: Nineteenth and Twentieth Centuries* (Harmondsworth, 1958), pp. 353-359; Hitchcock, *Early Victorian Architecture*, pp. 23-33, 144, 232.

3. "Statement of the Requirements of the Oxford University Museum," April 8, 1854, *Papers of OUM*. Completion date reported in *Building News*, V (22 October 1858), 1054.

4. "Oxford New Museums," Plan No. XIII Museum house, n.d., Original Plans (UM/P/3/7), Oxford University Archives.

5. For Pugin's smaller houses, see Phoebe Stanton, *Pugin* (London, 1971), pp. 163-166. For a formal discussion of Butterfield's and White's country vicarages, see Muthesius, *The High Victorian Movement*, pp. 66-82.

6. At the same time various proposals were made for re-siting the house. According to the firm's original plan the Curator's house was to be situated on South Parks Road just southeast of the Museum. Objections to the site were raised on the grounds that it was dangerously close to the chemistry laboratory and the unwholesome wall of Wadham College gardens. Consequently in December 1856 Woodward suggested an alternative site northwest of the Museum but this was voted down by the Museum delegates and the original site retained. "Report of Delegates,"

October 20, 1856, December 5, 1856, *Papers of OUM*; "No. XIII Museum House, n.d. (UM/P/3/7), Oxford University Archives.

7. "Report of Delegates," February 6, 1857, *Papers of OUM*.

8. "Museum House, Oxford, Alfred Robinson, 1921," Original Plans (UM/P/2/26), Oxford Univeristy Archives.

9. For Butterfield's parsonages, see Paul Thompson, *William Butterfield*, passim.

10. The original doorway was described in the *Building News*, VI (11 February 1859), 135.

11. *Works of Ruskin*, VIII, 108.

12. G. E. Street, "On the Revival of the Ancient Style in Domestic Architecture," *Ecclesiologist*, XIV (1853), 78.

13. Ibid.

14. For Street's vicarages in the 1850s, see Hitchcock, "G. E. Street in the 1850s," *JSAH*, XIX (1960).

15. The term "muscular" is taken from Eastlake, *Gothic Revival*, p. 319.

16. Quote from *Building News*, VI (11 February 1859), 135.

17. *Works of Ruskin*, VIII, 11.

18. The carving was described in *Building News*, VI (11 February 1859), 135.

19. Hughes, who was created Lord Dinorben in 1831, had inherited the Llys Dulas property from his father, the Rev. Edward Hughes, who had acquired it through marriage in the mid-eighteenth century. The elder Hughes discovered a rich seam of copper on the otherwise barren land. In 1774 he founded the Parys copper mine company and amassed a large fortune with which he purchased additional tracts of land and estates in Anglesey and North Wales including Kinmel Park in Denbighshire. At W. L. Hughes' death in 1852 the family property, save Llys Dulas, was inherited by his nephew Hugh Robert Hughes, who commissioned Nesfield and Shaw to rebuild the house at Kinmel Park in the 1860s and 1870s. Lady Dinorben, who had a long-standing quarrel with H. R. Hughes and with whom she proceeded to engage in a long and bitter legal battle, retired to Llys Dulas where she attempted with little success to dredge the last remnants of copper from the by then exhausted mine. For further information on the Hughes family and Kinmel, see Mark Girouard, "Kinmel Park," *Country Life* (4 September 1969), 542-545; and Girouard, *Victorian Country House* (Oxford, 1971), pp. 137, 183.

20. *Building News*, V (24 September 1858), 948; date given in Eastlake, *Gothic Revival*, no. 139.

21. See Hitchcock, *Architecture: Nineteenth and Twentieth Centuries*, p. 356.

22. Goodhart-Rendel, "The Victorian Home," *Victorian Architecture*, p. 79.

23. *Building News*, V (24 September 1858), 948.

24. In one of the ground floor reception rooms was a carved frieze of birds and flowers attributed to John Hungerford Pollen, who was collaborating with Deane and Woodward on other buildings at this time. I am indebted to Peter Howell and Helen Smith for telling me of Pollen's work at Llys Dulas, which has since disappeared.

25. *Building News*, V (24 September 1858), 948.

26. The O'Sheas were in England at the time, working on the firm's Oxford buildings.

27. Two of the four houses in question—Brownsbarn near Thomastown in County Kilkenny and St. Austin's Abbey in Tullow, County Carlow—were situated in the country and were built by a clerk of the works without the intervention of a contractor. The other two—Glandore in Monkstown and Clontra in Shankill—both just outside Dublin, were carried out by Gilbert Cockburn, the Dublin contractor who also built TCD, St. Anne's Schools, Llys Dulas, and the Kildare Street Club to Deane and Woodward's designs. See *Building News*, V (24 September 1858), 948.

28. Douglas Richardson, *Gothic Revival Architecture in Ireland*, p. 432.

29. C. P. Curran, "Dublin Plaster Work," *JRIAI*, LXX, Part 1.

30. *Building News*, V (24 September 1858), 948. There are also notations in Woodward's private sketchbook concerning the outbuildings at St. Austin's. Woodward Sketchbook: 7382, National Gallery, Dublin.

31. "G. N. Doyne Esq.," MS. 4824, National Library, Dublin.

32. Quoted from Eastlake, *Gothic Revival*, p. 319.

33. A brief discussion of the influence of French Early Gothic architecture in England in the late 1850s and early 1860s is in Muthesius, *The High Victorian Movement*, p. 144ff.

34. Information on the De Vesci family comes mainly from Andrew March, "Time Was," *Irish Times* (19 January 1970). The house is also mentioned in *Building News*, V (24 September 1858), 948.

35. "Proposed House at Monkstown for the Hon. W. J. Vesey, January 25, 1858," MS. 4824, National Library, Dublin.

36. For Lawson, see *DNB*, XI, p. 733.

37. *Dublin Builder*, IV (1 January 1862), 1.

38. *Building News*, V (24 September 1858), 948.

39. Ibid.

40. Mark Girouard, "Clontra, Co. Dublin," *Country Life* (29 May 1975), 1393. See also, R. I. Ross, "Dublin Bay's Little Villas," *Country Life*, CLIX (6 May 1976), 1182-1184; "The Other Dublin," *Architectural Review*, CLVI (November 1974), 325-326.

41. The paintings are dated and illustrated in Anne Pollen, *John Hungerford Pollen*, pls. 16-19.

42. Pollen and Woodward were collaborating at Kilkenny and Blickling in 1860-1861 (see Appendix) and probably devised the Clontra decorations at that time.

43. For Merton College Chapel and Blickling, see Anne Pollen, *John Hungerford Pollen*, pp. 190, 322.

44. *Building News*, V (24 September 1858), 948.

CHAPTER VII

1. "Notes of New Works," *Dublin Builder*, I (1 March 1859), 33, records that work began early in 1859; "The New Kildare Street New Clubhouse," *Dublin Builder*, II (1 July 1860), 292, notes that it was substantially completed in 1860; "The Kildare Street New Club-house," *Dublin*

Builder, III (15 August 1861), 600, gives a description of the interior when it was nearly finished. See also "Local Building News," *Dublin Builder*, I (1 April 1859), 43.

2. George Woods Maunsell, *Kildare Street Club* (Dublin, 1880), p. 3.

3. Ibid.

4. Raymond F. Brooke, *Daly's Club and Kildare Street Club, Dublin* (Dublin, 1930). All books and records of the club were lost in a fire in the club's old premises on November 11, 1860, just before the new building was completed.

5. According to the "Building Account KSC," in the Club's records the final expenditure came to £42,347/0/1. (I am indebted to Col. D. H. Boydell, Secretary of the Kildare Street Club, for this reference.) *Building News*, V (24 September 1858), 948; *Dublin Builder*, III (15 August 1861), 600.

6. *Dublin Builder*, I (1 March 1859), 33.

7. *Dublin Builder*, III (15 August 1861), 600.

8. *Building News*, V (24 September 1858), 948.

9. Dublin Builder, III (15 August 1861), 600.

10. G. E. Street, *An Urgent Plea*, p. 6. Street suggests: "The use of sash windows can be accomplished without sacrifice of reality or beauty . . . by detached shafts . . . whilst they prevent the weakness of effect always consequent upon large undivided window openings, they admit of . . . sash window frames behind, and independent of, the stonework." For Deane and Woodward's design, see *Dublin Builder*, III (15 August 1861), 600. For more concerning the "straight-sided arch," see Summerson, "The London Suburban Villa," *Architectural Review*, CIV (August 1948), 63-74; and Hitchcock, "Victorian Monuments of Commerce," *Architectural Review*, CV (1960), 61-74.

11. *Building News*, VII (20 January 1860), 44.

12. *Ecclesiologist*, XXIII (1862), 335.

13. *Building News*, VII (20 January 1860), 44.

14. Some of the capitals and bases of the ground-floor columns of the central hall were salvaged and are now at Pakenham Hall, Tullynally Castle, County Longford.

15. Richardson, *Gothic Revival Architecture in Ireland*, p. 428.

16. *Building News*, VII (20 January 1860), 44.

17. Ruskin, *Works of Ruskin*, XI, pl. 6.

18. *Dublin Builder*, I (1 November 1859), 144. The identical round-arched portico was also used by G. G. Scott in his design of 1860 in a "Byzantine-Italian" style for the India Office, which also clearly shows the influence of Deane and Woodward's TCD building. See n. 78, Chapter V.

19. *Building News*, VII (20 January 1860), 44.

20. C. P. Curran, *Studies* (1940), pp. 266-267.

21. Raymond McGrath, *Arts in Ireland* (January 1973), 27-29; Peter Harbison, *Irish Times*, July 22, 1976. Seamus Murphy, one of the last of the Dublin "stonies," who died in 1975, also maintained that the carving on the club was by the O'Sheas on the basis of information handed

down to him by word of mouth. (I am indebted to T. F. McNamara, who passed on to me a letter from Murphy concerning the Kildare Street Club carvings.)

22. "English vs. Irish Art Workmen," *Dublin Builder*, III (15 March 1861), 456.

23. *Dublin Builder*, I (1 November 1859), 144.

24. For Deane and Woodward's fountains and the firm of Purdy and Outhwaite, see Appendix.

25. Quote from *Dublin Builder*, I (1 November 1859), 144. Purdy and Outhwaite disappear from the Dublin directories in 1861. They went bankrupt a few months before the work on the club was completed. Harrison established his own business, "C. W. Harrison and Sons, Monumental Sculptors," at 178 Great Brunswick Street in Dublin, which still exists.

26. The O'Sheas were considerable celebrities by this time. It is therefore surprising that their names are not mentioned in connection with the work at the Kildare Street Club in contemporary notices. There is no evidence that they returned to Ireland after their work in Oxford. However, they may well have stepped in when the firm of Purdy and Outhwaite went bankrupt. Furthermore, the style of the carving inside the building suggests that some of this work is theirs.

27. *Dublin Builder*, III (15 August 1860), 600.

28. I am indebted to Peter Harbison for telling me about the sketches and to Mrs. Violet Sparrow, Harrison's granddaughter, for allowing me to photograph and reproduce them.

29. *Building News*, V (24 September 1858), 948.

30. *Ecclesiologist*, XXIII (1862), 335.

31. *Dublin Builder*, III (15 August 1861), 600.

32. Quote from *Ecclesiologist*, XXIII (1862), 335.

33. *MS. TOP. OXON*. D. 144.

34. Tuckwell, *Reminiscences of Oxford*, p. 48.

35. *MS. Acland*. d. 95. fol. 58.

36. Amy Woolner, *Thomas Woolner, R.A.*, p. 156.

37. *MS. TOP. OXON*. D. 144.

38. Letter from Woodward to Ruskin, n.d. [1857-1858], WCT 70, Newcastle.

39. Letter from T. N. Deane to J. Vernon, April 26, 1858, *Papers and Correspondence, Pembroke Estates*, Pembroke Estate Office, Dublin.

40. *MS. Acland*. d. 42. fol. 199.

41. Quotes from Letter from Woodward to Lady Trevelyan, August 28 [1860], WCT, 70, Newcastle.

42. Letter from Woodward to Lady Trevelyan, December 14 [1860], WCT 70, Newcastle.

43. *Art Journal*, XXIII (1861), 312.

44. *Dublin Builder*, III (1 August 1861), 593.

45. *MS. Acland*. d. 13. fol. 49; d. 65. fol. 131-135.

46. *MS. Acland*. d. 13. fol. 49.

47. *MS. Acland*. d. 72. fol. 21.

48. *MS. Acland*. d. 65. fol. 131, 133.

49. *MS. Acland*. d. 65. fol. 133.

50. *MS. Acland*. d. 65. fol. 135.

51. *MS. Acland*. d. 65. fol. 133.

52. *MS. Acland*. d. 65. fol. 135.

53. *Dublin Builder*, III (15 June 1861), 543.

54. Reprinted in *Transactions of the RIBA*, 1861-1862, p. 12.

55. *Art Journal*, XXIII (1861), 312.

56. *Dublin Builder*, III (1 February 1861), 416; ibid., V (1 May 1863), 72; *Builder*, XXIX (14 October 1871), 804.

57. In Dublin, Deane built a number of commercial buildings, notably Globe Insurance Co. office, 1868: *Dublin Builder*, V (15 January 1863), 4; Scottish Provincial Assurance Co., 1868: *Irish Builder*, XVIII (1 January 1867), 4, 5; *Builder*, XXVI (18 April 1868), 279; Munster Bank, 1872-1874: *Builder*, XXX (17 May 1873), 390; *Architect*, XIII (2 January 1875), 8; Scottish Widows Assurance Co., 1875: *Irish Builder*, XL (1 December 1899), 197; J. G. Mooney premises: *Irish Builder* (15 September 1872), 253, 259. In Oxford, aside from the Cowley House extension of 1862, he built the Meadow Buildings at Christ Church, 1864-1866: *Dublin Builder*, III (1 December 1861), 692; *Builder*, XX (29 November 1862), 856-857; ibid., XXIV (12 May 1866), 337, 346-347; Eastlake, *Gothic Revival*, p. 287; other work for Christ Church college; and the Clarendon Laboratory, 1869: *Builder*, XXVII (8 May 1869), 366-367, 369; Eastlake, *Gothic Revival*, p. 128. Deane also entered a design in the Law Courts Competition in 1866: *Building News*, XIV (28 June 1867), 442-443; ibid., XIV (15 March 1867), 186-187. In 1875 he was appointed Superintendent of National Monuments and Inspector of Ancient Monuments in Ireland and did a great deal of restoration work in Ireland. In 1878 he formed a partnership with his son Thomas Manly (1851-1933), who assumed much of the responsibility for the architectural practice from then on. In 1890 he was knighted for service to his country and profession. For T. M. Deane, see *Irish Builder*, XLIII (13 February 1901), 13, 27.

58. *Builder*, XXI (15 October 1862), 283.

59. Pevsner and Sherwood, "Oxfordshire," *Buildings of England*, p. 136.

60. Amy Woolner, *Thomas Woolner, R.A.*, p. 213.

61. C. Handley Read, "Sculpture in High Victorian Architecture," *The High Victorian Achievement*, 2nd conference report, Victorian Society, 1964, pp. 26-27.

62. For T. N. Deane's and the O'Sheas' work at Cowley House, see *Building News*, XII (21 October 1864), 793; *Jacksons Oxford Journal* (15 October 1864), 5; *Victoria History of the Country of Oxford*, III, 349.

63. Anne Pollen, *John Hungerford Pollen*, p. 287.

CONCLUSION

1. For Ruskin's list of the "noble characters" of architecture, see *Works of Ruskin*, VIII, 187.

2. Ruskin deals broadly with proportion, massing, and composition in "The Lamp of Power" in *Works of Ruskin*, VIII, 100-137.

3. Ruskin's definition of "surface Gothic" is in *Works of Ruskin*, X, 261-266.

4. The mode identified by Douglas Richardson as "Hibernian Monumental" is discussed at the end of Chapter V, above. For Richardson's own detailed treatment of the genre, see Douglas Richardson, *The Gothic Revival in Ireland*, pp. 381-384, 416-421, 423-425, 437-448.

5. Germann, *Gothic Revival in Europe and Britain*, p. 34.

APPENDIX

1. *MS. Acland*. d. 95. fol. 58-61, a letter from Woodward to Acland, includes sketches by Woodward for the arcaded windows of the library, the fireplace in the study, and a plan and references to alterations to an unidentified room in the house. The photographs are from the Minn collection in the Bodleian Library, Oxford (*MS. TOP. OXON*. D. 494. fols. 49, 58, 59, 67). The markings, "A," "B," "C," are on the original negatives. Minn identifies them as "A: Library"; "B: North Library"; "C: The Room referred to in fols." Here the "North Library" is referred to as the "Study."

2. E. T. Cook, *Life of Ruskin*, p. 447.

3. *MS. Acland*. d. 42. fol. 199, contains a reference to O'Shea's work on the chimneypieces.

4. *Building News*, VI (25 March 1859), 278. I am indebted to Howard Colvin, St. John's College, Oxford, for information on the history of the house.

5. An innovation deplored by the *Building News*, VI (11 February 1859), 135.

6. Tuckwell, *Reminiscences*, p. 48, also recalled that Mrs. Price had painted her drawing room at the same time. This, too, no longer exists.

7. *MS. Estates*. 413. Cathedral, fol. 189, Christ Church College Library, Oxford.

8. A. C. Sewter, *Morris and Co. Stained Glass* (New Haven and London, 1973), pp. 11-16.

9. S. A. Warner, *Oxford Cathedral* (London, 1924), pp. 95-96; *MS. Estates*. 143. Cathedral, fol. 188, Christ Church College Library, Oxford.

10. For Pollen's work at Blickling, see Geoffrey Fisher and Helen Smith, "John Hungerford Pollen and His Decorative Work at Blickling Hall," *National Trust Yearbook* (1975), 112-119. Pollen's drawings for the Hall decoration are in the RIBA Drawings Collection, London. The bookcases are attributed to Woodward in "Fine Art Gossip," *Atheneum*, no. 1756 (June 22, 1861), 836. Fisher and Smith, who were unaware of this notice when their article went to press, assigned the bookcases to Pollen.

11. For the property distribution of Dublin in the eighteenth and nineteenth centuries, see Maurice Craig, *Dublin 1660-1860* (Dublin, 1969).

12. For Sidney Herbert, first Baron Herbert of Lea (1810-1861), see *DNB*, IX, pp. 663-665. Quote from *The Tourist's Illustrated Hand-book for Ireland* (London, 1859).

13. "Application of Magistrates, Dundrum Sessions House," May 29, 1854, *Papers and Correspondence, Pembroke Estates*, Pembroke Estate Office, Fitzwilliam Place, Dublin. (Hereafter cited as *Pembroke Estate Office*.)

14. *Builder*, XII (22 September 1855), 450; *Building News*, IV (18 September 1857), 990; Papers concerning Dundrum Estates, *Pembroke Estate Office*.

15. Stefan Muthesius, *High Victorian Movement*, pp. 237-238, also relates it to the school-house type but erroneously claims that the courthouse was originally designed as a school.

16. "Schools," *Ecclesiologist*, VII (1847), 1-6. See also M. Seabourne, *The English School: Its Architecture and Organization* (London, 1971).

17. William White, in "Causes and Points of Failure in Modern Design," *Ecclesiologist*, XII (1851), 310-311, also made the same recommendations for schools and related buildings: "In schools and public buildings the want of definite distinctive character and expression is the fault most prevalent; but this is especially the case when any dwelling is attached, or a subordinate office of any kind . . . each chief or main portion of a group of buildings ought in itself to form a distinctive feature . . . if at right angles to each other they should be kept as distinct as possible."

18. William Butterfield, Two model designs for "School Rooms and Master's House," *Instrumenta Ecclesiastica*, II, 53.

19. For Inkpen Schools, see *Ecclesiologist*, XII (1851), 70. The building is also discussed by Hitchcock in "G. E. Street in the 1850s," *JSAH*, XIX (1960), 147, and *Early Victorian Architecture*, pp. 601-602.

20. Papers concerning Dundrum Estates, *Pembroke Estate Office*.

21. Ibid.

22. *Ecclesiologist*, XII (1851), 310: "A school often looks as if it were merely a room attached to a house, instead of the school being the chief feature, which it was necessary to furnish with a master's residence."

23. Entry in Letter Book for 1859, April 4, 1859, pp. 16-17, *Pembroke Estate Office*; S. G. Poyntz, Archdeacon of Dublin, *One Hundred and Fifty Years of Worship, 1824-1974* (Dublin, 1974), 23.

24. For Butterfield's brick schools of the 1850s, see Paul Thompson, *William Butterfield*, passim.

25. *Building News*, IV (18 September 1857), 990. St. Anne's Schools were built for £2000 and the contractors were Messrs. G. Cockburn and Son. The opening of the building is commemorated in a colored glass window over the back door which bears the inscription: "A.D. 1858."

26. With regard to style, the *Ecclesiologist*, XXIII (1862), 335, called it "a simple modification of Italian Pointed," while the *Building News*, IV (18 September 1857), 990, hailed it as "the first adaptation of the Early English style to street architecture."

27. For Molesworth Hall, which was also demolished in 1979, see *Irish Builder*, IX (15 May 1867), 125. In 1866, T. N. Deane was also engaged in designing a facade for the unfinished front of St. Anne's Church on Dawson Street. See *Dublin Builder*, VII (15 July 1866), 185.

28. *Dublin Builder*, III (15 February 1861), 436. I am indebted to Edward McParland for directing me to Patterson's ledger, which has been recently acquired by the National Trust Archive, Dublin. The following information on Patterson is from Nicholas Shaeff, one of the directors of the National Trust Archive: Benjamin Patterson was born c. 1837. In 1854 he was employed in the Valuation Office. He left the Office on July 14, 1855, and joined Deane and Woodward as

bookkeeper, probably working only part-time as he entered TCD in October 1855 as a part-time engineering student. In 1859 he took a Diploma in civil engineering and set up his own practice in January 1860 as "Benjamin Thomas Patterson, L.C.E., Surveyor," at 206 Grand Brunswick Street, Dublin. He continued as Deane and Woodward's bookkeeper until February 1861, when his salary from them was stopped. After Woodward's death Patterson was engaged to wind up the partnership accounts. In one of Woodward's sketchbooks (7382, National Gallery, Dublin), there are notations for "Mr. Gresson's house—wanted immediately" and "Miss Lowry's house—wanted immediately." Addresses for both appear in contemporary Dublin directories: Mr. Gresson at "Glencairn," Sandyford, outside Dublin. The property now belongs to the British Embassy and the house presently on the site was built in 1903 by Boss Croker. There was a small house, possibly by Deane and Woodward, on the site which was demolished at that time. Records of the property were destroyed in a fire at the Embassy in February 1972. (Information from Mr. Eric A. Townsend, administrator of Glencairn and Mr. R. W. Avery, assistant administrator.) Miss Lowry is listed at "Clooneven," Ballybrack. The house still exists but shows no trace of any work by Deane and Woodward.

29. "Arthur Guinness, Esq.," MS. 4824, National Library, Dublin.

30. I am indebted to Desmond Guinness and to Bryan Guinness, Lord Moyne, for this information.

31. Shanganagh Grove was bought by Sir John Galvin, c. 1964, and subsequently demolished by him to make way for a new housing development.

32. For William Stokes (1804-1878), see *DNB*, s.v. Stokes, William. Letter from Stokes to Henry Acland, November 27, 1861, *MS. Acland.* d. 65. fol. 135.

33. "Alterations at Carrickbrack House, Howth," MS. 4824, National Library, Dublin.

34. In Killanin and Duignan, *Ireland* (London, 1967), p. 40, there is a rather curious reference to the house that "Queen Victoria is said to have commissioned it (and never paid) for her 'whipping girl.' " Correspondence, 1855-1856, *Pembroke Estates Office*, Dublin.

35. Quote from Killanin and Duignan, *Ireland*, p. 240.

36. For Shaen, see Margaret J. Shaen, *William Shaen: A Brief Sketch* (London, 1912). For the subsequent history of the building, see W. Gordon Corfield, *The Phillimore Estate, Campden Hill, Kensington* (London, 1961), p. 40; "Northern Kensington," *Survey of London*, XXXVII (London, 1973), p. 64.

37. A. Trystan Edwards, *Good and Bad Manners in Architecture* (London, 1924), p. 138, fig. 31. The house is also listed in Eastlake, *Gothic Revival*, p. 395, who gives the erroneously early date of 1856.

38. "New Drinking Fountains," *Dublin Builder*, III (1 February 1861), 418-419.

39. "Fountain in Beresford Place," *Dublin Builder*, XL (1 June 1898), 83.

40. *Dublin Builder*, III (1 February 1861), 418.

41. This carving was executed by the firm of Purdy and Outwaite and was probably the work of Charles Harrison.

42. For the history of Kilkenny Castle, see Katherine M. Lanigan, *Kilkenny Castle* (Kilkenny, 1975); Killanin and Duignan, *Ireland*, p. 324; Leask, *Irish Castles* (Dublin, 1951), pp. 33, 57.

43. Lanigan, *Kilkenny Castle*, pp. 9, 14.

44. *Dublin Builder*, I (1 August 1859), 103; ibid., III (15 February 1861), 436. T. N. Deane exhibited a drawing of the proposed restoration of Kilkenny at the RHA in 1865; see notice in *Dublin Builder*, VI (15 June 1865), 147. The restorations were finished by 1866 when a notice appeared in *Dublin Builder*, VII (12 October 1866), 672.

45. The plans were recently deposited in the newly established National Trust Archive in Dublin.

46. Harrison's name is firmly associated with the work at Kilkenny, and some of the drawings referred to in Chapter VII relate to some of the carving in the Castle.

47. For references to Pollen's work at Kilkenny, see Curran, *Newman House and University Church*, p. 52; Anne Pollen, *John Hungerford Pollen*, p. 284.

48. For references to Pollen's fireplace design, see Anne Pollen, *John Hungerford Pollen*, p. 248. In the first panel the 3rd Earl is depicted purchasing the Castle from Hugh le Despenser; (2) the Chief Butler offers wine to the king; (3) Richard II acts as godfather to the 3rd Earl's son; (4) armorial bearings of Ormonde; (5) 12th Earl refuses to surrender his sword on entering the Irish House of Lords; (6) 2d Marchioness succors the poor during the great famine; (7) triumphal entry of Duke of Ormonde into Dublin as the first Viceroy after the Restoration.

49. Anne Pollen, *John Hungerford Pollen*, p. 248.

50. For the history of TCD Library, see Anne Crookshank, *The Long Room* (Dublin, 1976); Edward MacParland, "Trinity College Dublin," *Country Life*, CLIX (6 May 1976), 1166-1169.

51. *Board Minutes*, TCD, 15 November 1856, TCD Library, Dublin.

52. For McCurdy's proposal, see *Board Minutes*, TCD, 2 January 1858, TCD Library, Dubin.

53. *Board Minutes*, TCD, 21 December 1857, TCD Library, Dublin.

54. *Board Minutes*, TCD, 2 January 1858, TCD Library, Dublin. There are two watercolor drawings hanging in the Manuscripts Room of the Library at TCD showing the Long Room before and after Deane and Woodward's alterations. These may have been a form of presentation drawing by the firm for the Board of the college.

55. *Board Minutes*, TCD, 17 September 1859, TCD Library, Dublin, includes a note that the work was to be finished by July 1, 1861. Concerning the efforts to have the decision reconsidered, see *Board Minutes*, TCD, 21 January 1860, TCD Library, Dublin.

56. *Board Minutes*, TCD, 8, 9 June 1860, TCD Library, Dublin.

57. The best essay on the history of library design is the chapter on Libraries in Nikolaus Pevsner, *A History of Building Types* (Princeton, 1976), pp. 91-110.

58. Raleigh Trevelyan, "The Trevelyans at Seaton," *Country Life*, CLX (26 May 1977), 1397-1400. I am further obliged to Mr. Trevelyan for directing me to sources on the Trevelyans and Woodward's work at Seaton.

59. Sir Walter Calverley Trevelyan, *DNB*, s.v. Trevelyan, Sir Walter Calverley.

60. Biography of Pauline Trevelyan by Raleigh Trevelyan, *A Pre-Raphaelite Circle* (London, 1977).

61. Lady Trevelyan's friendship with Woodward, a much less well-known fact, has recently been brought to light by Raleigh Trevelyan.

62. Quote from Raleigh Trevelyan, *Country Life*, CLXI (26 May 1977), 1397.

63. *DNB*, s.v. Trevelyan, Sir Walter Calverley; Raleigh Trevelyan, *Country Life*, CLXI (26 May 1977), 1397.

64. Ibid.

65. Ibid.

66. Ibid. The date is also inscribed on the front of the building. Raleigh Trevelyan notes: "Obviously the building, if not Woodward's creation, was inspired by his work."

67. Ibid.

68. For a brief account of the suburban housing of the Land Societies and Artisans, Laborers and General Dwellings Company in London, see John Summerson, "The London Suburban Villa," *Architectural Review*, CIV (August 1948), 63-74.

69. Letter from Woodward to Lady Trevelyan, August 13 [1860], WCT 70, Newcastle.

70. Letter from Woodward to Lady Trevelyan, n.d. [September 1860], WCT 70, Newcastle.

71. *MS. 4824*, National Library, Dublin.

72. The best general essay on Victorian suburban housing is John Summerson, "The London Suburban Villa," *Architectural Review*, CIV (August 1948), 63-74.

73. Letter from Woodward to Lady Trevelyan, n.d. [September 1860], WCT 70, Newcastle.

74. Ibid.

75. Quotes from *Works of Ruskin*, VIII, 161.

76. Letter from Woodward to Sir Walter Trevelyan, September 3, 1860, WCT 70, Newcastle.

77. Letters from Woodward to Lady Trevelyan, n.d. [September 1860], and September 20 [1860], WCT 70, Newcastle. These letters contain several references to the cross but do not state its location. This, however, has been established by Raleigh Trevelyan. Woodward's sketches for the cross have not survived. It was erected in 1860 but the carving was never executed. Woodward communicated some of his ideas regarding the work to Lady Trevelyan. In a letter of September 1860 he suggested that he was considering ancient Irish churchyard crosses as prototypes. Concerning its execution he wrote, "I should have it carved by your Somersetshire man, but everything to be carved upon it should be settled by others, and nothing without definite meaning." We can see here that Woodward's well-known practice of allowing the workmen creative independence was not indiscriminate. It would seem that this freedom was only really accorded the O'Sheas and Charles Harrison, of whose competence he felt assured. During the same period the Trevelyans began discussing plans for building a church opposite the old manor house in Seaton. Woodward was consulted and replied in a letter of September 1860 to Lady Trevelyan:

> Have you a nice old church there? I hope you will not build a new one—I think there is a great deal too much new church building—my way would be to add space to the old (or rebuild of larger size even) and add curates to the rector (instead of multiplying rectors) and let them fill the empty stalls and sing in them on Sundays—Do you approve?

Woodward's attitude to church building is singular among Victorian Gothicists and perhaps explains why he never designed a church. Equally surprising is his attitude to restoration—so at variance with that of Ruskin, Morris, and other of Woodward's associates. As it turned out no further plans were made for building a new church in Seaton. Instead Trevelyan initiated an extensive program of restorations to the old village church which were carried out in the late 1860s by Edward Ashworth to disastrous effect.

78. Letter from Woodward to Lady Trevelyan, December 14 [1860], WCT 70, Newcastle.

79. Trevelyan, *Country Life*, CLXI (26 May 1977), 1400, claims that Calverley Lodge was executed "without doubt from Woodward's designs."

SELECTED BIBLIOGRAPHY

Tangential Bibliography is cited in the pertinent footnotes.

Manuscript Sources

Archives, Royal Insurance Group, Bread Street, London. Crown Life Assurance Company Board and Committee Minutes, 1855-1859.

Bodleian Library, Oxford. Acland Manuscripts. *MS. Acland.*

Bodleian Library, Oxford. *MS. TOP. OXON.* D. 144. Letters from D. G. Rossetti to Alexander Gilchrist, June 1861.

Christ Church College Library, Oxford College Muniments and *Estates MS.*

City Library, Cork. Thomas Crofton Croker Correspondence.

Companies House, Old Street, London. Crown Life Assurance Company Records. File 6854.

National Gallery, Dublin. Cat. Nos. 7381, 7384, 7385, 7386, 7387. Benjamin Woodward, Sketchbooks.

National Library, Dublin. MS. 4824. 24 Architectural Drawings of Residences in Dublin and Elsewhere in Ireland Designed by Messrs. Deane and Woodward, c. 1858.

National Trust Archive, Dublin. Benjamin Patterson, Ledger, 1860-1865.

National Trust Archive, Dublin. Kilkenny Castle Survey Plans and Proposals for Alterations.

Oxford University Archives, Oxford. UM/M. Papers of the Oxford University Museum.

Pembroke Estate Office, Dublin. Papers and Correspondence Concerning the Pembroke Estates.

Public Record Office, Chancery Lane, London. Works: 12/86/1. Foreign and War Office, Rules of Designs, Guidelines for Architects Entering in Competition.

Royal Irish Academy, Dublin. Exhibition Catalogues. Royal Hibernian Academy.

Royal Irish Academy, Dublin. RIA MS. 3.B.59. Benjamin Woodward, measured drawings of Holy Cross Abbey, Co. Tipperary.

Trinity College Library, Dublin. MS. 5203. A collection of 45 sheets of architectural drawings for a Museum, by Frederick Darley.

Trinity College Library, Dublin. MUN/MC/99/3. Plans and Sections for a Museum by John McCurdy.

Trinity College Library, Dublin. MUN/P/2. Trinity College Muniments.

SELECTED BIBLIOGRAPHY

Trinity College Library, Dublin. Register and Minute Books, Trinity College, 1851-1856.
University Library Newcastle-upon-Tyne. WCT 70. Trevelyan Papers.

PRINTED SOURCES

Acland, Henry, and Ruskin, John. *The Oxford Museum.* London, 1859.

Architect. London, 1869-1926.

Architectural Publications Society. *Dictionary of Architecture.* 9 vols. London, 1853-1892.

The Architecture of Ireland in Drawings and Paintings. Exhibition Catalogue. National Gallery of Ireland, Dublin, 1975.

Art Journal. London, 1849-1912.

Aslin, Elizabeth. *Nineteenth Century English Furniture.* New York, 1962.

————. *The Aesthetic Movement: Prelude to Art Nouveau.* New York and Washington, 1969.

Atheneum. London, 1828-1921.

Beckett, James C. *The Making of Modern Ireland 1603-1923.* London, 1952.

Bell, Malcolm. *Sir Edward Burne-Jones: A Record and Review.* London, 1898.

Bence-Jones, Mark. "A City of Vanished Waterways, Cork I," *Country Life,* CXLII (3 August 1967), 250-253.

————. "Boom Town of the Napoleonic Wars, Cork Harbour II," *Country Life,* CLVII (29 May 1975), 1421-1422.

————. "Two Pairs of Architect Brothers, Cork II," *Country Life,* CXLII (10 August 1967), 306-309.

Betjeman, John. *First and Last Loves.* London, 1952.

Blau, Eve Marion, "The Architecture of Deane and Woodward, 1845-1861," Yale University, Ph.D. dissertation, 1978.

————. "The Earliest Work of Deane and Woodward," *Architectura.* 2/1979, 170-192.

Board of Public Works, Ireland. Reports to Commissioners of Public Works. *Parliamentary Papers.* Annually from 1845.

Boase, T.S.R. *English Art, 1800-1870.* London, 1959.

Brandon, R. A., and Brandon, J. R. *Open Timber Roofs in the Middle Ages.* London, 1849.

Briggs, Asa. *Victorian Cities.* Harmondsworth, 1968.

Brooke, Raymond F. *Daly's Club and Kildare Street Club, Dublin.* Dublin, 1930.

Brunicardi, Niall. *Hawlbowline, Spike, and Rocky Islands in Cork Harbour.* Cork, 1968.

Builder. London, 1842—.

Building News. London, 1855-1926.

SELECTED BIBLIOGRAPHY

Burdett, H. C. *Hospitals and Asylums of the World*. London, 1891-1893.

Cavanagh, Michael. *Waterford Celebrities*. Cork, n.d. (c. 1900).

Civil Engineer and Architects Journal. London, 1837-1867.

Clark, Kenneth. *The Gothic Revival*. 1928; reprint Harmondsworth, 1962.

Clarke, Joseph. *Schools and School Houses*. London, 1852.

Cole, D. "Some Early Works of G. G. Scott." *Architectural Association Journal*, LXVI, 98ff.

C(oleman), J(ames). "Sir Thomas Deane, P.R.H.A." *Journal of the Cork Historical and Archaeological Society*. 2nd ser., XXI (1915), 180-186.

Colling, J. K. *Gothic Ornaments*. 2 vols. London, 1848-1853.

Colvin, H. M. *Biographical Dictionary of English Architects 1660-1840*. London, 1954.

Cook, E. T. *The Life of John Ruskin*. 2 vols. London, 1911.

———— and Wedderburn, Alexander (eds.). *The Works of John Ruskin*. 39 vols. London, 1903-1912.

Connolly, John. *The Construction and Government of Lunatic Asylums and Hospitals for the Insane (with Plans)*. London, 1847.

Corfield, W. Gordon. *The Phillimore Estate, Campden Hill, Kensington*. London, 1961.

Craig, Maurice. *Dublin: 1660-1860*. Dublin, 1969.

———— and Knight of Glin. *Ireland Observed*. Cork, 1970.

Croker, Thomas Crofton. *Songs of Ireland*. London, 1837.

Crone, John S. *A Concise Dictionary of Irish Biography*. Dublin, 1928.

Crook, J. M. *The British Museum*. Harmondsworth, 1972.

————. "The Pre-Victorian Architect: Professionalism and Patronage." *Architectural History*, 12 (1969), 62ff.

Crookshank, Anne. *The Long Room*. Dublin, 1976.

Curran, C. P. "Benjamin Woodward, Ruskin and the O'Sheas." *Studies*, XXIX (June 1940), 255-268.

————. "Dublin Plasterwork." *Journal of Royal Society of Architects of Ireland*, LXX, Part 1.

————. *Newman House and University Church*. Dublin, 1953.

D'Alton, E. A. *History of Ireland*, vol. V, 1782-1879. London, n.d.

Daubeny, C.G.B. *A Dream of the New Museum*. Oxford, 1855.

Dictionary of National Biography. London, c. 1885.

Dixon, Roger, and Muthesius, Stefan, *Victorian Architecture*. New York, 1978.

Dublin Builder. Dublin, 1859-1869.

Eastlake, Charles. *A History of the Gothic Revival*. London, 1872.

Ecclesiological Society. *Instrumenta Ecclesiastica*. London, 1847—. Second ser. 1856—.

Ecclesiologist. Cambridge, 1841-1845; London, 1846-1868.

Edwards, A. Trystan. *Good and Bad Manners in Architecture.* London, 1924.

Elmes, R. M., and Hewson, M. *Catalogue of Irish Topographical Prints and Original Drawings.* Dublin, 1975.

Ferrey, Benjamin. *Recollections of A. N. Welby Pugin.* London, 1861.

Ferriday, Peter. "The Oxford Museum." *Architectural Review* CXXXII (December 1962), 409-416.

———— (ed.). *Victorian Architecture.* London, 1963.

F.G.S. "The Oxford University Museum." *Macmillan's Magazine*, V (November 1861—April 1862), 527.

Fisher, G., and Smith, H. "John Hungerford Pollen and his Decorative Work at Blickling Hall." *National Trust Yearbook* (1975), 112-119.

Fowler, W. Warde. *The Museum and the Park: A Letter to the Rev. The Vice-Chancellor.* Oxford, 1901.

Fredeman, W. E. *Pre-Raphaelitism. A Bibliocritical Study.* Cambridge, Mass., 1965.

Fulton, H. *Remarks on Irish Collegiate Architecture.* Dublin, 1837.

Garrigan, Kristine Ottesen. *Ruskin on Architecture: His Thought and Influence.* Madison, 1973.

Germann, Georg. *Gothic Revival in Europe and Britain: Sources, Influences and Ideas* (trans. Gerald Onn). London, 1972.

Girouard, Mark. "Clontra, County Dublin." *Country Life*, CLVIII (29 May 1975), 1393.

————. "Kinmel Park." *Country Life*, CLII (4 September 1969), 542-545.

————. *The Victorian Country House.* Oxford, 1971.

Goodwin, K. L. "William Morris' 'New and Lighter Design.' " *Morris Society Journal*, II, No. 3 (Winter 1968), 24-31.

Goodhart-Rendel, H. S. *English Architecture Since the Regency.* London, 1953.

Great Exhibition of the Works of Industry of All Nations in London, 1851. *Official Descriptive and Illustrated Catalogue*, 3 vols. London, 1851.

Greater London Council. *Survey of London.* London, 1900—.

Green, J. F. "James and George Richard Pain." *Journal of the Architectural Association of Ireland* (Dublin, 1965), pp. 4-10.

Greswell, Richard. *Memorial on the (proposed) Oxford University Lecture Rooms, Library, Museums, etc.* Oxford, 1853.

Guinness, Desmond. *Portrait of Dublin.* New York, 1967.

Gwilt, J. *An Encyclopedia of Architecture.* New ed. revised by Wyatt Papworth. London, 1867.

Gwynn, Denis. "The College's First Year." *University College, Cork Record*, No. 12 (1951), pp. 2-27.

SELECTED BIBLIOGRAPHY

———. "James Roche: Father of Queen's College Cork." *University College, Cork Record*. No. 13 (1948), pp. 18-29.

———. "The Munster College Petitions in 1838." *University College, Cork Record*. No. 11 (1947), pp. 32-41.

———. "Sir Thomas Deane and the College Buildings." *University College, Cork Record* (Easter 1950), 26-30; (Summer 1950), 25-31.

———. "Sir Thomas Wyse and the Cork College." *University College, Cork Record*. No. 16 (1949), pp. 21-29.

Hamlin, A.D.F. *History of Ornament*. New York, c. 1916-1923.

Handley-Read, C. "Sculpture in High Victorian Architecture." *The High Victorian Achievement*. 2nd conference report, Victorian Society 1964, pp. 26-27.

Harcourt, A. Vernon. *The Oxford Museum and Its Founders*. Reprinted from the *Cornhill Magazine*. London, 1910.

Hatton, Richard George. *A Handbook of Plant and Floral Ornament*. New York, 1960.

Healy, John. *Maynooth College: Its Centenary History*. Dublin, 1895.

Henderson, Philip. *William Morris: His Life, Work, and Friends*. London, 1967.

Herbert, Robert L. (ed.). *The Art Criticism of John Ruskin*. New York, 1964.

Hersey, G. L. *High Victorian Gothic: A Study in Associationism*. Baltimore, 1972.

Hewison, Robert, *Ruskin and Venice*. London, 1978.

Hill, Birkbeck (ed.). *Letters of Dante Gabriel Rossetti to William Allingham*. London, 1897.

Hill, Henry H. "Cork Architecture." *Journal of Cork Historical and Archaeological Society*, XLIV (1939), 89-93.

Hiscock, W. G. *A Christ Church Miscellany*. Oxford, 1946.

Hitchcock, H. R. *Architecture: Nineteenth and Twentieth Centuries*. Harmondsworth, 1958.

———. *Early Victorian Architecture in Britain*. New Haven, 1954.

———. "G. E. Street in the 1850's." *JSAH*, XIX (1960), 145-171.

———. "High Victorian Architecture." *Victorian Studies*, I (1957), 47-71.

———. "Victorian Monuments of Commerce." *Architectural Review*, CV (February 1949), 61-74.

Hollis, C. *The Oxford Union*. London, 1965.

Houghton, Walter E. *The Victorian Frame of Mind 1830-1870*. New Haven, 1957.

Hussey, Christopher. "Foreign Office's Threatened Glory." *Country Life* (6 April 1964), 272-275.

Illustrated London News. London, 1943—.

Irish Builder. Dublin, 1869—.

Jamieson, John. *The History of the Royal Belfast Academical Institution, 1810-1860*. Belfast, 1959.

SELECTED BIBLIOGRAPHY

Jones, Owen. *The Grammar of Ornament.* London, 1856.

Jordan, Robert Furneaux. *Victorian Architecture.* Harmondsworth, 1966.

Journal of the Royal Institute of British Architects. London, 1842—.

Journal of the Royal Society of Antiquaries of Ireland. Dublin, 1850—.

Kaye, B. *The Development of the Architectural Profession in Britain.* London, 1960.

Kerr, Robert. "Ruskin and Emotional Architecture." *Journal of the Royal Institute of British Architects.* 3rd ser. 7 (1899-1900), 181-188.

Killanin, Lord, and Duignan, Michael V. *The Shell Guide to Ireland.* London, 1967.

Lancaster, Osbert. "The Seventh City of Christendom." *Cornhill Magazine*, 161 (May 1944), 7-14.

Lanigan, K. M. *Kilkenny Castle.* Kilkenny, 1975.

Lang, S. "The Principles of the Gothic Revival in England." *JSAH*, XXV (1966), 240-267.

Leask, H. G. "Pugin In Ireland." *The Irish Times*, 26 July 1963.

Leeds, E. T. *Celtic Ornament in the British Isles Down to A.D. 700.* Oxford, 1933.

Leeds, W. H. *The Traveller's Club House.* London, 1839.

Leon, Derrick. *Ruskin the Great Victorian.* London, 1949.

Lewis, Samuel. *A Topographical Dictionary of Ireland.* 2 vols. London, 1837.

McDowell, Robert Brandan (ed.). *Social Life in Ireland 1800-45.* Dublin, 1957.

McGrath, Raymond. *Arts in Ireland.* (January 1973), 27-29.

Mackail, J. W. *The Life of William Morris.* 2 vols. London, 1899.

Macleod, Robert. *Style and Society: Architectural Ideology in Britain 1835-1914.* London, 1971.

MacNamara, T. F. "The Architecture of Cork, 1700-1900." *Yearbook of the Royal Institute of the Architects of Ireland.* Dublin, 1960, 15-39.

MacParland, Edward. "Trinity College Dublin." *Country Life*, CLIX (6 May 1976), 1166-1169; (13 May 1976), 1242-1245; (20 May 1976), 1312-1313.

Madsen, S. T. *Sources of Art Nouveau.* Trans. R. Christophersen. New York and Toronto, 1956.

Maguire, J. F. *The Industrial Movement in Ireland, As Illustrated by the National Exhibition of 1852.* Cork, 1853.

Mansergh, Nicolas. *The Irish Question 1840-1921.* Rev. ed. London, 1965.

Maunsell, G. W. *Kildare Street Club.* Dublin, 1880.

Maxwell, Constantia. *A History of Trinity College, Dublin, 1591-1892.* Dublin, 1946.

Meehan, Denis. *Window on Maynooth.* Dublin, 1949.

Moody, T. W., and Beckett, T. C. *Queen's Belfast, 1845-1949: The History of a University.* 2 vols. London, 1959.

Morrah, H. A. *The Oxford Union 1823-1923.* London, 1923.

Murphy, Seamus. *Stone Mad.* London, 1966.

SELECTED BIBLIOGRAPHY

Muthesius, Stefan. *The High Victorian Movement in Architecture 1850-1870*. London, 1972.

————. "The 'Iron Problem' in the 1850s." *Architectural History*, 13 (1970), 58-63.

Neale, J. P. *Views of Seats of Noblemen and Gentlemen in England, Wales, Scotland, and Ireland*. 1st ser. 6 vols. London, 1822-1823.

O'Donoghue, D. J. *The Geographical Distribution of Irish Ability*. Dublin, 1906.

O'Donovan, Diarmuid. "John Hogan, The Irish Sculptor." *Festival of Cork Souvenir Program* (11 May 1958), 41-45.

O'Hart, John. *Irish Pedigrees*. London, 1849-1861.

Parkinson, P., and Simmonds, P. L. *The Record and Descriptive Catalogue, Dublin International Exhibition 1865*. London, 1866.

Patmore, Coventry. "Walls and Wall Paintings at Oxford." *Saturday Review*, IV (26 December 1857), 62.

Pender, Seamus (ed.). *A Census of Ireland Circa 1659*. Dublin, 1939.

Petit, S. F. "The Queen's College, Cork: Archival Sources, 1849-50." *University College, Cork Record*, No. 51 (1976), 25-26.

Pevsner, Nikolaus. "Art Furniture of the 1870s." *Architectural Review*, III (1952), 43-50.

————. *A History of Building Types*. Princeton, 1976.

————. *Pioneers of Modern Design*. Middlesex, 1960.

————. *Ruskin and Viollet-le-Duc: Englishness and Frenchness in the Appreciation of Gothic Architecture*. London, 1969.

————. *Some Architectural Writers of the Nineteenth Century*. Oxford, 1972.

————. *Studies in Architecture and Design*. London, 1968.

Physick, J., and Darby, M. *Marble Halls*. Exhibition Catalogue, Victoria and Albert Museum, 1973.

Pollen, Anne. *John Hungerford Pollen 1820-1902*. London, 1912.

Poyntz, S. G. *One Hundred and Fifty Years of Worship 1824-1974*. Dublin, 1974.

Pugin, A. C. *Specimens of Gothic Architecture*. London, 1831.

Pugin, A.W.N. *An Apology for the Revival of Christian Architecture*. London, 1841.

————. *Contrasts or, A Parallel Between the Noble Edifices of the Fourteenth and Fifteenth Centuries, and Similar Buildings of the Present Day*. London, 1841.

————. *The Present State of Ecclesiastical Architecture in England*. London, 1843.

————. *The True Principles of Pointed or Christian Architecture*. London, 1841.

Richardson, Douglas. *Gothic Revival Architecture in Ireland*. New York, 1978.

Rosenberg, J. D. *The Darkening Glass, or Portrait of Ruskin's Genius*. Cambridge, Mass., 1963.

Ross, R. I. "Dublin Bay's Little Villas." *Country Life*, CLIX (6 May 1976), 1182-1184.

————. "The Other Dublin." *Architectural Review*, CLVI (November 1974), 325-326.

Rossetti, William. *Ruskin, Rossetti, and Pre-Raphaelitism: Papers 1854-1862*. London, 1899.

Saint, Andrew. *Richard Norman Shaw*. New Haven and London, 1976.

Scott, G. G. *Personal and Professional Recollections*. London, 1879.

———. *Remarks on Secular and Domestic Architecture Present and Future*. London, 1858.

Seaborne, Malcolm. *The English School, Its Architecture and Organization*. London, 1971.

Sewter. A. C. *Morris & Co. Stained Glass*. New Haven, 1973.

Shaen, Margaret J. *William Shaen: A Brief Sketch*. London, 1912.

Sherwood, P., and Pevsner, N. *Oxfordshire, the Buildings of England*. Middlesex, 1974.

Sproule, J. (ed.). *Irish Industrial Exhibition of 1853*. Dublin, 1854.

Stanton, Phoebe. *Pugin*. London, 1971.

Steegman, John. *Victorian Taste: A Study of the Arts and Architecture from 1830-1870*. Cambridge, Mass., 1971.

Stirling, A. M. *A Painter of Dreams*. London, 1916.

Street, A. E. *Memoir of George Edmund Street*. London, 1888.

Street. G. E. *An Urgent Plea for the Revival of True Principles of Architecture in the Public Buildings of the University of Oxford*. Oxford and London, 1853.

———. *Brick and Marble in the Middle Ages: Notes of a Tour in the North of Italy*. London, 1855.

———. *Some Account of Gothic Architecture in Spain*. London, 1865.

Strickland, Walter G. *A Dictionary of Irish Artists*. Dublin, 1913.

Summerson, John. *Architecture in Britain 1530-1830*. Harmondsworth, 1953.

———, et al. *Concerning Architecture*. London, 1968.

———. *Heavenly Mansions*. New York, 1963.

———. "The London Suburban Villa." *Architectural Review*, CIV (August 1948), 63-74.

———. *Victorian Architecture; Four Studies in Evaluation*. New York, 1970.

Taylor, Nicholas. *Monuments of Commerce*. London, 1968.

Thompson, John D. and Goldin, Grace. *The Hospital*. New Haven, 1975.

Thompson, Paul. *William Butterfield*. London, 1971.

———. *The Work of William Morris*. London, 1967.

The Tourist's Illustrated Hand-book for Ireland. London, 1859.

Trevelyan, Raleigh. *A Pre-Raphaelite Circle*. London, 1977.

———. "The Trevelyans at Seaton." *Country Life*, CLXI (26 May 1977), 1397-1400.

Tuckey, Francis H. *The County and City of Cork Remembrancer—Or Annals of the County and City of Cork*. Cork, 1837.

SELECTED BIBLIOGRAPHY

Tuckwell, William. *Reminiscences of Oxford*. London, 1901.

Turner, T. Hudson. *Some Account of the Domestic Architecture of the Middle Ages*. Oxford, 1851-1853.

Unrau, John. *Looking at Architecture with Ruskin*. Toronto and Buffalo, 1978.

Vernon, H. M., and Dorothea K. *A History of the Oxford Museum*. Oxford, 1909.

The Victoria History of the County of Oxford. Vol. III. London, 1939—.

Warner, S. A. *Oxford Cathedral*. London, 1924.

Watkinson, Raymond. *Pre-Raphaelite Art and Design*. London, 1970.

Webb, Alfred. *A Compendium of Irish Biography*. Dublin, 1878.

Wheeler, Henry, et al. *Architectural Conservation, An Irish Viewpoint*. Dublin, 1975.

White, Grove. "Historical and Topographical Notes of Mallow, Buttevent, Doneraile and Castletownroche." *JCHAS* (1905-1917).

Wilkinson, George. *The Practical Geology and Ancient Architecture of Ireland*. London, 1845.

Woodward, E. L. *The Age of Reform 1815-1870*. Oxford, 1938.

Woolner, Amy. *Thomas Woolner, R.A. His Life in Letters*. London, 1917.

Wyatt, M. D., and Waring, J. P. *The Byzantine and Romanesque Court in the Crystal Palace*. London, 1854.

————. *Specimens of the Geometrical Mosaic of the Middle Ages*. London, 1848.

INDEX

INDEX

[216]

ILLUSTRATIONS

2. Benjamin Woodward (1816-1861).

1. Sir Thomas Deane (1792-1871).

3. Thomas Newenham Deane (1828-1899).

4.   Queen's College, Cork. Anonymous lithograph, c. 1850.

5.   Queen's College, Cork. College Quadrangle from southeast.

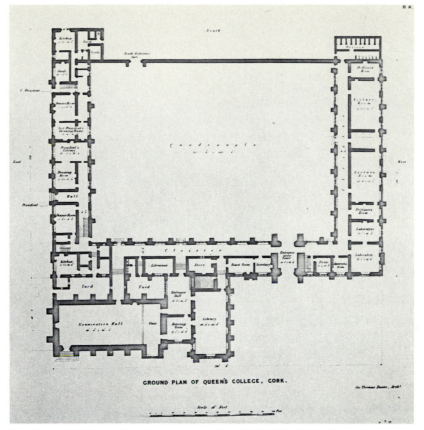

GROUND PLAN OF QUEEN'S COLLEGE, CORK.

6. Queen's College, Cork. Ground plan. Board of Public Works Ireland,
   Sixteenth Report (1848), p. 532.

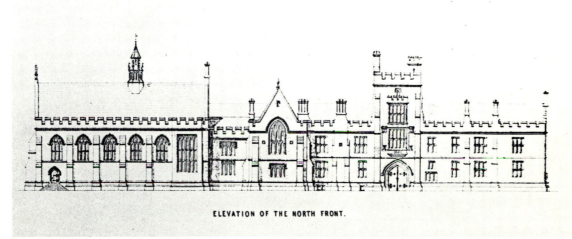

ELEVATION OF THE NORTH FRONT.

7. Queen's College, Cork. Elevation of north front. Board of Public Works Ireland, *Sixteenth Report* (1848), p. 532.

8. Queen's College, Cork. President's residence.

9. Queen's College, Cork. Vice-President's residence.

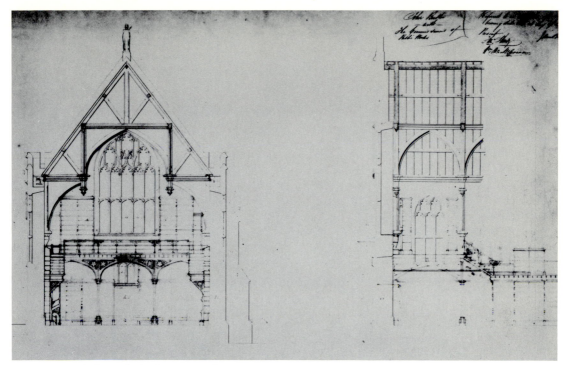

10.   Queen's College, Cork. Sections of Examination Hall showing roof construction.

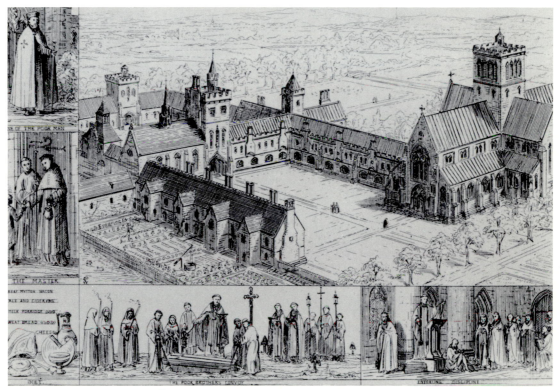

11.   A.W.N. Pugin, "Ancient Residences for the Poor," *Contrasts*, 1841.

13. Queen's College, Cork. Detail of south front of gate tower.

12. Queen's College, Cork. Label stop from cloister.

14. Queen's College, Cork. Label stop from cloister.

16.   Queen's College, Cork. Drawing for fireplace in Library, by Benjamin Woodward.

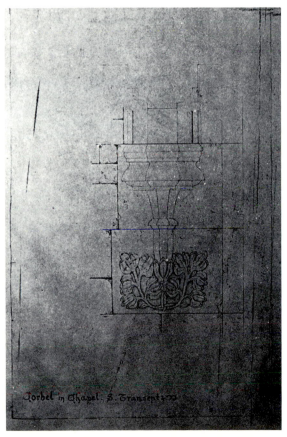

15.   Benjamin Woodward, measured drawing of Holy Cross Abbey, County Tipperary. Chancel.

17.   Benjamin Woodward, measured drawing of Holy Cross Abbey, County Tipperary. Detail of the Waking Bier.

18. Queen's College, Cork. Corbels on cloister.

19. Queen's College, Cork. Interior of Library looking south.

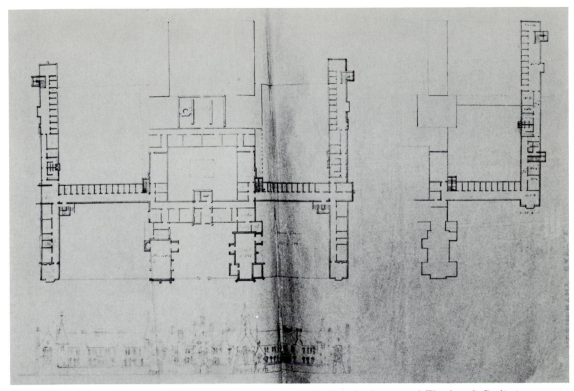

20. Killarney Lunatic Asylum, Killarney, County Kerry, 1847-1850, by Deane and Woodward. Preliminary plan (?).

21. Killarney Lunatic Asylum, Killarney. Entrance block south front.

24. Killarney Lunatic Asylum, Killarney. Interior Catholic Chapel.

22. Killarney Lunatic Asylum, Killarney. South front.

23. Killarney Lunatic Asylum, Killarney. Central administration block from north.

25. Cork Town Hall Design, 1851, by Deane and Woodward. Lithograph, 1851.

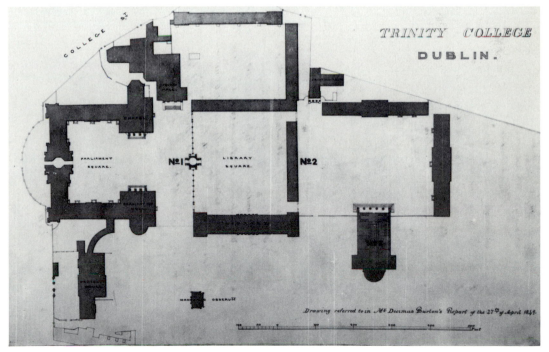

26. Decimus Burton, site plan for proposed museum, 1849.

27.   Trinity College Museum, Dublin (TCD), 1852-1857, by Deane and Woodward. North front.

28.   TCD. South front.

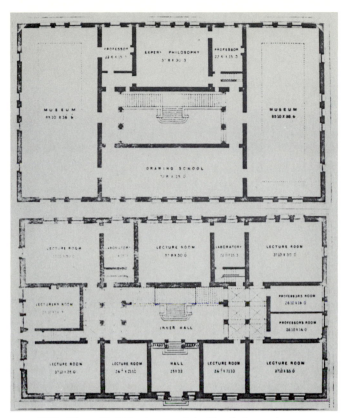

29.   TCD. Plan. *Civil Engineer and Architect's Journal,*
      1855, 48.

30.   Palazzo Dario, Venice, *Builder*, 1851,
      202.

31.   Casa Visetti, Venice, *Builder*, 1851,
      330.

33. Garden facade, Traveller's Club, Pall Mall, London, 1829-1832, by Charles Barry. *Building News*, 1858, 1151.

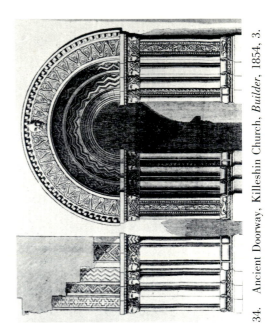

34. Ancient Doorway, Killeshin Church, *Builder*, 1854, 3.

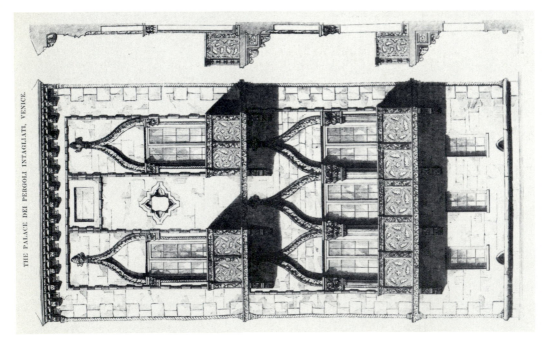

THE PALACE DEI PERGOLI INTAGLIATI, VENICE.

32. Palazzo dei Pergoli Intagliati, Venice, *Builder*, 1851, 170.

36. TCD. Interior, stairhall from east.

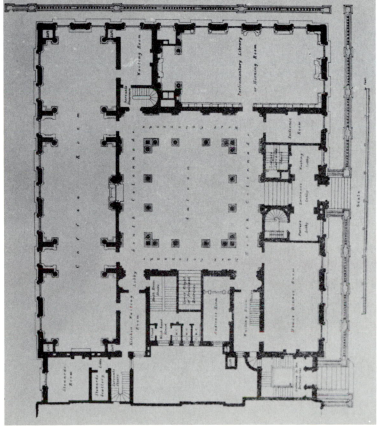

35. Plan Reform Club, Pall Mall, London, 1838, by Sir Charles Barry. *Civil Engineer and Architect's Journal*, 1840, 409.

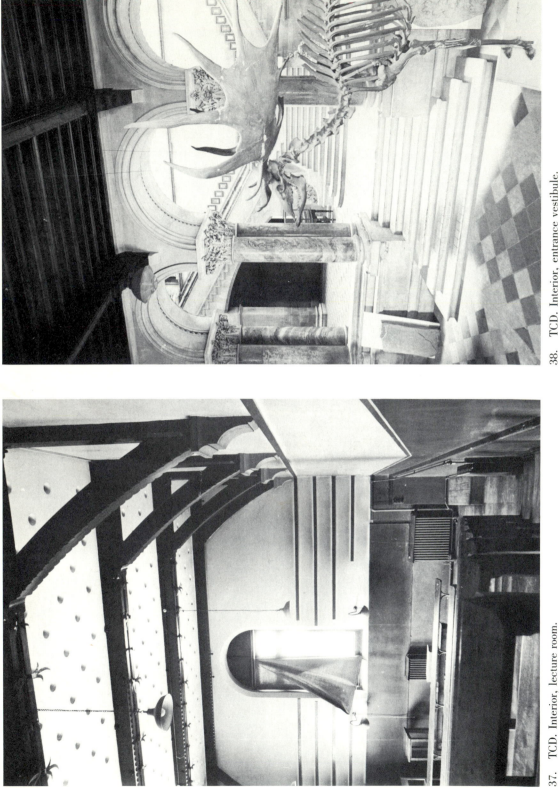

38. TCD. Interior, entrance vestibule.

37. TCD. Interior, lecture room.

40. TCD. Interior, stairhall looking into entrance vestibule.

39. Wall Veil Decoration.
Ruskin, *Stones of Venice*, I
(1851), pl. 1.

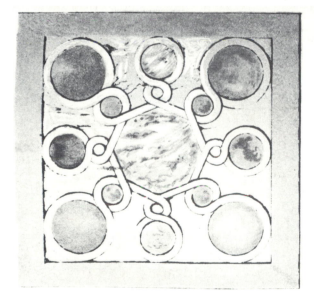

42. Archivolt in the Duomo of Murano. Ruskin, *Stones of Venice*, II (1853), pl. V.

41. Pierced ornaments from Lisieux, Bayeux, Verona, and Padua. Ruskin, *Seven Lamps* (1849), pl. VII.

43. TCD. Detail, north front.

44. TCD. Pier and capital detail, north front.

45.   TCD. Sketch for exterior windows, by Benjamin Woodward.

46.   TCD. Photograph of building under construction, c. 1855.

47. TCD. Interior capital.

48. TCD. Interior capital.

49. TCD. Stairhall from west.

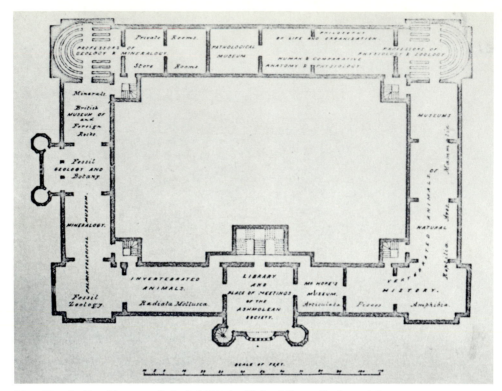

50. Plan for New Museum, Oxford, 1853, by Richard Greswell. Ground floor.

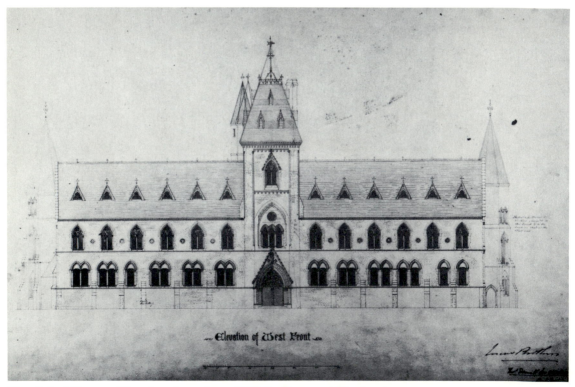

51. Oxford Museum. Elevation of west front, 1855, by Deane and Woodward.

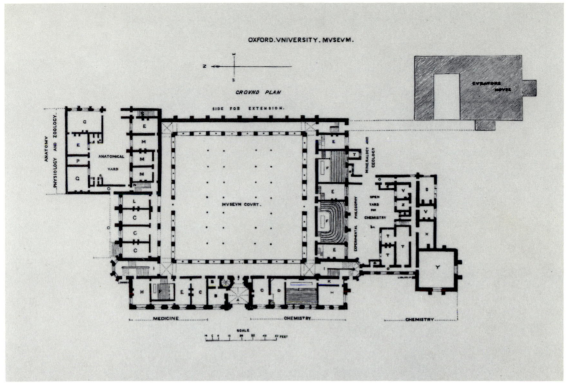

52.   Oxford Museum. Plan of ground floor.

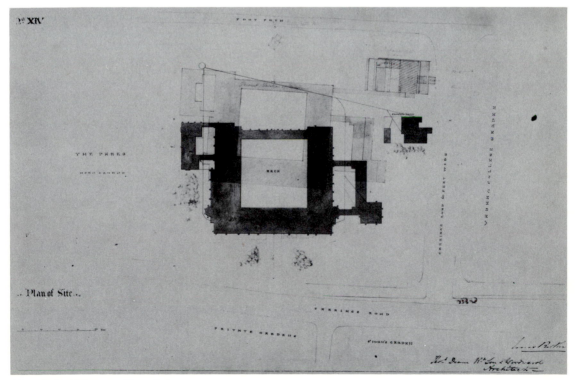

53.   Oxford Museum. Plan of site.

56. Oxford Museum. Sketches for Chemistry Laboratory, by Benjamin Woodward.

54. Oxford Museum, 1854-1860. From southwest. *Illustrated London News*, 1859, 438-439.

55. Proposed University Museum, Oxford. *Builder*, 1855, 319.

59. Oxford Museum. Sketches for alterations to southwest tower, by Benjamin Woodward.

57. Oxford Museum. West front.

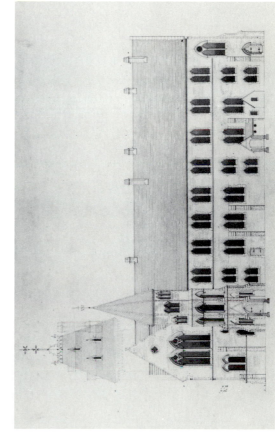

58. Oxford Museum. South elevation.

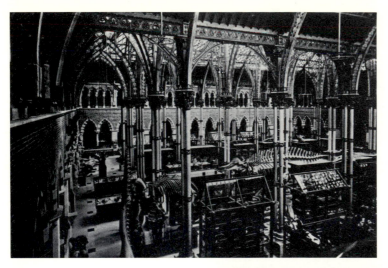

60. Oxford Museum. Interior court.

61. Oxford Museum. Hope
Entomology Department.

62. Proposed Museum for Oxford,
1852, by
G. E. Street.
An Urgent Plea. . . ,
1853.

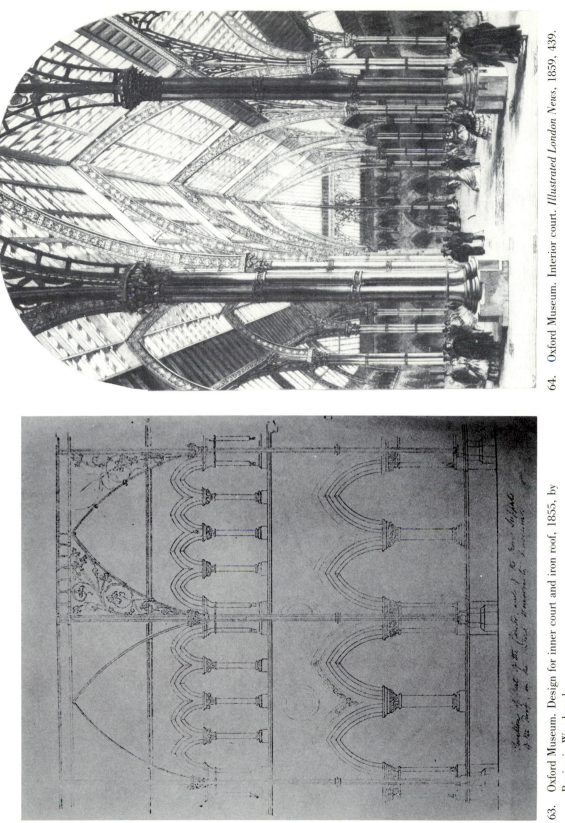

64. Oxford Museum. Interior court. *Illustrated London News*, 1859, 439.

63. Oxford Museum. Design for inner court and iron roof, 1855, by Benjamin Woodward.

65.   Oxford Museum. Wrought iron capitals, inner court.

66.   Oxford Museum. Wrought iron capitals, inner court.

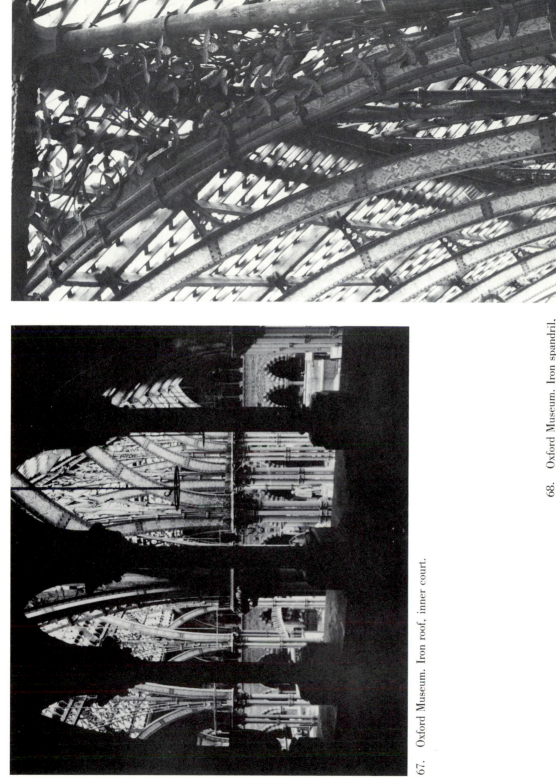

67. Oxford Museum. Iron roof, inner court.

68. Oxford Museum. Iron spandril, inner court.

69. Oxford Museum. Capital in lower level, inner court.

70. Capital, Ducal Palace, Venice. Ruskin, *Examples of the Architecture of Venice*, pl. I.

71. Oxford Museum. Sketch for capitals of inner court, by Benjamin Woodward in letter to W. B. Scott, 1859.

72. Oxford Museum. Capital in lower level, inner court.

73. Oxford Museum. Capital in lower level, inner court.

74. Oxford Museum. Capital in lower level, inner court.

75. Oxford Museum. Capital in lower level, inner court.

76. Oxford Museum. Capital in lower level, inner court.

77.   Oxford Museum. Upper corridor, inner court.

78.   Oxford Museum. Capitals in upper gallery, inner court.

79.   Oxford Museum. Corbel in lower level, inner court.

80.   Oxford Museum. Corbel in lower level, inner court.

81.   Oxford Museum. Capitals in entrance hall.

82.   Oxford Museum. Design for unexecuted mural in inner court, c. 1858.

83. Oxford Museum. Painted
frieze in Hope Entomology
Department.

84. Oxford Museum.
Wooden desk and stool.

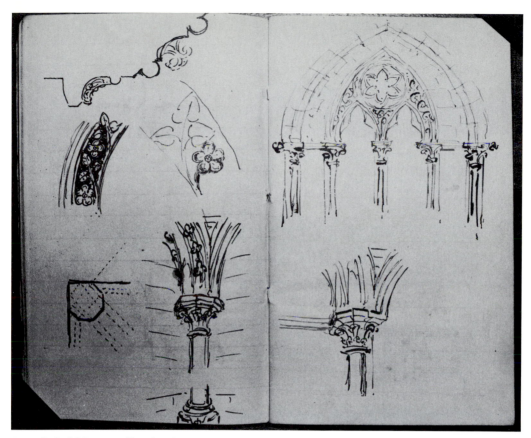

85.   Oxford Museum. Sketches for exterior decoration, by Benjamin Woodward.

86.   Oxford Museum. Second floor window, west facade.

87.   Oxford Museum. Sketch for carving on exterior window, 1859, by James O'Shea.

88. Oxford Museum. Design for carving on entrance porch, 1859, by John
Hungerford Pollen.

89.   Oxford Museum. Inner court showing statues.

90.   Government Offices Competition Design, 1857, by G. G. Scott. *Building News*, 1857, 162.

91. Oxford Union Debating Hall. 1857, by Benjamin Woodward. From the east.

92. Oxford Union. Interior.

93. Oxford Union. Interior. *Illustrated London News*, 1863, 348.

94. Oxford Union. Interior, detail of wrought-iron work.

95. Government Offices Competition Design, 1857, by Deane and Woodward. *Illustrated London News*, 1857, 348.

96. Government Offices. Sketches for windows, by Benjamin Woodward.

97. Government Offices. Sketches for stair tower windows, by Benjamin Woodward.

98. Government Offices. Sketches for arcades, by Benjamin Woodward.

99. Portion of design for War Office facade of Deane and Woodward's Government Offices Design, by John Hungerford Pollen. *Builder*, 1857, 563.

100. Crown Life Assurance Company Office, New Bridge Street, Blackfriars, London, 1856-1858, by Deane and Woodward. (Demolished.) *Building News*, 1858, 723.

101. Crown Life Assurance Company Office, New Bridge Street, London. Engraving, c. 1830, by Thomas Shephard.

102. Crown Life Assurance Company Office, New Bridge Street, London. Details. *Building News*, 1865, 447.

103. Crown Life Assurance Company Office, Fleet Street, London, 1865, by T. N. Deane. (Demolished.) *Building News*, 1865, 503.

104. Crown Life Assurance Company Office, Dame Street, Dublin, 1871, by T. N. Deane.

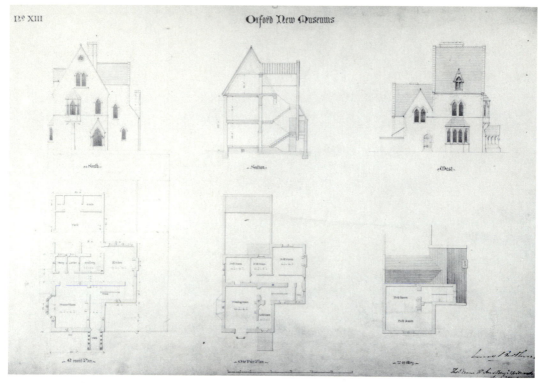

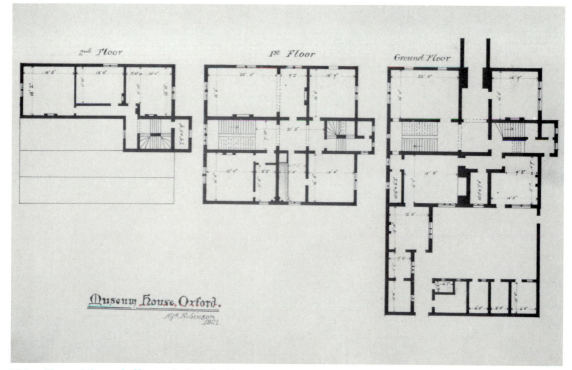

105. Design for Curator's House, Oxford Museum, Oxford, 1855, by Deane and Woodward.

106. Plans of Curator's House, Oxford, by Deane and Woodward.

107.   Curator's House, Oxford, 1857-1860, by Deane and Woodward. (Demolished.)

108.   Curator's House, Oxford. From southwest.

109. Llys Dulas, Anglesey, Wales, 1856-1858, by Deane and Woodward.

110. Llys Dulas, Anglesey. Exterior, balcony and window on front.

111.　Brownsbarn, near Thomastown, County Kilkenny, 1858-1864, by Deane
and Woodward. West front.

112.　Brownsbarn, County Kilkenny. From southeast.

114. Brownsbarn, County Kilkenny. Interior, staircase.

113. Brownsbarn, County Kilkenny. From north.

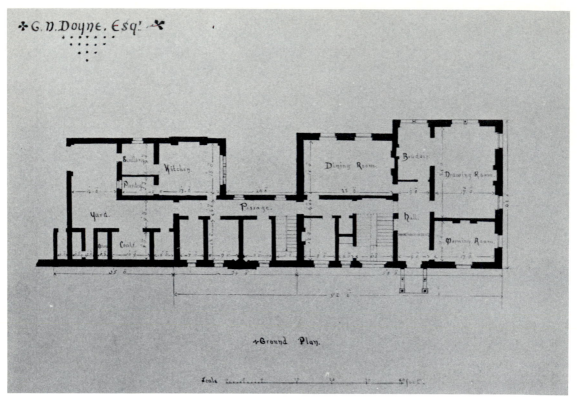

115.   St. Austin's Abbey. Plan, 1858, by Deane and Woodward.

116.   St. Austin's Abbey, Tullow, County Carlow, 1858-1859, by Deane and Woodward. Garden front.

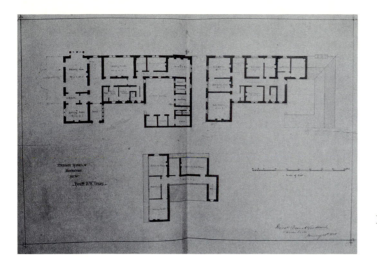

117. Plans for Glandore, Monkstown,
County Dublin, 1858-1859, by
Deane and Woodward.

118. Glandore, County Dublin. From north.

119. Glandore, County Dublin. From south.

120. Clontra, Shankill, County Dublin, 1858-1862, by Deane and Woodward. From south.

121. Clontra, County Dublin. From west.

122. Clontra, County Dublin. From east.

123. Clontra, County Dublin. Entrance stairhall.

124. Clontra, County Dublin. Central hall.

125. Clontra, County
Dublin. Drawing
room, looking south.

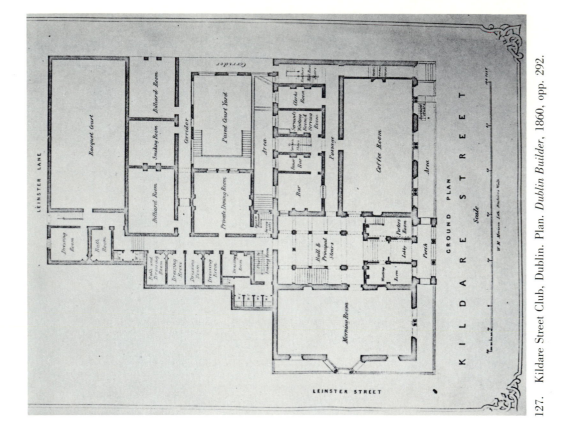

127. Kildare Street Club, Dublin. Plan. *Dublin Builder*, 1860, opp. 292.

126. Kildare Street Club, Dublin, 1858-1861, by Deane and Woodward. From northwest.

129.   Kildare Street Club, Dublin. Portico capital.

128.   Drawing by Charles Harrison for carving on Kildare Street
Club, Dublin. Portico capital.

130. Drawing by Charles Harrison for carving on Kildare Street Club, Dublin.

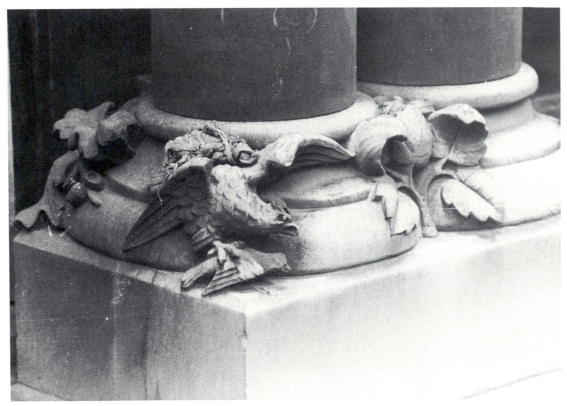

131. Kildare Street Club, Dublin. Carving on bases of exterior columns.

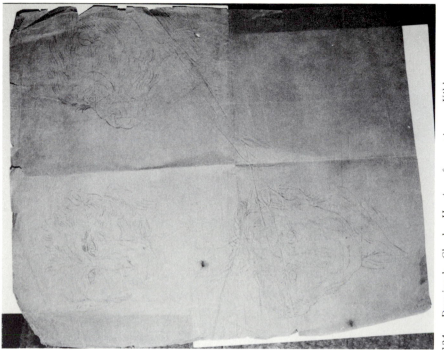

134. Drawing by Charles Harrison for carving on Kildare Street Club.

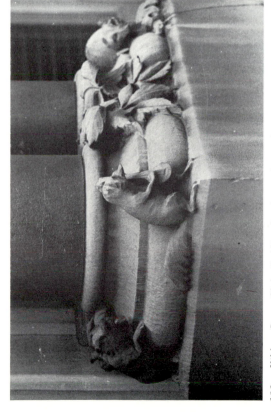

132. Kildare Street Club, Dublin. Carving on base of exterior column.

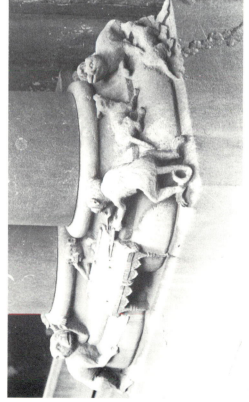

133. Kildare Street Club, Dublin. Carving on base of exterior column.

135. Kildare Street Club, Dublin.
       Racquet court roof.

136. Kildare Street Club,
       Dublin. Stairhall.

138.   Medallion of Benjamin Woodward,
        1861, by Alexander Munro,
        in the Oxford Museum.

137.   Kildare Street Club, Dublin.
        Stairhall.

139. 40-41 Broad Street, Oxford.
Study and library extension,
1857, by Benjamin Woodward.
(Demolished.)

140. Middleton Hall, St.
John's College, Oxford,
1859, by Benjamin
Woodward.

141. Dundrum Police Court and Barracks, Eglinton Terrace, Dundrum, County Dublin, 1855-1857, by Deane and Woodward. From southwest.

142. Dundrum Schools, County Dublin. From northwest.

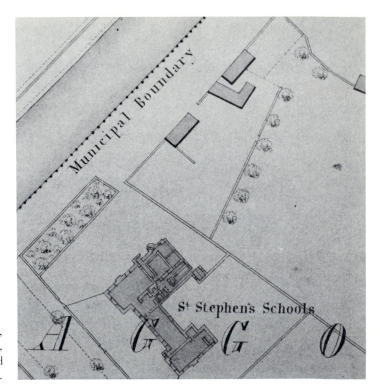

143. St. Stephen's Schools,
Northumberland Road, Dublin,
1859-1861, by Deane and
Woodward. Site plan.

144. St. Stephen's Schools, Dublin. Main front.

145. St. Stephen's Schools, Dublin. Master's house.

146. St. Anne's Parochial Schools, Molesworth Street, Dublin, 1856-1858, by Deane and Woodward.
(Demolished.)

147.   House for Arthur Guinness, Shanganagh Grove, Ballybrack, County Dublin, c. 1860, by Deane and Woodward. Watercolor drawing of proposed house.

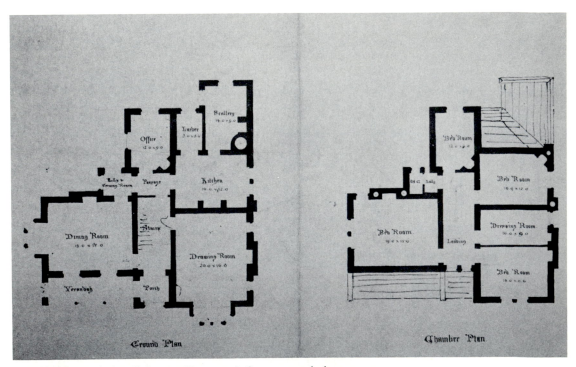

148.   House for Arthur Guinness, Shanganagh Grove, ground plans.

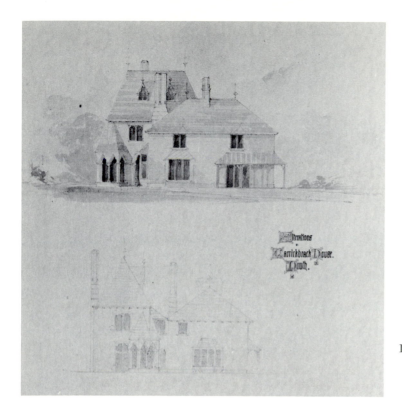

149. Proposed alterations to
     Carraigbraec House, Howth,
     County Dublin, c. 1860,
     by Benjamin Woodward.

150.   28 Fitzwilliam Place,
Dublin, 1855-1856 (alterations), by
Deane and Woodward.

151. 15 Upper Phillimore Gardens (center), Kensington, London, 1859-1861, by Benjamin Woodward.

152. Drinking Fountains in Beresford Place and Parkgate Street, Dublin, 1860, by Deane and Woodward. *Dublin Builder*, 1861, 419.

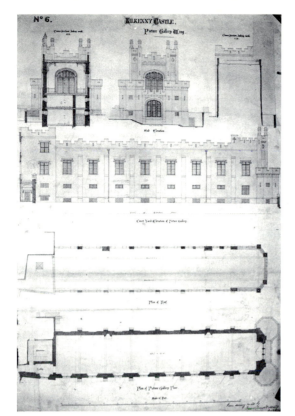

153. Survey drawing of east wing, Kilkenny Castle, County Kilkenny, c. 1858, by Deane and Woodward.

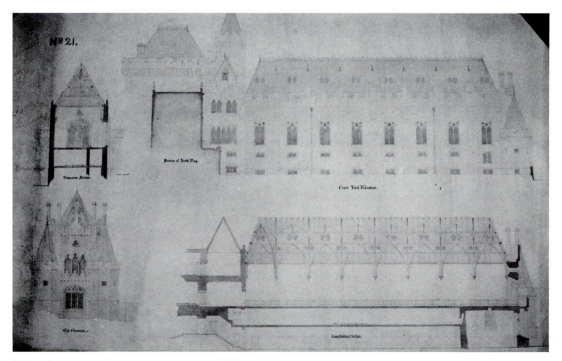

154. Design for alterations to east wing, Kilkenny Castle, 1858, by Deane and Woodward.

155.   Kilkenny Castle, County Kilkenny. East wing.

156.   Kilkenny Castle, County Kilkenny. Stairhall, northeast corner of east wing.

157.   Kilkenny Castle, County Kilkenny. Picture Gallery from north.

158.   Kilkenny Castle, County Kilkenny. Detail of roof in Picture Gallery.

159.   Trinity College Library, Dublin.
Watercolor drawing of Long Room
before alterations, c. 1860, by Deane
and Woodward.

160.   Long Room, Trinity College Library, Dublin, 1860-1862, by Deane and Woodward.

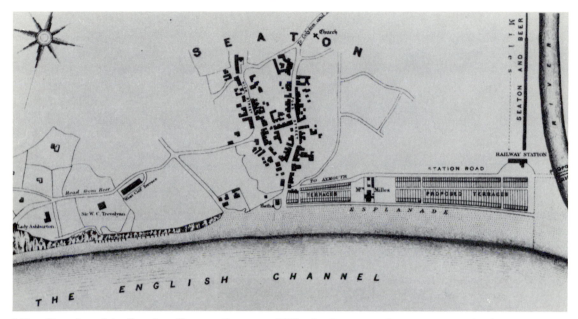

161. Part plan of the Trevelyan Estate at Seaton, c. 1860, showing proposed terraces on espalande.

162. Design for semi-detached houses, c. 1860, by Benjamin Woodward.

163. Design for semi-detached houses, c. 1860, by Benjamin Woodward.

164. Design for terraces, c. 1860, by Benjamin Woodward.

165. Design for terraces, c. 1860, by Benjamin Woodward.

166. Calverley Lodge (now Check House), Seaton, Devon, 1866-1867, by Charles Edwards.